INSIDE
THE
BELTWAY

INSIDE THE BELTWAY

OFFBEAT STORIES, SCOOPS, AND SHENANIGANS FROM AROUND THE NATION'S CAPITAL

JOHN McCASLIN

WND BOOKS
A Division of Thomas Nelson Publishers
Since 1798

www.thomasnelson.com

From GRIZZLY COUNTRY by Andy Russell, copyright © 1967 by Andy Russell. Used by permission of Alfred A. Knopf, a division of Random House, Inc.

From FAT MAN IN A MIDDLE SEAT by Jack W. Germond, copyright © 1999, 2002 by Jack W. Germond. Used by permission of Random House, Inc.

Published in Nashville, Tennessee, by WND Books.

Library of Congress Cataloging-in-Publication Data

McCaslin, John.
   Inside the Beltway : offbeat stories, scoops, and shananigans from around the Nation's Capital / John McCaslin.
      p. cm.
   ISBN 0-7852-6191-5
1. Washington (D.C.)—Politics and government—1995–   I. Title.
F201.M38   2004
975.3'041'0922–dc22   2004011322

Printed in the United States of America
04 05 06 07 08 QW 7 6 5 4 3 2

For Kerry, who keeps me writing.

Contents

CONTENTS

Introduction

L IKE OTHER EVERYDAY POLITICAL OBSERVERS, Mississippi lawyer J. Kevin Broughton was intrigued by the tremendous swell of support behind the latest Democratic newcomer, former Vermont Governor Howard Dean.

So much so that Broughton, a Republican who previously hung his shingle in Washington, D.C., wasn't shy about infiltrating a Dean for president "meet-up" in Jackson. What occurred next could only happen in America.

"I'm basically now head of Central Mississippians for Dean," said a bewildered Broughton.

The handful of Dean supporters on hand included a political consultant who had been state chairman of Al Gore's 1988 presidential campaign, a retired Army colonel, a local broadcaster, and a pair of middle-aged women. They were a nice enough bunch, and (honest lawyer that he is) Broughton decided to come clean.

"I disclosed that I was a Republican, interested in seeing Dean take Mississippi's delegates and win the nomination. I had to take charge of the meeting," he explained. "They were all talking about how Bush lied about WMDs [weapons of mass destruction] and how sick it was that Arnold [Schwarzenegger] got elected [governor] in California.

"'Listen,' I said, 'it'll be a four-man race at most by Super Tuesday. Dean will be one . . . [but] we'll have an incredibly low turnout. We need 25 percent of the black vote, and that will get us the 30 to 32 percent plurality that will take the delegates.'

"Blank stares," the lawyer recalled. "I'm trying to walk them through the mechanics of winning a primary. 'Look, let's divide up the counties in the middle third of Mississippi. Each of us can contact the Democrat county chairs, and get the voter and donor lists.'

"The retired colonel said, 'Kevin, tell us what it is that has disaffected you with the current administration.'

"'Not a darn thing,' I said, finally getting through. 'My motivation may be different than yours, but our goal is the same, at least until summer. Your guy can't be president if he doesn't win the nomination. I want him to get the nomination.'"

Before he knew it, Broughton was crowned chairman of the Dean club. They met again the next week.

As it was, despite this unprecedented joining of minds in central Mississippi, the once "unbeatable" Dean spiraled out of control. Voters in several key primary states soon declared him unsuitable for the presidency. Broughton and his loyal band of Mississippi Democrats were even more perplexed the day Dean signed off from his $41 million campaign with a reverberating "Yee-Haw!" heard round the world.

You couldn't write a better script in Hollywood. Or pen a better column.

ENCOUNTERING REAL-LIFE CHARACTERS like the Mississippi infiltrator is the rule, not the exception, when walking the most rewarding news beat in Washington—that of political columnist.

I've proudly penned the purely anecdotal "Inside the Beltway" column, published in the *Washington Times* and syndicated by the *Chicago Tribune,* for over a dozen years. Prior to that, as you'll gather from these many memorable stories, I toiled just as happily as news broadcaster and photographer, wire stringer, and White House correspondent.

Amazingly enough, as I enter my twenty-fifth year in the news business, each subsequent assignment is more thrilling than the last. How many people can say that about their jobs?

It was by the grace of God, outside church one miserable morning, that I stumbled upon journalism as a possible profession. Arithmetic and all else technical, I knew from experience, didn't run in my family. So during four years of college I steered towards the only language I knew, English, with minor concentrations in geography and girls. I preferred the latter two subjects, but neither was offered as a major.

While pursuing that degree in letters, I'd met Elizabeth Ray, the tattletale mistress of Capitol Hill, on the heels of her scandalous affair with Ohio Congressman Wayne L. Hayes, chairman of the House Administration Committee. She was thirty-four; I was just shy of my twentieth birthday.

A childhood friend had passed away, and I'd returned home from Old Dominion University to attend his funeral at St. Mary's Catholic Church in Alexandria. When who, in the midst of my mourning, should saunter out of the priests' rectory but the voluptuous Ray. How did I know it was she?

After leaving the FBI to raise three sons, my mother became parish secretary of St. Mary's, the oldest Catholic Church (founded in 1795) in the commonwealth of Virginia. I used to call her "Sister Wanda" because she orchestrated every baptism, wedding, and funeral short of sprinkling the holy water. Mom had whispered to me in confidence that Ray, after spilling her soul in the newspapers, was calling on the priests for spiritual guidance and counseling.

The other reason I knew it was the ex-mistress was because she had just bared her shapely soul in *Playboy.*

As luck would have it, my journalism professor had given our class the assignment of interviewing a "pillar of the community"—an alderman, judge, or police chief would suffice. As I stood there observing this statuesque blonde bending over to unlock her shiny white Corvette—tagged "Liz 1"—I saw no better pillar in my community.

Hours after her glossy image was eagerly passed around my dormitory, Ray was seated at my kitchen table. Not sure what to make of her son's first "scoop," my mother nervously served coffeecake, then chased my two brothers back upstairs.

"I wasn't qualified for secretarial work," Ray began. "I've never even learned to type."

Bingo, there's my lead.

It was the last thing I remembered her saying, although she went on to describe how disenchanted she'd become with the "permissiveness" of Washington (go figure). She also revealed that she was moving to New York City to study acting under Lee Strasburg and, if all went well, pursue a career in show business.

Fortunately, I was taping the interview (I still have the cassette). The entire time she spoke I debated in my head whether to get her to autograph my *Playboy*. But with Sister Wanda busy scrubbing clean dishes at the kitchen sink, I didn't dare ask.

"Get it published!" my professor exclaimed two days later. It was my first exclusive—pasted on the front page of the university's *Mace & Crown* beneath the headline, "I've Never Even Learned To Type."

I knew how she felt, but the time had come for me to learn.

I had been bitten by the same journalism bug that, without warning, lands on other budding reporters. Most bid goodbye to proud parents and beeline for the big-city lights. NBC News anchor Tom Brokaw was one such product of the nation's heartland, writing that when he drove clear of the cornstalks, he never looked back.

What, on the other hand, if one bitten by this bug had grown up in the shadow of the Washington Monument and returned home after college to seek fame and fortune?

"You need to go some place and get experience," said a producer at CBS.

"As in New York?"

"As in Kansas City. Actually, I know of an opening in Pittsburgh."

I knew of another place—another editor—I'd come to know only in print and photographs. Before I would ply my trade in Washington, inside the Beltway, I would follow my family roots there, to where my great-grandfather drove stakes into enough ground to call himself a rancher. It seemed a natural, if not totally unlikely, place to launch my own career.

And so, Mom fought back tears on that hot summer's day in 1980 when, instead of Pittsburgh, I packed my bags for Montana—aiming to enter the Fourth Estate through its trapdoor.

Chapter 1

Grizzly Politics

THE SECRET SERVICE "war wagon" climbed the narrow, twisting road until it reached Logan Pass, elevation 6,664 feet. The lone passenger in the back seat resembled the ordinary Joe beneath his camouflage hat. For once, Ronald Reagan's right-hand man wasn't riding in style. A White House limousine would stick out in the Montana landscape anyway.

As George Herbert Walker Bush stepped out to scan the horizon, his bodyguards—their job to take a bullet for the president and vice president of the United States—began to unload a large cache of weapons. They wouldn't be taking any chances, not given the recent bloodshed. Considering the awesome strength of the terrorists known to be hiding in these woods, no weapon would be too powerful.

G. GEORGE OSTROM, self-proclaimed "oldest living reporter," grew up on an arid cattle ranch on Montana's Flathead Indian Reservation. It proved to be too arid. When George was seven, his father loaded up everything the family owned and moved it and them to a remote mining camp called "Hog Heaven."

"My dad told me I could be anything I wanted to be—except a miner," says George. "Out of a one-room school's few students we produced a surgeon, a

1

chemist, a corporate president, the president of the University of Montana, a female executive, and a school teacher—my sister. My brother Ritchey pulled four years in the Korean War and then embarrassed me by making it through the University of Montana in three. My youngest brother was killed fighting Chinese invaders in North Korea."

Young George fared better during his three-year stint with the Army—parachuting into the German occupation and hiking safely back out. He continued leaping from airplanes in college, but as a U.S. Forest Service smokejumper.

When John F. Kennedy moved from Capitol Hill to the White House, George moved from Montana to Capitol Hill, toiling as legislative assistant—handling wilderness legislation mostly—for Montana Senator Lee Metcalf. But his feet never took to the concrete sidewalks of Pennsylvania Avenue, and like his father before him, George didn't think twice about loading up the family if it meant finding heaven.

In 1967, he formed a partnership to buy a remote fly-in ranch on Canada's wilderness border with Montana, just west of Glacier National Park. He named it "Moose City," although bears outnumbered the moose. George shared the ranch with the University of Montana's wildlife research center, which couldn't have picked a better time to take an interest in grizzly bears: *ursus arctos horribilus.*

On a single August night that same year, two college girls, who camped a considerable distance apart in Glacier Park, were savagely mauled by enraged grizzlies. Nothing like it had ever occurred in the park's fifty-seven-year history, the pair's gruesome demise documented by Jack Olsen in his best-seller, *Night of the Grizzlies.* George, a columnist and photographer for Montana's Pulitzer-prized *Hungry Horse News,* covered the twin-maulings for *Time-Life* and snapped many of the photos in Olsen's book.

Seven years later, in 1974, his woodland tales and photographs now delighting readers from *Sports Afield* to the *Saturday Evening Post,* George purchased Montana's smallest newspaper, the *Kalispell Weekly News.* In six years' time he turned it into Montana's largest weekly, surpassing many dailies with a circulation that stretched from Kalispell and the surrounding Flathead Valley to my mail slot in Virginia. The newspaper was popular for two reasons: George's unsurpassed wildlife portraits and his unparalleled wit.

I felt I already knew the legendary Montana editor, his trademark goatee and black cowboy boots, when I walked through his front door on a cool summer's day in 1980 and inquired in a southern drawl I never knew I had if he knew where I might find a job.

SCOTT BREWSTER, A LIEUTENANT stationed at Montana's Malmstrom Air Force Base near Great Falls, and his father-in-law, Robert T. Shanahan of Mount Laurel, New Jersey, were enjoying a splendid day of trout fishing along the banks of St. Mary River.

The date was July 24, 1980, the height of tourist season in Glacier National Park; but given one million acres of fishing holes to wade through, the two men had all the river they could see to themselves.

LIKE ALL SEASONAL EMPLOYEES of Glacier National Park, after orientation sessions on housekeeping, cooking, and steering the park's venerable red tourist buses, Kim Eberly and Jane Ammerman, working for the summer at Lake McDonald Lodge, were warned about grizzly bears.

A forestry student at the University of Montana, Eberly already knew more than most. His brother Bill, a Glacier Park seasonal ranger and biologist, was attacked and mauled by a chocolate grizzly the previous fall while counting cutthroat trout at Ole Lake.

Hiking along a backcountry trail with fellow biologist Chris Tesar, Bill came upon a sow and her two cubs as they were feasting on huckleberries. (George always said that good huckleberry years are best for everybody because bears get fat without raiding people places.) Well aware of a mother bear's instinct to protect her young, the pair of biologists darted for nearby trees.

Grizzlies are among the fastest animals of their size, and most are large.

And unlike people, they run fastest with their noses pointed uphill. Tesar clambered to relative safety, but the brittle branches of Eberly's chosen pine gave way, dropping the biologist to within jaw-range of the mother bear. Sinking her teeth deep into his leg, the sow pulled the ranger out of the tree, dumping him, in most unladylike fashion, into the thick brush below.

As quickly as she loosened her grip, Eberly sprang to his feet and tried scurrying up a second tree—only to be pulled out again, this time by his shoulder. Now landing in a creek, he hoped to look up and find the sow returning to her cubs. Instead, he was staring straight into the beast's mouth—her bloodstained canines ready to penetrate again.

Dropping from his perch, Tesar yelled out to his friend. Again, Eberly got on his feet and was able to reach a third tree, where this time Tesar met him. Tearing off his shirt, Tesar tied the bleeding biologist high into the tree's branches and quickly radioed for help. He then began massaging Eberly to keep him warm (Eberly's own shirt had been ripped from his body) until the "thump-thump-thump" of a rescue helicopter was heard. While a lone armed ranger stood guard, Eberly was lifted out of the tree and flown to Kalispell Regional Hospital where, like other lucky ones before him, he was sewn back together.

Had the grizzly been angry, or hungry, Eberly would likely have been toe-tagged at the morgue—if he had any toes left to tag. Fortunately, as George says, it was a good huckleberry year.

Recovering from the encounter, Eberly pleaded with a reporter from Kalispell's *Daily Inter Lake:* "When you write this, please don't make it sound like a 'mugger' bear story. They are just so beautiful, so gorgeous."

Without question, grizzly bears are among the most magnificent of God's creatures. Still, not a single visitor today steps foot inside Glacier Park without being handed a written warning: "You Are Entering Grizzly Country."

AN ESTIMATED ONE THOUSAND OR SO grizzlies—identified by long, crescent-shaped claws, bulging shoulder humps, and dished faces—lumber and slumber (depending on the season) in and around three heavily-forested regions of the contiguous forty-eight states: Glacier National Park, Montana's Bob Marshall Wilderness Area, and Yellowstone National Park in Wyoming.

The majority, however, roam around Glacier, one of the largest intact ecosystems in the United States.

A virtual garden during the warmer months, the Montana park is split down its middle by the Continental Divide, providing resident grizzlies— and encroaching hikers—two geologically-diverse halves: the lush "west side" with snow-capped peaks, alpine meadows, and a sweeping canopy of larch, fir, and Englemann Spruce; and the equally breathtaking but more arid "east side," with jagged spires, scrub trees, and windswept grasslands.

Linking the two is one of the most scenic, hair-raising ribbons of asphalt anywhere: "Going-to-the-Sun-Road."

––––––––––––––

IT WAS JULY 23, 1980, almost Christmas Eve. Glacier Park employees traditionally celebrate Christmas on July 25 because nobody but snow owls roost there for the actual holiday. With the immortal enthusiasm of young adults, Eberly, of North Lawrence, Ohio, and Ammerman, a college student from Stillwater, Minnesota, drank in the spectacular vistas as they climbed Going-to-the-Sun bound for the ideal camping spot along the park's eastern edge.

There was another reason to be in high spirits. Eberly's parents had just arrived from Ohio and set up camp at Old Man Lake, a Glacier jewel nestled in the park's Two Medicine Valley.

Leaving the serene setting of Lake McDonald Lodge, considered one of the finest examples of Swiss architecture in the United States, Kim and Jane's two-or-so-hour journey took them past Sacred Dancing Cascades— a series of rapids and waterfalls teeming with cutthroat and bull trout— beneath the hemlock canopy of Avalanche Gorge, and through the shadow of Heaven's Peak.

Soon they came upon Bird Woman Falls, the Weeping Wall (most weeping, or snowmelt, occurs in June and July), and the base of the Garden Wall with its "ten-month" icicles. They climbed several thousand more feet, onto the summer snowfields of Logan Pass and the Continental Divide, where they no doubt took in the impressive view of Jackson Glacier, one of the largest chunks of ice this side of Alaska. The pair then headed down again, this time into the park's east side—past Rising Sun, Virginia Falls, through the grasslands of Two Dog Flats, and finally into the practically people-less village of St. Mary.

Given the ideal stretch of weather (it snows every month in Glacier), the two seasonal employees had likely encountered several of the park's permanent residents, cautiously stepping into the warm, forever fleeting sunlight, only to be photographed by hordes of *Homo sapiens* driving Winnebagos from Wisconsin.

———————

NEVER, EVER FEED A BEAR. It could prove deadly for you and the bear. Granted, if you are about to become the bear's meal then by all means give up your last Twinkie and hope the beast likes eating dessert first.

When my grandfather, "Grand Si" Larson, patrolled Flathead County as a sheriff's deputy during the 1950s and 60s, he'd snap pictures of assorted bear hind-ends protruding from Montana trash dumpsters and send them to his grandkids back east. I knew as a boy that something was wrong with those pictures: bears, after all, are supposed to lick honey from beehives, not jars. In Grand Si's day, bears "hooked" on human leftovers were often left to forage until the following hunting season.

Today, bears that overstep their natural bounds are immediately trapped and relocated or else shot on the spot. Suffice it to say, if there's a garbage dump anywhere near the backcountry there's a bear within sniffing distance.

Such was the case shortly after my arrival in Montana in 1980. For three days the National Park Service tried to trap a cinnamon grizzly foraging an illegal dumping ground near St. Mary. Witnesses described the bear as "underweight," or approximately 250 to 300 pounds (adult grizzlies generally weigh 400 to 900 pounds), and in poor health. But the bear proved to be "trap-shy," as rangers described it, and given a lack of federal manpower—and concern that children might get snared instead—the trap was rolled away.

The bear, of course, stayed put. Soon, reports came in that several campsites in the vicinity were rampaged, while two or so more miles up the road three pigs on a pair of farms were almost swallowed whole by one or more beasts. The few residents living near St. Mary were convinced the pillager was the same grizzly that had been frequenting the dumping ground. Glacier's rangers were contemplating for a second time how to trap the elusive animal the same afternoon Kim and Jane arrived to set up camp.

SEARCHING FOR THE IDEAL, undesignated campsite to pitch their tent, the couple settled on a secluded sandbar in the middle of Divide Creek, the babbling border between Glacier Park and the Blackfeet Indian Reservation.

A mile or so away, the St. Mary Campground sat empty, one of four of Uncle Sam's campsites "closed" that summer because of budget cuts. Another five hundred yards downstream a privately run KOA campground was half full. Not that it mattered. Kim and Jane, both nineteen, sought—and found—seclusion. During a more playful moment that night, one of them took a stick and scratched Kim's name in the sandbar along with the word "Rose."

Little did they know it would be their epitaph.

FLY TIED, ROBERT SHANAHAN SCANNED the shimmering water for telltale signs of trout. Montana is famous for several varieties, none more exciting to catch than the native rainbow. It was approaching the noon hour, the sun about as high as it gets all year. Glancing upstream, Shanahan didn't detect any fins slicing the surface, but he did spot what appeared to be a tent, albeit crumpled up and entangled in a branch near where the creek enters the river. Forgetting about the trout for a moment, the angler began to make his way upstream. Soon, another object, blue in color, caught his eye. This looked to be a sleeping bag, lying in the brush of the creek bed.

What the fisherman stumbled upon next would have turned stomachs in the urban jungles of his native New Jersey.

GRIZZLY BEARS IN THE EARLY DAYS of Glacier, George writes in *Glacier's Secrets,* his second volume of photographs, were hunted as policy. As a boy in the 1930s, he had seen dozens of giant grizzly rugs decorating the balconies of Glacier's lodges and chalets.

"As late as the fifties and sixties it was rare to see a live one," George notes. When the Endangered Species Act "brought federal protective action, the big bears began a comeback and management problems arose. Today, there is an educated estimate of four to five hundred grizzlies in and around Glacier Park. We see them often."

So often that George and his otherwise law-abiding Thursday hiking partners—the "Over-the-Hill Gang," he calls his famous mountain troupe—have admitted to packing, illegally mind you, high-power handguns whenever traipsing through Uncle Sam's park.

"With the thought we did not want to curl up and play dead while a grizzly killed one of our friends or family," George explains. "My .357 magnum was in a camera case labeled 'Cannon.' Not entirely deceitful."

Today, George knows to stay away from unpredictable pockets of Glacier, like the far north country surrounding Kintla and Kinnerly Peaks, where his aging gang was once hounded by grizzlies.

"If you can get good grizzly photos without a telephoto lens," he reasons, "I don't want to go."

ANDY RUSSELL WAS BORN IN 1915 in Lethbridge, Alberta, just north of the Montana border. Once asked to submit a resume, he simply wrote: "Limited formal education, considerable Rocky Mountain variety."

He'd spent his entire life as a trapper, hunter, guide, outfitter, and naturalist. And, like George, he shot a mean camera. Today, Russell's grizzly bear photographs remain some of the most daring ever taken.

Shortly after my arrival "out West," George and his charming "first wife" Iris, as he calls her, invited me into their Kalispell home for a meal and bear stories. I quickly learned that if turned to the chapter on grizzly bears, George becomes a talking encyclopedia. My heart literally pounded as I listened to one terrifying tale after another—grizzly encounters to grisly remains. George himself was a character in many of the stories, and unlike others who went to the "big alpine meadow in the sky," he lived to tell about it. When the hour grew late, George walked over to his bookshelf and pulled down a worn copy of Andy Russell's 1967 book, *Grizzly Country*.

"There's plenty more bear stories in here," he said. "You keep it."

In awe as I was of George, it was an incredible gift. I opened it up to read "G. George Ostrom, Sept. 1967" scribbled on the first page, just days after the Night of the Grizzlies. Today, the book has a prominent place on my own bookshelf, and every so often I'll pull it down to read my favorite passage.

"Levi was cutting trail along a mountain slope in the midst of his wilderness territory one hot day in June," Russell writes of a humorous (it makes me laugh, at least) encounter his trapper friend, Levi Ashman, had with a big grizzly. "He was suffering from thirst and climbed down into a wooded canyon for a drink. He was accompanied by a dog, a cross-bred husky-German shepherd someone had given him. When Levi lay flat drinking from the stream, the dog let out a great roar and took after something in the timber across the creek. Before Levi could do more than lift his head, a returning procession split the creek in a cloud of spray, the dog leading with a large and very angry grizzly bringing up the rear.

"Levi was not a young man any more, but this did not slow his enthusiastic squirreling up a tree. There he clung to the slim bole of a lodge-pole pine, while the dog and the bear played Ring-Around-a-Rosy at its base.

The bear eventually wearied of chasing the dog in the hot sun and left, whereupon Levi slid down to terra firma.

"The dog greeted this belated arrival of reinforcement with great joy and, emitting another enthusiastic roar, promptly took off after the grizzly again. Following Levi's profane instructions, the dog came back even faster, again closely pursued by the irate bear. Once more Levi went up the tree."

By way of winding up his story, Levi said: "By the time that damn fool dog got it into his thick head, I wasn't about to come down and help him fight that grizzly, and the grizzly decided to leave for good. I was sure tired of camping in that tree. It didn't have a branch for forty feet and was slippery as a barber's pole."

"I'll bet you tied the dog up in camp after that," Russell said to his friend.

"Hell no!" Levi snorted. "I shot the son-of-a-bitch! Dog like that can get a man killed."

SHANAHAN SCRAMBLED AS FAST AS waders could carry him up the creek bank. When he reached St. Mary Lodge, staff immediately radioed park ranger Jerry Ryder, who spread urgent word to Blackfeet tribal police, the Glacier County sheriff's office, and the FBI—two hours away by siren in Great Falls.

Not knowing what type of crime scene he had on his hands—or in whose jurisdiction it lay—Ryder waited for additional armed rangers and tribal officers before making his way upstream. One of the first things he noticed was that whoever bunked down in this unlikeliest of campgrounds knew they were in grizzly country and took precautions to keep the bears away. A food cache tied ten feet up in a tree—twenty-five or so yards from the campsite—remained untouched. The same can't be said for Kim and Jane.

Based on evidence scattered along the creek, federal and tribal authorities speculated the bear wandered into the camp by chance, the *Daily Inter Lake* reported: "Angered by the site of the tent, the grizzly ripped through the nylon exterior and first grabbed the woman by her head, ripping off her scalp. The scalp later was found in the tent downstream."

Tribal policeman Ken Arnoux, among the first to arrive on the scene, guessed Jane passed out after the initial attack, at which time the bear turned its fury on Kim.

"Marks on forearms indicate Eberly may have been fending off attacks," the newspaper's chronology continued. "He was either dragged, knocked across or ran across the creek from the tent. His body was found about thirty feet from the campsite."

Bite and claw marks covered Kim's body. His left calf was entirely eaten. His wallet and identification, still tucked into the pocket of his pants, was found floating nearby. Arnoux speculated that as Kim was being mauled, Jane regained consciousness and started running for her life downstream.

"The bear overtook her about sixty feet away from the campsite, killed her and ate about a third of her body," said the Kalispell paper. "Her left arm was eaten to the bone and right breast, shoulder, abdomen, and buttocks were also eaten."

BILL POWELL HAD A HUNCH. Shortly after midnight, twenty or so hours after the maulings, the Blackfeet officer drove his pickup truck to the blackened banks of St. Mary River and turned off the lights. Sure enough, by the light of the moon thirty minutes later, he spotted the eerie outline of a bear navigating the riverbank. His heart racing, Powell immediately turned on the lights, which sent the wily bruin running.

Reaching the shoreline, the officer hollered into the still night air. At a distance of some two hundred yards, the grizzly—which had reached the far side of a sandbar—spun around and let out a tremendous roar. Squeezing the bear into the sights of his 7mm Seiko rifle, Powell fired a first shot (grizzlies rarely go down with one slug). The beast let out another roar, and Powell fired again. This time, the bear fell. And to be sure it didn't get up, he fired a third time.

Hearing the shots, tribal officers and park rangers raced through the darkness to the river, where flashlights revealed that the bear was still breathing. The animal was shot several more times. Frightfully enough, it lay bleeding next to the road leading to the KOA campground. Officers realized something else as they crowded around the bear awaiting its last breath: it matched, almost perfectly, the description of the cinnamon bear frequenting the St. Mary dump—underweight, in poor health, and (they would eventually learn) suffering from a stomach ulcer the size of a silver dollar. No wonder the grizzly was so mean.

A subsequent autopsy of the bear found human hair in the stomach that matched both victims and the hair found in bear scat near the site of the maulings. Measurements of the bear's canines also matched the teeth marks in what remained of Kim and Jane's bodies.

Later that day, the National Park Service dispatched a helicopter to Two Medicine Valley, where rangers would break the implausible news to Eberly's parents that, for the second time in under a year, one of their sons was mauled by a grizzly bear.

Except this grizzly, if not the other, was a "mugger."

Chapter 2

Out of Montana

BILL PATTERSON HIRED ME because George Ostrom asked him to. "We'll give you a month and see how you do," said the owner of Kalispell's KOFI radio station, a clear-channel affiliate of the old Mutual Broadcasting Network.

I understood Patterson's concern. While George was polite enough that initial summer to publish a few of my photographs—mountain goats licking the salty cliffs of "Goatlick," buffalo stampeding across Mission Creek, and the occasional car wreck and house fire ("We're trying to teach John that a good newsman sleeps with his camera," George wrote in one 1980 caption)—my journalism portfolio didn't consist of two pages. That would soon change.

SOMETHING INTANGIBLE WAS IN THE AIR that Night of the Grizzlies." Two attractive nineteen-year-old coeds savagely mauled on the same summer night in August 1967, by different bears, in separate campgrounds, miles apart.

One mauling perhaps, but two?

Michele Koons of San Diego worked at Lake McDonald Lodge, her beautiful smile greeting tourists in the gift shop. A rising sophomore at California Western University, she was camping with friends near Trout Lake when the beast came calling.

Blue-eyed Julie Helgeson, a pompom girl in high school, was a sophomore at the University of Minnesota and worked in the laundry room at East Glacier Lodge. She bid farewell to her parents who'd been visiting for two days and left on her first—and last—camping trip.

Nine years would pass before a Glacier grizzly took another life, a twenty-one-year-old Illinois woman mauled in September 1976 while otherwise snug in her sleeping bag at Many Glacier (my parents honeymooned there in 1953).

Now, four years later, it wasn't just the maulings of Kim Eberly and Jane Ammerman that had Flathead Valley old-timers dubbing 1980 the "Year of the Grizzlies." There was an unusual amount of bear activity during the summer, and it was still only September. "Bear season," so to speak, was still in effect. Autumn is the time of year when grizzlies like to add a few pounds to their big frames, to hold them over for the winter.

Sustenance was on the mind of a grizzly, for instance, that broke into two outbuildings at the Belly River ranger station. Coming up empty-handed, the bear showed its displeasure by breaking every window in the station office.

Laurence Gordon wasn't afraid of bears—or so he said. The former commercial airline pilot from Dallas, Texas, who had piloted reconnaissance planes during Vietnam, was warned more than once that hiking alone in Glacier was the dumbest trail a person could go down.

But the muscular Gordon, a born-again Christian who read scriptures from a pocket Bible, put his faith in the Lord. He obtained a four-night back-country permit at St. Mary, where only two months before Eberly and Ammerman met their fate. The thirty-three-year-old hiker told park rangers that he planned to camp September 25 at Many Glacier, then take the Ptarmigan Tunnel to Elizabeth Lake—prime grizzly habitat closed several times that summer due to "bear activity" (more specifically, a blonde-striped grizzly and, even more dangerous, a sow with three cubs).

Not once, but twice, rangers tried to instill in Gordon the importance of the "buddy system" when venturing into Glacier's remote and rugged wilderness. Bears weren't the only dangers to worry about. Hikers frequently stumble off ledges, break legs, drown, even get struck by lightning. But Gordon wasn't listening. The last time rangers saw the bearded gent, he was trudging north with only a backpack and cedar walking stick—and God as his hiking partner.

MIKE HOEFT USED TO SNAP the filters off of his cigarettes before lighting them. An avid outdoorsman towering well above six feet, "Hoofer," as I called him, could climb mountains with the surefootedness of a goat—hardy traits that didn't prevent us from almost getting killed one night while trespassing onto Uncle Sam's property.

It was one of those spur-of-the-moment road trips, its itinerary scribbled on a wet bar napkin, to photograph sixty-foot snowdrifts and feel earth-shaking avalanches. Without even a change of clothes, we left Moose's Saloon at last call, drove east out of Kalispell over Marias Pass and the Continental Divide, then north for forty miles onto the Blackfeet Indian Reservation. Arriving in the Indian village of Babb, we turned west onto the only road leading to Many Glacier, a spectacular Glacier Park jewel that wouldn't open for another month—or until the snow thawed enough so you could find the front door.

It was just after three o'clock in the morning, about as close to nowhere as a person can get, and we were mushing along the reservation road buried in snow and marked "closed for the season." Suddenly, Hoeft spotted headlights in his rearview mirror that, to his amazement, grew larger and brighter by the second. Whoever was rapidly gaining on his faded maroon Volvo station wagon, he observed out loud, wasn't afraid of dying.

Moments later, I was horrified to report that it was a large-bodied pickup truck, loaded with Blackfeet Indians, one waving a rifle out of the passenger window. Ironically, I'd just spent the previous hour keeping Hoeft awake by observing that trappers were scarce in these parts during the 1800s because it was almost impossible to keep a trading station open. Now, the modern-day descendants of these once-proud warriors were barreling down the wrong side of an icy road, the giant wheels of their pickup truck churning up snow like it was popcorn.

Just when I thought we were destined for the "happy hunting grounds," as Blackfeet refer to heaven, Hoeft, to my utter amazement, swerved his wagon in the direction of the truck, presenting the startled driver two split-second options: back off into our tracks or else plunge over a cliff into frozen Sherburne Lake.

We played Cowboys and Indians like this for several terrifying minutes: Hoeft weaving his unarmed wagon from side to side, Blackfeet speeding up then retreating, and yours truly sliding further into the seat, expecting a bullet to slice through the window at any second. I'd never been so scared in all my life—and never so relieved to skid past a U.S. government "Closed—Do Not Enter" sign.

To my astonishment, the Indians slid to a halt exactly where their reservation ended. It was as if we'd entered another country.

Which isn't to say we didn't cower all night (all they needed to do, after all, was follow our tracks in the snow) in the boarded-up bunkhouse we crawled into for refuge. Hoeft, who grew up in Wisconsin, lived in the none-too-fancy quarters a previous summer as a seasonal employee at Many Glacier. Now he was a newspaperman for Kalispell's *Daily Inter-Lake,* and one of the best in the trade. (As life would have it, years later I was sitting in a small chapel on the Oneida Indian Reservation in northern Wisconsin, witnessing Hoeft marry Patty Ninham, the most beautiful Native American bride I ever laid eyes on. Her tribal ancestors sided with Americans to fight the British during the Revolutionary War. In fact, there is a Ninham Mountain in upstate New York named for one of Patty's "patriotic" forebears. Today, Hoeft is the opinion page editor for the *Green Bay Press-Gazette* in Wisconsin, and remains one of the best in the business).

SUPPOSEDLY IN COMPETITION WITH ONE ANOTHER, reporters in the Flathead Valley preferred sticking together when covering a beat as big as Delaware. Whether toiling in newspapers, radio, or television, we kept each other company at town hall meetings in Whitefish and Bigfork and racing to snowslides at Hungry Horse and East Glacier.

For one assignment, Hoeft and I agreed to meet at Moose's Saloon, raised our long-neck beer bottles to Laurence Gordon, then drove the thirty-five miles to West Glacier and the federal board of inquiry examining his grizzly death. The Bible-toting Texan became Glacier's third bear-related fatality in two months' time. Indeed, it was the Year of the Grizzlies.

STANDING FLAT-FOOTED, A GIANT GRIZZLY can have a reach of thirteen feet. That was the estimated range of the bear that treed three Minnesota hikers on September 30, 1980, near Glenn Lake. Unable to reach the trio's trembling limbs, the massive mammal ripped through their backpacks instead.

At dusk several days later, park rangers climbed into a helicopter and lifted a bear trap to Glenn Lake. On the way back, they spotted what appeared to be a disheveled campsite along the shores of nearby Elizabeth Lake. Unfortunately, with darkness rapidly setting in, whatever was down there would have to wait until morning.

The next morning, October 3, park ranger Bill Conrod and his wife, Cheryl, strapped on their backpacks (and one would assume a gun or two) and set out for Elizabeth Lake. Given that bears were the couple's closest neighbors, they immediately sensed something was wrong. And the fact that Gordon was nowhere to be found didn't help matters.

Additional rangers were called in, and just before 1:00 P.M. what was left of the Texan—a pelvic bone, two leg bones, and skull (its eye sockets, I announced over the radio, were "licked clean")—was discovered in a stand of willows some one hundred yards from the campsite.

It appeared to rangers that Gordon attempted to swim out into Elizabeth Lake to escape his four-legged pursuer. But either he couldn't swim fast enough, or else he grew exhausted from treading water.

Two days after Gordon's bones were found, a mid-sized blonde bear weighing 379 pounds was shot by park rangers stalking the beast by helicopter. How they were able to determine it was the "guilty" grizzly was nothing short of miraculous, and a sight I shall never forget.

After Hoeft and I arrived at the board of inquiry hearing, I snapped a photograph (later published by George) of Glacier Park ranger Reed Dietring holding Gordon's Bible in the palm of his hand (the purple ribbon marked September 26, the last day the hiker communicated with God—at least from earth).

In his other hand, the ranger clutched the skull of the suspect grizzly. As regional National Park Service Director Ken Ashley of Denver looked on in amazement, the ranger lowered the skull's razor-sharp canines into two holes discovered in Gordon's Bible. It was a perfect fit.

But there's an even eerier ending to this grizzly tale. A camera found among Gordon's earthly possessions showed all thirty-six frames exposed. When rangers later developed the film they were shocked to see that Gordon's last two photographs revealed his ransacked campsite. Rangers theorized that Gordon was off enjoying a day hike and returned to find his belongings scattered about. The theory was he snapped the last two frames on his roll to show the folks back home in Texas what happens when a grizzly comes calling and nobody's home.

But this grizzly tale still isn't over.

In the very last frame, rangers swore they spotted a terrifying outline through the trees in the background. Its eyes were glued on Gordon.

WHEN MY BROTHERS AND I were growing up in Virginia, my grandmother, "Grand Notie" Larson, used to send us brightly colored T-shirts lettered, "Where the Hell is Kalispell?"

You seldom see these shirts anymore. I knew the town's tranquility was doomed the summer I moved there, when I clipped an article from the *New Yorker* magazine's "The Talk of the Town":

> Everybody's had the dream of being a cowboy, and I've just lived mine out. Where else could you live in the eighteen-eighties and get paid for it? I just came off a picture called *Heaven's Gate,* directed by Michael Cimino. We were shooting near Kalispell, Montana, in the Flathead River Valley. It's green, with streams and mountains. Now, I'm partial to the whole, entire West, because I've spent my whole, entire life there, and I like Arizona and New Mexico and Colorado and Wyoming, but if any place could look like heaven it's got to be Kalispell, Montana.

Soon, people came to see for themselves. Especially Californians. Many decided to stay. As Don Henley once sang, "You call some place paradise, kiss it goodbye."

I spent two years growing the ugliest beard ever hung in Kalispell, then signed on as news director of twin radio stations a dozen miles north in Whitefish, home to the state's largest ski resort, Big Mountain. Besides news, KJJR-AM/KBBZ-FM owner Benny Bee recognized the importance of high school athletics. So, one or two nights each week I'd find myself seated on wooden bleachers alongside Benny and usually a surprise commentator—a banker, car dealer, or any other potential advertiser the station was trying to schmooze. Needless to say, there were never any dull moments as three of us broadcast Whitefish Bulldogs basketball games.

"Mac, you're not going to believe who I've got lined up to do color for tonight's game," Benny boasted before the start of one Lady Bulldogs game. This time he had reason to brag.

For several decades now, pro-basketball legend Phil Jackson has lived, fly-fished, and ridden his motorcycle around the Flathead Valley. During the early 1980s, Jackson was between his championship days with the New

York Knicks (he played forward alongside Walt Frazier, Willis Reed, Jerry Lucas, and future senator and Democratic presidential candidate Bill Bradley) and coaching the Chicago Bulls to an astounding six NBA championships. Most recently, he's been head coach of the Los Angeles Lakers.

For this particular game, the Whitefish girls were tipping off against the visiting Dillon Beavers, who'd traveled 325 miles to play sixty minutes of basketball. Knowing the majority of kids in Whitefish, Benny handled the play-by-play, Jackson provided the color, while I checked microphone connections and mentioned what the weather was doing outside (the weather is always a relevant topic in Montana, especially when you don't have anything else to talk about).

Yet none of us could utter a single word—about basketball or blinding blizzards—after Benny, who'd been impressed the entire game with the rebounding skills of the Dillon girls, blurted out, "You know, gentleman, you've got to be impressed with the size of these Beavers!"

Two baskets were scored, one by each team, and nobody in radio land heard it. One Whitefish chamber official, listening to the game on his car radio, said he had to pull onto the side of the road because he couldn't see through his tears. Doctors tell us that laughter is the best medicine, and I don't recall a single day in the two years I worked for Benny that he didn't make me laugh.

Ronald Reagan around that same time paid a presidential visit to the Montana metropolis (population 56,690) of Great Falls, and Benny sent me across the Continental Divide to cover his appearance. Through my good friend Jerry O'Leary, White House correspondent then for the *Washington Times*, I was able to land a backstage interview with White House Chief of Staff James A. Baker III, who was kind enough to make some news: fingering Jimmy Carter for the nation's inflation. My resulting UPI dispatch crossed the national wires, my first political scoop of any significance.

Vice President George Bush twice visited the Flathead Valley during the early 1980s, but my favorite repeat visitor was the ever-controversial Interior Secretary James Watt. Sporting his white cowboy hat, Watt practiced reverse psychology on the "greenies" by posing before the sacred trees and waterfalls of Glacier Park while announcing his unpopular environmental initiatives.

For instance, on July 15, 1983, I filed this UPI story:

GLACIER NATIONAL PARK—Secretary of Interior James Watt, in the midst of a July snowstorm, said his agency would not attempt to measure its successes by how many acres have been added to the park system, "but in how well we do in protecting the resource of the parks we have." National Parks Director Russell Dickenson brought a few jeers from the crowd, estimated at up to five hundred people, when he introduced Watt as "the man who loves parks."

Watt, who would resign in three months' time, wasn't in the mood that day for any one-on-one interviews. Still, I'd promised Benny that I'd approach the secretary and ask him to record a station promotion I'd typed up. The only chance I saw was when Watt ducked into the bathroom.

There we stood, side by side, staring at a white porcelain wall. There was no place for him to turn. The next day, under the headline, "Watt Promotes Watts," the *Great Falls Tribune* reported:

WHITEFISH—When KJJR listeners tune to the radio station's more powerful 10,000-watt voice today, they will hear Interior Secretary James Watt. Watt was approached by John McCaslin, the station's newsman, and asked if he would read a cleverly worded promotion. There were so many "watts" in the promotion that Watt himself tripped over the lines and had to repeat them several times before getting them right.

"Hi, this is Interior Secretary Jim Watt. I think one would have to agree that if anyone knows about watts, it's me. Congratulations to KJJR Radio of the Flathead Valley, who are now broadcasting at a full ten thousand watts. Imagine that! Ten-thousand Watts. Sounds like hog heaven."

What the newspaper didn't report was that before editing the tape for promotional purposes, I'd broken my pledge to the secretary by airing on that evening's newscast each of Watt's hilarious takes—riddled with the secretary's tripping over the pronunciation of his own last name. Not once did it occur to me that he would be tuning in. No sooner did his car arrive at Glacier Park International Airport for the flight back to Washington than he was on the telephone.

Not only was I embarrassed, I felt ashamed—suddenly counting myself among a relentless, unforgiving pack of reporters that dogged Watt from coast to coast. All I could do was apologize. Then, several days before he resigned—"removing a millstone from around the neck of President Reagan," I wrote for UPI—a photograph of Watt and me taken outside the men's restroom in Glacier Park arrived in the mail.

"Thanks for breaking me into radio," he wrote on the picture, which still hangs in my office today. Few reporters—and fewer environmentalists—cared for Watt. But he'd taught me two very valuable lessons: integrity and forgiveness. (A dozen years later I sat in U.S. District Court in Washington, watching Watt be sentenced for his alleged role in an influence-peddling scandal at the Department of Housing and Urban Development. With his wife, Leilani, at this side, Watt was spared a jail sentence by Judge Royce C. Lamberth. Nevertheless, he was placed on five years' probation, fined a maximum five thousand dollars, and ordered to perform five hundred hours of community service for a single misdemeanor count of withholding documents from a grand jury.)

"It seems to me that what you did there is out of character," Judge Lamberth said. "You have had a life of great integrity, and it's a shame to see what happened here."

"I made a serious mistake," an emotional Watt replied. "I would not wish this experience on my worst enemy."

Facing $950,000 in legal bills, Mrs. Watt a few weeks later appealed in a mass mailing for donations: "Just like Oliver North and John Poindexter before him, my husband became a victim of the liberals' determination to destroy Ronald Reagan's legacy. So we've sold our home and cashed in Jim's retirement fund."

The day I received her letter I picked up the phone and called Watt's home in Jackson Hole, Wyoming. The former secretary answered. After I told him how envious I was that he was back in the Rocky Mountains, he said he'd be happy if he never stepped foot inside Washington again.

―――――――――

WITHOUT QUESTION, "bear" was my favorite story line, or "slug," during four unforgettable years in Montana. The majority of my bear tales, which numbered in the dozens, had happy endings. I was always delighted when one or two would get published in the major newspapers in Washington because my mother would get to read them.

One of my favorites surrounded a fisherman named Tony Malone, who hooked a grizzly rather than a trout.

Fishing pole in hand, Malone stumbled upon the bear by walking along Kintla Creek in Glacier Park. In the blink of an eye, the grizzly stood up, charged the fisherman, and bit him on the ear and wrist. Malone, being a Montanan, knew exactly what to do when placed in that uncomfortable position: play dead.

Convinced its prey is no longer breathing, a grizzly will usually leave its victim where he or she dropped them and then come back to eat them later. Such was the case with Malone. Giving the fisherman up for dead, the grizzly turned its attention to sniffing the fishing gear—only to get a fishhook stuck square in its nose.

Suddenly feeling as much pain as the fisherman, the agitated bear stood on its hind legs, snapped the fishing line, and stormed off into the woods—fish hook, believe it or not, still dangling from its nose.

Another UPI story of mine was published in the *Washington Post* under the headline, "Charging Grizzly Bear Repulsed by Umbrella." Granted, few men in Montana carry umbrellas (it just doesn't look right above a cowboy hat). But one Montana outdoorsman who owes his life to his umbrella is Dave Reynolds who, when hiking with three companions, came upon a large sow and her cubs.

"We watched her for three or four minutes," Reynolds recalled. "Then she caught site of us, laid her ears back, woofed, and charged."

As his friends clambered up nearby trees, a terrified Reynolds stood his ground. Just when the grizzly was almost on top of him, he popped open his umbrella and quickly ducked behind it.

Crouched there like that, Reynolds had no way of knowing the bear's reaction. But as his visibly impressed friends told him later, when the umbrella sprang to life the bear stopped dead in its tracks, carefully approached the umbrella, sniffed it, then quickly ran away—confused cubs in tow.

Another favorite bear tale, carried by newspapers as far away as Chile, surrounded a Glacier Park ranger who'd been hounded all night by an unusually aggressive black bear. (Encounters with long-clawed grizzlies are said to be twenty times more deadly than run-ins with short-clawed black bears, which generally only weigh 150 to 300 pounds—about the size of a grizzly cub). What made this story so intriguing was that the ranger was forced to spend the night in an outhouse.

The black bear first treed ranger John Heiser while he was setting up camp at Ole Lake. Before long, the bruin grew tired of stalking the unarmed ranger and headed off into the woods to dig up some roots. Sore from sitting in the tree, Heiser jumped down and happily crawled into his sleeping bag. Soon, the bear returned, sending the sleepy-eyed Heiser scurrying for the outhouse. (The ranger described his sleeping quarters as "fairly new, roomy, and not uncomfortable," but what else was he going to say with everybody from Kalispell to Santiago laughing at him?)

Heiser didn't poke his head out of the outhouse until daybreak. That afternoon, armed rangers arrived and, to my surprise, shot the bear. A strict new bear policy, implemented after the deaths of Eberly, Ammerman, and Gordon, allowed rangers to take such drastic action if it was determined a bear—grizzly or black—had no fear of man.

Out of Montana

SHORTLY BEFORE MEMORIAL DAY 1983, I was happy to receive word that Billy Dwyer, a friend of mine from Virginia, would be passing through Montana on his way to Alaska. I was even more surprised to learn that his travel companion, thirty-eight-year-old Maureen Dursi, had recently left the Catholic convent. After hanging up her habit, "Mo" decided to visit a relative in Anchorage, and Billy agreed to load into his van what few belongings the ex-nun had and get her there.

Just as George "oriented" me with Glacier's carnivores three years earlier, I kept my visitors wide-eyed beyond midnight with bear tales. I even pulled a scrapbook off the shelf and showed my guests pictures of Laurence Gordon's skull—licked clean.

The fact that Mo and Billy would be hiking the next day to remote Avalanche Lake only spurred me on. I recommended they tie "bear bells" to their backpacks, so the grizzlies could hear them coming and scamper off the trail. Mo, I noticed, was squirming in her chair.

"Do you know the difference between black bear scat and grizzly bear scat?" I asked her. "Grizzly bear scat has bells in it."

She didn't laugh.

"Talk out loud, clear your throat, whistle. Sing if you have to," I continued into the wee hours of the morning. "Just never, ever, surprise a bear."

Of course, the chances of ever coming nose-to-nose with a grizzly bear are extremely remote, even in Glacier. I'd hiked in the park from spring to autumn for almost four years' running and never spotted a grizzly outside of my binoculars or rearview mirror. But I didn't tell them that.

"WHAT IS THIS, SOME KIND OF JOKE?" I asked myself, discovering Billy and Mo's backpacks, heavily scratched and caked in mud, dumped on my living room carpet. I walked onto the second-floor balcony and through the rising steam spotted the pair in the hot tub below. A twelve-pack of "Lucky" beer was next to Billy. Grabbing a pair of trunks, I headed down to hear about the day's hike.

"You weren't kidding about those grizzly bears," Billy said as I climbed into the bubbling water.

"You see one?" I asked, playing along with his charade.

"See one? We were treed!"

On closer examination, Billy appeared dazed.

"Show him your arm, Mo," he said.

They'd promised Glacier rangers that they would proceed directly to the hospital to get Mo's arm X-rayed. But en route, they figured they'd better alert me, and, while they were at it, why not pick up a case of beer and jump in the hot tub?

Later that night, Mo's arm wrapped tightly in a sling, Billy had the undivided attention of every stool in Moose's Saloon as he recalled the day's chilling events. At one point, he got down on all fours (a brave act in and of itself, given Moose's floor is covered in sawdust to soak up all the tobacco juice) and mimicked the grizzly that terrified them.

Around 4:30 that afternoon they spotted the sow, thirty yards in front of them on the trail near Avalanche Lake. Stopping dead in his tracks, Billy, as I instructed the night before, loudly cleared his throat. Then, rather than singing, he yelled out, "Mo, we got a griz!"

"The two knew they were in danger," reporter Jackie Adams wrote in the *Hungry Horse News,* "because a local friend, John McCaslin, had shown them clippings about the 1981 grizzly death of Laurence Gordon when they arrived."

Dropping their backpacks, Billy and Mo ran for their lives. In seconds, the bear reached their starting point, scooping up their discarded packs and shaking out the contents. Finding nothing worth munching on, "She dropped the pack and started after us," Mo told Adams.

Billy, who'd taken the lead, glanced behind him at one point and was shocked to find that Mo was missing. He was even more shocked to see her standing a considerable distance behind him—literally frozen in fear. With no time to spare, Billy retreated to her side, only to hear the ex-nun say, "Billy, we need to pray."

Preferring to pray in a tree, Billy scanned the horizon for something to climb, but what few trees there were at the high altitude had no low branches. He grabbed Mo's arm, and the two scrambled onto an ice field, hoping the bear didn't wish to get her feet cold. Few things (short of umbrellas) will change the course of a grizzly in pursuit, and ice isn't one of them. So Billy stripped off his bright red shirt and threw it onto the snow, hoping to momentarily distract the bear. It didn't.

Mo, all but exhausted by now, slipped and fell onto the ice, severely jamming her wrist. Billy again came to her aid and, fearing the end was near, tried climbing the closest pine tree. He could get up, she couldn't. Just when the pair's predicament couldn't get any worse, Billy spotted a lone birch tree well off in the distance. Able to get there before the bear, Billy climbed up first, then reached down and pulled up Mo.

From their twenty-foot perch, the petrified couple watched as the grizzly, now circling the trunk of the tree, repeatedly raised her large nostrils into the air and sniffed (bears have extremely poor eyesight), trying to pinpoint the whereabouts of the humans. Then, an amazing thing happened. The wind picked up, and whatever scent the bear detected went with it. After what seemed like an eternity, the bear gave up and disappeared into the woods.

Cold, tired, and beaten, Billy and Mo jumped out of the tree, waded through an ice-cold stream (another of my half-serious suggestions "so the bear can't follow your tracks"), then beat a path through thick brush to rejoin the trail and retrieve their packs. As luck would have it, they encountered a group of five hikers and warned them about the grizzly. Together, all seven retreated at a fast clip. Shortly after word of the treeing reached park headquarters, the Avalanche Lake trail was closed.

The very next morning, a reporter for the *Washington Post* telephoned Bill and Mary Ellen Dwyer at their Virginia home. The scribe had read my UPI account of the near-mauling, which I had dictated from Moose's, and wanted their reaction to their son's narrow escape. (Unfortunately, given we shut down the saloon, Billy hadn't yet broken the news to his parents.)

Hearing over the telephone how frantic his mother was, and realizing how close Billy and Mo came to entering the happy hunting grounds, I never again made light of grizzly bears.

ABOUT THE SAME TIME Billy and Mo pulled safely into Anchorage, Vice President Bush grabbed his fishing pole and headed down a trail on Logan Pass in search of trout. Four heavily armed Secret Service agents tagged along, with an untold number of park rangers hiding behind trees. After catching one fish, which he threw back, Bush returned to Lake McDonald, where his wife Barbara and Wyoming Senator and Mrs. Alan Simpson were setting up camp.

After a hearty Montana supper and lots of laughter around the campfire, the Washington couples retired to their tents and drifted into peaceful slumber. To me, it seemed particularly dark that night, although I normally wasn't in the middle of the woods at such a late hour. I knew better. Then again, the VIP campers had unprecedented protection. Park rangers in green trucks continuously patrolled the outer perimeter of the campsite. Closer in, Secret Service sentries posted themselves in strategic positions, listening all night to strange noises one only hears on camping trips. The closest agent to the "offical" tent sat atop a picnic table, his loaded Uzi submachine gun resting atop a box of condiments. For once, it wasn't two-legged terrorists the agents were worried about confronting.

"Grizzly bears are awkward to deal with politically," George could have told them, "because they are higher up on the food chain than we are."

Chapter 3

Historic Datelines

ROBERT E. LEE grew up in Alexandria, and so did my closest childhood friend, Brendan O'Leary. The latter was born with so much reporters' ink in his blood he didn't want any more and went into sales. His great uncle, Mike Flynn, was editor of the old *Washington Times-Herald*. His second cousin, William McAndrew, was president of NBC News. His grandfather, Jeremiah Aloysius O'Leary Sr., covered Congress for the *Washington Star*. His father, Jeremiah Aloysius O'Leary Jr., was State Department and White House correspondent for the old *Washington Star* and the *Washington Times*. I first knew him as Santa Claus.

Jeremiah Sr. was fifteen when he began his newspaper career, spending an impressive forty-five years in the House and Senate press galleries, gazing down on the likes of great statesmen named Sam Rayburn and Russell B. Long.

Jeremiah Jr. launched his own incredible journey at 6:30 one morning, filling every paste pot in the *Star* newsroom. The salary for a "copy boy" in 1937 was ten dollars for a six-day week (the highest-paid reporters during the Depression were getting seventy-five a week), and Jerry considered himself the luckiest kid in the world.

Like his father, Jerry climbed the ladder to cover some of the biggest historical events of his lifetime. When his country called during World War II and Korea, he was a Marine rifleman and battlefield correspondent, earning four Battle Stars, a Bronze Star, and a Purple Heart. Foremost, though, he was a newspaperman. And few could write a story like Jerry.

"One of my greatest assignments came when I was still a teenager," he recalled in 1987, his fiftieth year in the trade. "The job was to help two older reporters cover the seventy-fifth anniversary observance of the Battle of Gettysburg in that small Pennsylvania town where so many Americans died at the high tide of the Confederacy.

"More than six thousand veterans of both the Blue and the Gray, all in their nineties or older, came to the old battlefield for their last muster. I was put to interviewing scores of the old-timers. It has occurred to me since that my lifetime has overlapped the lives of men whose grandfathers fought in the American Revolution."

If he'd ever run out of story ideas, which he never did, Jerry could have written about his own life. As a young scribe he danced the Big Apple with Eleanor Roosevelt at the White House; when Prohibition ended in 1933 he sipped the first legal beer in Washington ("President Roosevelt gave a case of Yuengling to the White House press corps, which was then about the size of a Marine rifle squad," he wrote); he was arrested in Cuba by Fidel Castro's thugs; played dangerous tricks on Papa Doc's Tonton Macoute killers in Haiti; and he was besieged by angry rednecks at the University of Mississippi during the desegregation riots of 1962.

On another unforgettable day, Jerry was standing a dozen steps away when Jack Ruby forever silenced Lee Harvey Oswald.

"I was not free just to mourn quietly, or scream with rage," he'd written of the assassination of John F. Kennedy, the first Irish-Catholic to assume the Oval Office. "It was my job to rush to Dallas, and for the next ten days I became as intimately acquainted as a reporter could be with Oswald, Ruby, Dallas Police Chief Jesse Curry, homicide squad Captain Will Fritz, a small army of FBI and CIA agents, the families of Oswald and Ruby, and a cast of characters who knew them both.

"For half an hour I found myself with custody of the Mannlicher

Carcano rifle used by ex-Marine Oswald to blow off the back of President Kennedy's head. And it came to pass that I acted as a pallbearer for Oswald because only his mother, his brother, and a handful of reporters turned out for the burial of the sullen loser who murdered President Kennedy for reasons he took with him to the grave."

THANKS ENTIRELY TO JERRY, I segued from Whitefish to the White House, the widest, most undeserved leap in modern journalism. Better yet, I was back home along the cobblestone streets of "Old Town" Alexandria, its eighteenth century blocks sketched square by a young surveyor named George Washington.

Five years later, in 1754, the father of our country recruited his first military command on the steps of Alexandria's Gadsby's Tavern, and held his final military review there in 1799. He kept a townhouse one block from the tavern, so whenever he made last call he didn't have to gallop the dozen miles home and answer to Martha at Mount Vernon.

Never losing its fighting spirit, Alexandria was the first "Southern" city to fall during the Civil War. Early on the morning of May 24, 1861, Colonel Elmer E. Ellsworth, a friend of Abraham Lincoln's, rowed boatloads of blue bellies across the Potomac River, marched them up King Street, and ordered Marshall House innkeeper James W. Jackson to lower the extra large Confederate flag flying atop his hotel.

Lincoln's wife, or so the story is told, complained to her husband that she could see the large rebel banner from her White House window. Republican Senator Benjamin F. Wade of Ohio told the *New York Herald* that he, too, spied the huge flag through a White House looking glass. The senator told Lincoln that such a display should not be tolerated, and the president reportedly replied, "I don't think it will wave there too long."

Still clad in his nightshirt, the sleepy-eyed Jackson grabbed his rifle when told Ellsworth had burst through the hotel lobby and climbed onto the roof to haul in the flag. Ellsworth got the banner he was after, along with a bellyful of shot on his way down. And so began the Civil War. Ellsworth was the first Yankee casualty, the innkeeper the first secessionist to die—duly shot in the nose by Sergeant Francis Brownell, then repeatedly bayoneted by the 11th New York Fire Zouaves.

In fact, the gaily-dressed Zouaves, sporting white gloves, white leggings, baggy trousers, jackets with red trim, and French-style red forage caps, were so unaccustomed to drawing blood they had difficulty withdrawing their saw-toothed bayonets from Jackson's warm body. The innkeeper's young daughter, who stepped out of her bedroom to investigate the commotion, ran back and told her mother, "Father is on the floor outside with broomsticks sticking out all over him!"

JERRY LIVED FOR MUCH OF HIS NEWSPAPER CAREER in an old brick house on the same block where the innkeeper was speared. I grew up around the corner. I have numerous memories of Jerry as a State Department correspondent, circling the globe with Secretary of State Henry A. Kissinger. Upon his return, Brendan and I would pick him up at Andrews Air Force Base and, whether asking for it or not, get briefed on foreign affairs during the ride home. We knew about Richard Nixon's inroads with the Chinese before senior White House officials read about it in the newspaper. And what White House Counsel John Dean, another one of our neighbors, didn't tell us about Watergate, Jerry did.

One of my favorite stories surrounded a junket Jerry didn't take with Kissinger. A colonel in the Marine Corps Reserves during the Vietnam War (White House officials and reporters often addressed Jerry by his rank, "Colonel"), he happened to have weekend duty at Andrews on the same day Kissinger flew back into Washington. Dressed in full military uniform, Jerry greeted the perplexed Kissinger at the bottom steps of his airplane, declaring with the straightest face he could muster, "The coup was successful, and I am in charge here!"

"Over these years," Jerry wrote in his farewell column, "I have known presidents and paupers, bartenders and cops, murderers, dictators, assassins, Hollywood stars, and hundreds of newspaper people, who have always fascinated me."

His final years in the newspaper field were spent at the White House, covering Presidents Carter, Reagan, and Bush. Before the latter president rode down Pennsylvania Avenue into the sunset, he and Jerry threw horseshoes together on the south lawn. He lived long enough to see Bill Clinton strut into town and considered himself lucky that he didn't have to cover him.

During Reagan's trip to Montana in 1983, Jerry told me two things: one, my mother wished I would come home; and two, covering the White House "is no different than covering the Kalispell City Hall. In fact, it's easier because every word the president utters is transcribed for you. You don't have to take so many notes." That is, unless it's April 2, 1984, and you're standing next to the pitcher's mound as President Reagan throws the season-opening pitch to Baltimore Orioles catcher Rick Dempsey. (I actually observed that Reagan was standing several feet in front of the mound.)

It turned out to be an historic day, I'd write in my White House "pool" report. Reagan, seated on the bench next to Hall of Famers like Cal Ripken Jr., Eddie Murray, and Jim Palmer, made baseball history by becoming the first president to watch a major league game from a dugout. (In 1988, the Gipper broadcast an inning and a half of baseball, becoming the first president to call play-by-play while in office.)

I lost count of how many states Reagan had stumped in during his 1984 reelection campaign, but I was fortunate at the young age of twenty-six to accompany him to many. The aging "colonel," as I too was now calling my lifelong friend, said he needed the rest. I knew better, as did the senior editors at my newspaper. Jerry was handing me the opportunity of a lifetime.

Actually, were it not for Geraldine Ferraro, the widely popular Reagan could have accomplished his reelection campaign from the Oval Office. But it was the first time in history that a woman graced a U.S. presidential ticket, and the president's strategists figured the New York congresswoman gave running mate Walter Mondale at least a glimmer of hope.

In the end, the guy-gal ballot captured only the District of Columbia and one state—Mondale's Minnesota. On the Electoral College scoreboard, it was Reagan-Bush 525 to Mondale-Ferraro's 13. By every definition, a slaughter.

Before my apprenticeship under the colonel drew to a close, he saw to it that I was introduced to every major player in town who wasn't sitting in the Orioles dugout on opening day. I used to do double-takes whenever Marine Lieutenant Colonel Oliver North and Jerry saluted each other in the bowels of the West Wing. But mostly my eyes were glued to Fawn Hall, North's soon-to-be infamous secretary. Had I paid less attention to her and more to what was on her desk, I might have caught the first glimpse of the Iran-Contra affair.

My biggest thrill was covering Reagan on "pool" assignments, when select reporters accompanied the president to more intimate affairs. One Saturday morning, White House press secretary Larry Speakes hurriedly phoned me at home and asked if I might be able to accompany the Reagans on a hastily arranged trip. For security reasons, he couldn't say where, only that "it's a beautiful day and Nancy wants to get out of the White House."

I remember UPI reporter Ira Allen and me peering out of the window of the Marine helicopter trying to learn our destination. Finally, I spotted Thomas Jefferson's Monticello—tucked beautifully into the green hills of Charlottesville, Virginia (as well as the tails side of nickels). Seconds later, we touched down on the estate's sweeping lawn.

Monticello's curator, his wife, and daughter were the only ones on hand to greet the presidential party and offered to provide the Reagans with a private tour of the mansion and its grounds. But the president, perhaps because it was an election year, insisted on joining a tour in progress. I'll never forget the expression on the face of an African-American gentleman, clad in a red-white-and-blue jogging outfit, when the larger-than-life Reagan burst through Monticello's French doors.

"Where the hell did you come from?" the man exclaimed, totally surprised.

I LEFT THE WHITE HOUSE the same day as Reagan's trusted counselor Edwin Meese III, both of us bound for the Justice Department—he to replace William French Smith as attorney general, me to return to reality.

Ironically, just as I found myself reporting from the same Montana sheriff's office where Grand Si was deputy decades before, I now was walking the same corridors my father did for nearly four decades as a G-man under J. Edgar Hoover. Days into my new beat, I purposely requested an interview with William Bradford Reynolds, assistant attorney general for civil rights, so I could see Hoover's office again.

When I visited the same office as a boy, I remember J. Edgar asking me if I'd let him have my red-and-green-plaid sports jacket. He explained he'd always wanted one like it, but in reality Hoover never allowed his agents to wear anything more colorful than gray.

My father grew up on a farm on "Norway Ridge," the New York-Pennsylvania state line practically slicing through the dairy barn where his father, Herbert McCaslin, milked fourteen cows in a row. Dad's mother, the former Elizabeth Walsh, was principal of a school for the blind when she met my grandfather and became a farmer's wife. When my grandparents lost their first child to "the plague" before the start of World War I, the local undertaker refused to handle the burial. So a neighbor farmer, his own son deathly ill, stepped in to dig the grave, and when that neighbor's boy died, my grandfather grabbed his shovel and returned the favor.

In 1941, at age twenty-three, my father reported to FBI headquarters in Washington. He didn't own a car, so he hitched a ride south. He was already an expert shot, so the FBI taught him how to properly conceal his government-issued .45 caliber pistol, then promptly posted him in Little Rock, Arkansas, a state he couldn't even pronounce.

No sooner did he cross the "Ar-Kansas" line than the Japanese let loose on Pearl Harbor. Dad was immediately ordered to find every Japanese American living in the poor state, and fortunately there weren't many. One concerned farmer tipped-off the FBI that a Japanese "houseboy" was working on a prominent family's rice plantation. Dad drove practically to the Mississippi River and told me he ended up "liking the little fellow." (Fortunately my father wasn't tracking Ma Barker, because throughout his life he's always found something good in everybody). He returned to Little Rock without the Japanese servant, but only after the plantation owner promised to take the law into his own hands if he ever caught wind of any espionage.

My father impressed his boss enough that he was soon transferred to New York City, where the FBI had him living undercover in a rooming house operated by a German couple suspected of espionage. Dad pretended to be a newspaper hawker at the Brooklyn Navy Yard, but rather than peddling papers, he'd go straight to the FBI office where he worked on other counterespionage. In the evening he'd return home to the boarding house, where the German fellow always had a croquet mallet waiting for him. Dad ended up liking the German, too, and wrote in his final report that the only spying he ever saw the man undertake was on his wife.

While Dad was still in New York, a genuine southern belle he dated from the tiny Arkansas town of Cotton Plant came north for a visit. The two were on a bus tour of the city when the driver pulled up to the tomb of Ulysses S. Grant. In a sweet accent that would melt any red-blooded northerner, the woman politely asked if she might step off the bus for a moment. As my father and the other passengers watched in disbelief, she then marched to Grant's tomb and spit on his grave.

Dad said he knew there and then that she would never be my mother.

Two agents Dad worked closely with during the thirty-seven years he spent with the FBI were former FBI assistant director Ray Wannall, who headed the bureau's intelligence division, and Hoover's top aide, Cartha "Deke" DeLoach, godfather to my younger brother Mark. All three agents greatly admired Hoover and have defended his spirit in their retirement.

In 2001, Wannall published *The Real J. Edgar Hoover: For the Record*, which he invited me to review. In the book, Wannall complained that Hoover has been "vilified and misrepresented" ever since his death—baseless allegations ranging from racism to homosexuality.

While nobody has ever proven that Hoover was a closet gay, his body-guard and chauffeur, FBI agent James E. Crawford, countered in Wannall's book of the racism charges: "I'm so tired of people saying that Mr. Hoover discriminates against the blacks. When we would stop for dinner at a restaurant, Mr. Hoover was frequently told they would not serve me. . . . He would say, 'We won't eat here, either,' and he and whoever was with him would leave and eat at a place that would serve all of us."

"For a man of his time," DeLoach added in his own book, Hoover "was remarkably free of such prejudices."

The No. 3 man in the bureau during the tumultuous 1960s, DeLoach was outranked only by Hoover's deputy, Clyde Tolson. In his narrative, *Hoover's FBI*, DeLoach shed more light on the assassinations of John F. Kennedy and Martin Luther King, organized crime and communism, even Hoover's disputed sexual preferences. But my favorite passage is when DeLoach discloses how Hoover managed to remain in office for so long.

"In January of 1965, he would turn seventy, the mandatory retirement age for civil servants," DeLoach pointed out. "The very idea of retirement terrified him."

So DeLoach himself was dispatched to the Oval Office to try and persuade President Lyndon B. Johnson to waive the government's mandatory retirement age, easily accomplished with a mere stroke of his pen.

"After I'd finished, Johnson shook his head. 'Do you realize what you're asking me to do?' I told him I thought I did. 'I don't think you do. If I waive mandatory retirement, Edgar will stay in there until he dies.'

"'I want you to give the old man what he wants,' I said finally.

"Johnson shook his head and sighed. 'All right,' he said. 'I suppose I'd rather have the old bastard inside the tent pissing out, than outside the tent pissing in. Go into the next office and dictate to Mildred what you want me to say in an executive order.'"

Hoover remained in office until the day he died.

THE TOP EDITOR AT MY NEWSPAPER the day I took over the Justice Department beat was Arnaud de Borchgrave, a correspondent of nineteen wars, including the two most recent conflicts where he was dug-in on the south sides of Baghdad and Tora Bora.

Arnaud was Paris bureau chief for *Newsweek* for twenty-three years and during that time was impressed with another promising young reporter named Ben Bradlee, who he would recommend becoming *Newsweek's* European correspondent. The rest is history. Some believe Arnaud accepted the top position at the *Washington Times* so he could go head-to-head with Bradlee and the *Washington Post* one last time.

Besides being a battlefield correspondent for much of his life, Arnaud fought in World War II. In fact, he never stopped tracking Nazis after the war ended. Even as late as 1985 there wasn't a week that went by that Arnaud didn't ask me for a progress report on the notorious Josef Mengele, Auschwitz's "Angel of Death."

The Justice Department's Office of Special Investigations, led by chief Nazi hunter Neal Sher, undertook the U.S. government's role in uprooting aging Nazis from America's cities and farms, where they'd been living otherwise normal lives. Sher personally supervised the denaturalization and deportation of dozens of such war criminals, while also helping to uncover the Nazi past of Austrian President Kurt Waldheim.

It was Mengele, though, that consumed Arnaud. And every time he'd ask in his Belgian accent for a progress report I'd have to pick up the phone and call Sher. And every time, Sher, granted I got past his secretary, would give me the same terse reply: "If there was something to report—and believe me, there isn't—it would have to come through the Justice Department press office, not me."

But Arnaud was relentless, which boggled my mind. I constantly reminded myself that it had been forty years since the mad doctor had vanished. What were the odds that he would be found so many years later? Yet Arnaud, who keeps a separate Rolodex for every country in the world, smelled a rat. And it was Mengele.

On May 31, 1985, acting on a tip that for all I knew came from the editor himself, West German police raided the home of Hans Sedlmeier, who was rumored to have kept in touch with Mengele well after the war's end. Searching the man's personal belongings, police found several letters from a person they suspected might be Mengele. They were postmarked "Brazil."

Several days later, my telephone rang.

"Do you like Chinese food?"

I couldn't believe my ears. And I didn't dare tell Neal Sher that I was allergic to MSG.

We met at a crowded restaurant on K Street in Washington, and for most of an hour we chatted about newspapers. He explained that his son was vaguely interested in journalism, and he appreciated the opportunity to hear firsthand about the life of a newspaperman. I answered every question, and then the check came.

As Sher read his fortune cookie, I finally got the nerve to say, "Look, I can't go back to the newsroom and face Arnaud without something on Mengele. At least tell me what continent you think he's on."

The OSI director smiled and let me turn on my tape recorder.

"The trail's gotten hot," were his exact words, which became the lead of my story. No sooner did the newspaper hit the streets the next morning, however, than UPI saw fit to send a story across the wires saying "contrary" to what had been reported in the *Washington Times*, "the trail for Mengele is cold."

I was furious—both at UPI and at Sher, who obviously didn't confirm to the wire reporter what he'd told me. The late Woody West, one of my senior editors who hailed from Montana, stopped by my desk and told me to keep my chin up. Days like this go with the territory, he said. No sooner did Woody walk away than an "URGENT" bulletin crossed the wire. It was datelined Sao Paulo, Brazil, where authorities had unearthed human remains thought to be Mengele's but buried in a grave marked "Wolfgang Gerhard."

"Bring me Mengele!" Arnaud roared.

"But I'm getting married on Saturday," I reminded him.

"So, come back on Friday."

Instead of driving to my bachelor party, I was flying to Brazil—on the same plane, ironically, as Sher, who was ignoring me again. Still, I owed him big time.

I'd never seen so many skyscrapers and stumbled amidst such confusion as I did in Sao Paolo, all of it written and spoken in Portuguese. Hyperventilation setting in, I glanced out the window of my taxi only to experience one of those freak coincidences. There was Timothy O'Leary, eldest and tallest son of Jerry, his head sticking out above everybody else's on a pedestrian-choked sidewalk. Unlike his brother Brendan, Tim followed his family roots into the Fourth Estate (today, he's an award-winning editorial writer for the *Dallas Morning News)*, and was I ever glad to see him.

Based in Buenos Aires, Tim had been on assignment in Paraguay and got wind of the potential Mengele discovery. He'd just checked into his hotel, several miles away from mine, then stepped outside to hail a cab. Seconds later he was telling my driver in Portuguese where we needed to go, and the three of us sped off to the coastal region of Embu.

What remains remained of Mengele—assorted small bones and tattered cloth—that authorities hadn't shoveled into plastic bags and carted off for testing were thrown into a plastic tub and left there. Were they the "leftovers" of anybody else, it would have been sacrilege. I still have a photograph of a jubilant Brazilian police investigator, Jose Antonio de Mello, hoisting Mengele's hairy skull into the air as if he were peddling coconuts.

Locals told us that the mystery man buried in Gerhard's grave suffered a stroke six years earlier while swimming in the ocean. I'm not sure what compelled me to do what I did next while standing there eyeing the discarded remains (later positively identified as Mengele), but I never saw reason to acknowledge it publicly until sixteen years later.

"What is it about roving reporters and the bizarre souvenirs they snatch?" I wrote in my December 3, 2001, column. "British scribe Richard Lloyd Parry, of the *Independent,* strolled into the bathroom of Osama bin Laden's abandoned compound in Afghanistan and grabbed from the hook the terrorist leader's striped gray and black cotton boxers, with a label reading Angelo Petrico, size XXL.

"Explained Mr. Parry: 'How many can claim to own the underwear of the world's most dangerous man?'

"Meanwhile, Matt Labash, senior writer for the *Weekly Standard* in Washington, acquired his unusual souvenir while on assignment in Florida, where he happened by the Palm Beach Flight Training center where terrorist Mohamad Atta rented planes to practice up for his flight into the World Trade Center. Mr. Labash not only slid into the cockpit of Atta's rental, he retrieved with the flight center's permission Atta's laminated flight-safety checklist. 'I had never understood the murderabilia market until that moment,' Labash said. 'Why would anyone want the clown paintings of John Wayne Gacy or the nail clippings of serial killer Roy Norris?'

"Perhaps," I opined, "for the same reason someone would want the remains of Nazi war criminal Dr. Joseph Mengele."

"WHAT IS THIS?" asked Arnaud, rubbing the contents of the film canister between his fingers. Other top editors of the newspaper, gathered around the conference table for the Friday afternoon news meeting, looked on with curiosity.

"It looks like hashish," Arnaud said.

"It's Mengele," I winked. "You wanted him, I brought him to you."

Chapter 4

Byrd's-Eye View

DUST HUNG LOW in the autumn evening air as a steady stream of cars bounced along a dirt road outside Centralhatchee, on Georgia's border with Alabama. Where the dust ended, a teenage boy clad in camouflage pointed every vehicle but ours to a field. Peering through the window of our rental car, two angular men, cigarettes dangling below their unshaven chins, weren't sure what to make of the unexpected visitors.

"Where're you boys from?" one of the men inquired.

"Virginia," I replied, sounding every bit the boy from Dixie.

"Virginia?"

"Fredericksburg klavern," I lied.

"You boys are a long way from home. We're gonna have to take a look in the back."

Trying not to resemble the Annapolis yuppie that he was, Kevin Gilbert eyed me nervously. His loaded camera bag was in the trunk with the rest of our luggage.

We'd covered dozens of stories together, the photographer and I, standing in the White House Rose Garden and on the sidelines of the Super Bowl.

Through his assorted lenses, Kevin captured award-winning expressions of U.S. presidents and Third-World dictators, sports heroes and famished children. He even snapped my wedding pictures at St. Mary's Church and handed me the rolls of film as his gift. But this was the first assignment we ever approached undercover.

"I like your hat," one of the men came back to say, not finding anything that concerned him in the trunk.

I picked up the bright red cap, emblazoned with the Confederate flag, only an hour before at a Centralhatchee bar and bait shop. It was there, over several bottles of beer, that Kevin and I mapped out our plan of infiltration. When we were ready to roll, he stashed his purple watchband in his pocket, then debated whether to lose his Docksiders. And in case I didn't hear him the first time, he reminded me he'd just become a father.

"Pull up yonder and park," said the boy, who couldn't have been more than fourteen.

The festivities wouldn't begin for another hour, but the aura of a church social was already taking hold of the men, women, and children gathered at the secluded farmhouse. It promised to be unlike other Ku Klux Klan rallies in these parts. This time attendees were told in writing that their identities would be kept secret. To make certain, several hooded figures were posted at strategic locations around the farm's perimeter.

On the front porch of the two-story yellow frame house, a young man and his girlfriend swayed in a swing. In a more peaceful place and time they might have passed for Andy Taylor and Helen Crump, except the law-abiding Hollywood sheriff wouldn't be caught dead at this segregated social (then again, black folks didn't show their faces in Mayberry, either).

Other men sat uncomfortably in straight-back chairs scattered around conversations on the front lawn. Their wives and daughters, meanwhile, crowded around a large table carried from the kitchen, unsealing plastic containers of fried chicken and deviled eggs while spreading the latest gossip of Heard County.

Soon, a Cadillac sedan pulled up driven by a gentleman who looked like he could be a banker or country lawyer. On the floor of his car were two half-gallon jars of iced tea, which he handed through the window to his wife. Next to the tea was a two-gallon can of gasoline. From the back seat, a young boy tugged on the man's cuff-linked sleeve.

"When are the fireworks going to start, Daddy?"

"Fireworks are later, son. Fireworks are later."

Editors made that the headline of my story.

The invitation to the local rally touted "nationally known" Klan leaders, souvenirs, and refreshments: "Come one, come all—bring family, children, and friends. White public only invited. News media barred from this event."

Off to the side of the house in a hayfield, a dozen men and a tractor soon raised a large wooden cross, draped in gasoline-soaked burlap. As they stood admiring the risen crucifix, a large sedan pulled into the meadow, and four neatly dressed men climbed out. One clutched a briefcase, as if he'd come to sell crop insurance.

Ed Stephens was grand dragon of Georgia's Invisible Empire, Knights of the Ku Klux Klan, considered by the U.S. Justice Department to be one of the most violence-prone racist groups in the country. On his heels was Imperial Wizard Jim Blair, dressed totally in black.

An Alabama auto mechanic and the highest-ranking Klansman in the Invisible Empire, Blair had spoken with me by telephone only two days before while I was in Montgomery interviewing an official with the Southern Poverty Law Center. During our conversation, the wizard mentioned he'd be attending a Klan rally that very week outside Centralhatchee. I don't think he ever expected me to show up, particularly with a photographer in tow, but he didn't say not to. As quickly as I hung up, I called Kevin, who flew into Atlanta the next afternoon.

While publicity in previous years aided the Klan, mainly helping to attract new recruits, it also brought organized opposition and increased prosecution. To its credit, the Reagan administration during its first term handed down more Klan-related indictments than any previous administration. Pretty impressive, considering the Klan had been around well over one hundred years.

As a result of the negative publicity, amendments to the Invisible Empire's constitution and bylaws now forbade news agencies access to "private" cross-burnings like this one.

Blair's arrival signaled the official start of the rally, and given the "fireworks" were about to begin, Kevin and I figured we'd better introduce ourselves. Blair, it turns out, couldn't have been more polite. He firmly shook our hands, huddled with his fellow leaders, then came back to say we could stay—"to send our message to Washington."

Then he asked, "Where'd you get your hat?"

We grabbed our notebooks and cameras from the car, with the instructions we were not to identify or photograph anybody who resisted.

"We feel real good about the people who've joined up in the last year," Stephens told me. "Our new membership includes county commissioners and judges, who've given us the punch we need in politics. But we won't disclose their identities. Only Jim Blair knows who the highly secretive ones are."

Blair concurred: "We need 'secret' members as much as we need 'open' members."

During the 1980s, the Klan was beginning to follow the path of other militant white supremacist groups—taking some of its membership underground. This new period of secrecy was called the "Fifth Era." Blacks and Jews, at the same time, were no longer the favorite targets of this hardcore, frustrated breed of Klansmen. The new enemy was the "system," or federal government.

"The Fifth Era of the Klan is supposed to go back underground, return to its highly secretive ways of the post-Civil War period—in essence a return to being the terrorist group that it was when it was founded," Bill Stanton, of the SPLC, had told me in Montgomery.

That same summer, an official with the Bureau of Alcohol, Tobacco, and Firearms warned a meeting of the National Sheriff's Association in Dallas: "Ladies and gentlemen, fellow law enforcement officers, you have become a prime target of the white supremacists. They are surveilling you at work;

they are observing your activities at home; and if it serves their purpose or you become a threat, they have made plans to kill you."

Sure enough, only a few weeks later, a federal grand jury in Raleigh, North Carolina (a Klan-heavy state where Kevin and I headed to next), indicted five KKK members on charges of conspiring to steal U.S. military explosives and weapons, including rockets.

The SPLC first began monitoring hate activity in 1981, responding to a "resurgence" of the Klan. Today, the center's Intelligence Project tracks the activities of more than six hundred racist and neo-Nazi groups and dozens of militias and other extremist antigovernment groups in the United States. Just six months before the Oklahoma City bombing, the SPLC warned Attorney General Janet Reno "that the new mixture of armed militia groups and those who hate was a recipe for disaster."

Little did Reno know the recipe would soon boil over.

There were very few, if any, "extreme" Klansmen at the Centralhatchee rally, as far as Kevin and I could tell. There was no talk of declaring war on Uncle Sam or the "system."

Instead, these otherwise ordinary country folk were content in calling for a return to Jim Crow segregation. One overfed girl who looked to be about thirteen grabbed the microphone being passed around the cross and complained that she was forced to share a school locker "with this nigger girl." To help right the wrong, she implored the crowd to "help bring prayer back to the classroom."

"Amen," replied a middle-aged woman, asking God to "uplift the white race by blessing our Sunday school teachers and public officials."

I couldn't believe the twisted logic I was writing down.

When it came time for the grand dragon to speak, he ranted against men with earrings and women with tattoos.

"American citizens have lost their masculinity," Stephens scolded. "I'm not telling you to hate, I'm telling you to hate God's enemies."

And with those words, the cross was lit.

WHEN WEST VIRGINIA SENATOR Robert C. Byrd was asked on national television to describe the kind of person who would attend a KKK rally, the onetime powerful majority leader replied in two words: "white niggers."

For those who didn't hear him the first time, he repeated himself.

The most senior of all Democrats on Capitol Hill, Byrd later apologized for his poor choice of words. And he was forgiven, just as he was decades earlier when it became known that in his previous life Byrd was a "Kleagle"—an official recruiter of the KKK.

Byrd reportedly pocketed ten bucks for every racist he robed. He explained that he joined the Klan in the 1940s because the white-sheeted ghosts breathed excitement, promoted traditional values, and protected America from communism.

Then again, any God-fearing, law-abiding man like Byrd who has demonstrated a change of heart and apologized for his past should be forgiven, right? That's the American way. And Byrd certainly was forgiven— enough to outlast ten presidents during his Capitol Hill watch.

But the pardoned, unfortunately, didn't go out of his way to remind other Democrats about forgiveness when they led the 2002 leadership coup against Senate Majority Leader Trent Lott of Mississippi. One would have thought it was Lott, not Byrd, who once hid beneath a hood.

Instead, Lott's crime consisted of inserting his racially insensitive foot into his mouth while singing "Happy 100th Birthday" to Senator Strom Thurmond (yet another lawmaker forgiven for his segregationist rhetoric of the past). Yet the Republican Lott, who apologized beyond sufficiently, couldn't be forgiven, and for one primary reason: politics.

From what I've gathered of the two leaders, and I've written about both extensively, Lott and Byrd don't have a racist bone between them. In fact, I've probably penned more paragraphs about Byrd than any other senator in my own two decades covering Capitol Hill. Several things impress me about the West Virginian.

For starters, he never leaves home without a copy of the Constitution in his pocket. Without question he is Congress's foremost authority on the rule of law and government. And when given the floor of the Senate he becomes a talking history book.

Laying the groundwork for often rancorous debate, Byrd somehow bolsters his position by meshing the lives of his longsuffering constituents in the "hills and hollows" of West Virginia with ancient Roman scholars and a cast of other characters he resurrects. It doesn't matter that the Romans never heard of Medicare or George W. Bush. "Desultory ramblings," I call them.

Like the day he warned Republicans how history would remember advocates of House Speaker Newt Gingrich's "Contract With America."

"I am reminded of Croesus, who was defeated by Cyrus the Great in the battle of Thymbra in 546 B.C.," he exclaimed.

Byrd once explained of his incredible grasp of history: "Lots of people jog, they jog to build their bodies, keep their muscles in good tone, and strengthen their limbs. I jog my memory, jog my mind, read as much as I can. If one doesn't retain what he reads, it is a considerable waste of time. Through self-discipline, I try to remember certain salient things that I read. I'm selective in my reading, don't read novels, although there are some great novels. I read mostly history and great literature."

Thus, there's no trepidation when pronouncing long-forgotten names like Polybius, Diodorus, Dionysius of Halicarnassus, Cornelius Neopos, Gaius Sallustius Crispus, and Titus Livius. These "blood brothers" of the silver-haired Byrd would never have embraced Gingrich's contract. In fact, Byrd wondered why Republicans were in such a hurry to pass the unproven contract. "Eternity," after all, was on their side.

"Would senators like to know how long eternity is?" he asked. Nobody raised any hands, but I knew to grab my notebook.

"I take this handkerchief in my hand," Byrd said, retrieving the prop from his pocket. "Let us suppose that a bird flew over Mount Everest once a minute, drawing this handkerchief across Mount Everest just as I am drawing it across this microphone, and that the bird could live forever.

"When Mount Everest had been worn down to a level with the sands of the sea—by the bird dragging the handkerchief across the top of Mount Everest—eternity would have just begun."

Once, Byrd uncovered a gigantic loophole in a Republican balanced-budget amendment—so large that it was "big enough for Attila, the king of the Huns and the scourge of God, to drive his seven hundred Scythian horsemen through."

And pity the congressional page not up to snuff on his or her American history.

"I often ask the young pages who serve us, 'Who is Nathan Hale?' If an American history book does not tell us about Nathan Hale, I do not think it is much of a history book," Byrd will say.

Sometimes, the Senate leader will ask pages to show him their history books, so he can make certain Hale (for those who don't remember, Captain Hale gave his life while spying on the British during the Revolutionary War) earned his rightful chapter. If a book doesn't teach about Hale, Byrd does:

"Nathan Hale said: 'I only regret that I have but one life to lose for my country.'"

Byrd began his schooling eighty-two years ago, and Hale was among his first heroes, along with Francis Marion (the "Swamp Fox"), Nathanael Greene, Daniel Morgan, George Washington, Benjamin Franklin, and James Madison.

"I will never forget those [history] books," Byrd says. "They shaped me. They shaped my attitude. They shaped my outlook."

What Byrd chooses to remember of his own life is equally amazing. The day he celebrated his fiftieth anniversary of filing for political office he recalled paying a ten-dollar filing fee and getting handed "receipt No. 5333."

Byrd obviously knows his numbers. Once, New Hampshire Republican Senator Robert C. Smith dared argue that no president had ever submitted a balanced budget to Congress. The West Virginian immediately rose to his feet and with incontrovertible certainty countered that President Jimmy Carter not only submitted a balanced budget, he could remember what room he was in and what he was eating for lunch the day the budget arrived on Capitol Hill.

"I sat over in Room 211 on a weekend," Byrd told the astonished Smith.

"Brought my little paper bag with some coal miner's steaks—slices of bologna."

Byrd rightfully gets summoned on stage when the topic turns to term limits. He was, after all, elected to the House of Representatives in 1953 and the Senate in 1958. (Byrd cast his historic 17,000th vote in the Senate on April 1, 2004.) Once, when the body fell two votes short of forcing a vote on a constitutional amendment to limit terms like his to twelve years, the elder statesman asked:

"For to whom is the inexperienced legislator to look for guidance if all of his colleagues are inexperienced? Moses would not have led the Israelites from Egypt through the wilderness to bring them to view the Promised Land—he led them for forty years [I did some quick math and realized that forty years was the exact span of time Byrd had led his West Virginians]—if there had been a limit on service. He would have been out a long time ago."

Byrd isn't the first lawmaker to hog his seat. Senator Byron Dorgan of North Dakota recalled the day he first set foot in the Capitol Hill office of Claude Pepper, the oldest member of Congress when he died in 1989 at the age of 88. On Pepper's wall, Dorgan said, "I saw something I have not forgotten."

Behind Pepper's desk "was an autographed picture of Orville and Wilbur Wright making the first airplane flight. And it was autographed, 'To Congressman Claude Pepper,' by Orville Wright. Then, hanging just above that was a picture of Neil Armstrong setting his foot on the moon, autographed, 'To Congressman Claude Pepper.'"

I got a kick out of eighty-year-old Tennessee Congressman James H. Quillen when he explained why he wasn't seeking an eighteenth term in office. "Leaving is a sad day for me, but thirty-four years is long enough," Quillen said. "My career in the House has convinced me that term limits are appropriate, and I think seventeen terms should be the limit."

Above everything else, Byrd over the years has been criticized for bringing home to his constituents more than their fair share of bacon. And for that he feels no shame.

"I have no apologies to make for serving my people," he says. "I know who sends me here. I grew up in West Virginia when we had only four miles of divided four-lane highway in the whole state. This money, so-called 'pork,' doesn't go overseas. It goes to help people in West Virginia—their schools, their highways on which to get to work. And those highways I helped to build with that kind of 'pork' have saved a lot of lives."

Byrd, few people know, was in a head-on collision on West Virginia State Road 2 in which the driver of the other car was killed.

"I know West Virginia," he says, "and what is one man's pork is another man's job."

Wrapping up thirty minutes of floor debate, Republican Senator James M. Inhofe announced, "I am going back to Oklahoma, where real people are." He dared suggest that Byrd "take a trip back to West Virginia," to hear what his folks have to say.

The Democrat's cheeks turned fire-red.

"May I say to my friend, he does not need to instruct me about going to West Virginia," Byrd shot back. "When I came here, I was a little wet behind the ears, too, but I have never said to a senator you ought to go back to your own state and see what the people think. Leave me and my fellow West Virginians to ourselves."

And most senators do.

Chapter 5

Bubba and Sundance

THE *Arkansas Democrat-Gazette,* the newspaper of record in Bill Clinton's home state, opined before Election Day 1992 that President George H.W. Bush had been "less than successful," H. Ross Perot was a "strange man," and Clinton was "a master politician, but what principles, if any, inform his politics?"

To make a long "non-endorsement" short, the Little Rock editors said they could not recommend their locally-grown governor for the nation's highest shelf.

"There is something almost inhuman in his smoother responses that sends a shiver up the spine," they wrote. "It is not the compromises he has made that trouble so much as the unavoidable suspicion that he has no great principles to compromise."

An honest assessment—and fair enough warning—to the American public from the people who knew Clinton best.

But the star-struck Washington press corps, which all but spit-shined the candidate's shoes at every campaign stop, ignored the hometown paper. They had no choice, having already heralded the sweet-talking Arkansas governor as the Second Coming. It was too late to publish disclaimers now.

In a subsequent lead editorial shortly before Clinton assumed his coveted throne, the Arkansas newspaper considered it its final duty to rebuke one of the nation's most prestigious newspapers—the *Washington Post*—for its outrageously lopsided reporting during that 1992 presidential campaign.

The Little Rock editors reminded the Washingtonians that "news should be reported—not made, or tilted." (For anybody confused as to which direction the *Post* leaned, the editorial was headlined: "The Clinton Tilt").

Even my liberal friends (in Washington you're bound to have a few) became nauseated after reading one 1,700-word *Post* puff piece praising candidates Clinton and Al Gore as the "New Heartthrobs of the Heartland."

Post publisher Katherine Graham might have been snoozing that summer on Martha's Vineyard, but the *Columbia Journalism Review* was rudely awakened—scolding her Washington newspaper as "indeed giving the appearance of cheerleading for Clinton."

"Fawning" was the word I used.

One *Post* article called attention to Clinton and Gore's "star power" and resulting "passion inspired by celebrity."

Bill and Al are "Butch and Sundance," the newspaper proclaimed, going together "like a flannel lumberjack shirt and blue jeans. They match! They fit together in a photograph the way George Bush and Dan Quayle never could."

If nobody else, the cheerleading from Hope to Hollywood to the Hay Adams Hotel drew the ire of the *Post's* ombudsman, Joann Byrd: "If the *Post* is an example, news coverage at the end of the campaign was lopsided—very lopsided," she wrote.

(In 1999, near the end of Clinton's two tumultuous terms in the White House, David Broder, the *Post's* Pulitzer prize-winning columnist, confessed that he wished he'd paid closer attention to newspaper colleagues in Arkansas when they bid good riddance to their governor. Speaking before the Freedom Forum in Washington, Broder remarked: "Those of us in the national press corps dismissed much too easily the insights the Little Rock press corps had from their years of covering then-Governor Clinton.")

Not long after Clinton took office, I wiggled my way into the annual share-holders' meeting of the *Washington Post* Company, held in a conference room on the ninth floor of the newspaper. With his mother and longtime editor Ben Bradlee looking on, *Post* publisher Donald Graham called the proceedings to order. He'd hoped to begin the morning's business by accepting nominations for the company's board of directors. Instead, one of the *Post's* shareholders, former D.C. councilman and Methodist minister Douglas Moore, rose from his seat and inquired how many blacks sat on the twelve-person board.

Pausing for a moment, Graham replied: "One African American."

To which the minister expressed his hope to Mr. Graham that the makeup of the board would one day more appropriately reflect Washington's majority minority. But that's not why I sneaked into the meeting.

Another shareholder stood up to express alarm about "so-called massage parlors" that advertise in the *Post*. He wondered, "How much revenue does the *Post* Company derive from these ads?"

"My best estimate," Graham replied, "is that the *Post* makes around $250,000 a year in advertising revenue from spas, massage establishments, and health centers."

Graham said the *Post* dropped one "advertiser" after a police raid on the establishment turned up evidence of prostitution. (I had to laugh because, as I had already written in my column, the ad for the massage parlor appeared in the *Post* the very same day the paper reported that police raided the establishment.)

Graham, for whatever reason, then saw fit to add that "pro-life" adver-tisements that periodically run in the *Post* often generate more negative comment and outcry from readers than do ads for massage parlors.

"We're talking apples and peaches," the shareholder replied. "This has nothing to do with abortion and anti-abortion." As much as I enjoyed the dialogue, that's not why I was there.

As for the newspaper's cheerleading for Clinton and Gore, Graham was finally asked about a poll conducted by the Freedom Forum revealing that a wide majority of Washington newspaper editors and reporters considered themselves liberals or moderates. (The survey of 139 Washington journalists found 89 percent voted for President Clinton in 1992.)

"I take the matter very seriously, and I saw the Freedom Forum survey," Graham assured the stockholder. "And I, too, took note of the results and thought a good deal about them. I care deeply about the fairness of this newspaper.

"I do not want the news reporting of the *Washington Post* to be unfair or inaccurate because of biases on the part of anyone in the process," he continued. "The executive editor of the *Washington Post,* Len Downie, is so extreme in his pursuit of this goal . . . he doesn't vote because he doesn't want to be judging the qualifications of any candidate. He thinks it might affect his own judgment on these things."

"BUTCH AND SUNDANCE" NOTWITHSTANDING, Clinton in his first bid for the White House received only 23.8 percent of the eligible vote—the lowest share for a president-elect since John Quincy Adams in 1824 (Clinton received 23.9 percent of the vote in 1996, the second-lowest share since Adams).

Many of his supporters turned out to be women. In fact, one star-struck lady journalist was deemed unable to keep her hands off of Clinton during the campaign and soon found herself relegated by her editors to another campaign bus.

Cheryl Russell, editor of a consumer trends monthly called the *Boomer Report,* went so far as to say "every woman I know is having sex dreams about Bill Clinton."

"I don't recall anyone having sex dreams about Michael Dukakis," she added.

Even CBS anchorman Dan Rather couldn't contain himself when signing off from an exclusive interview with the newly-elected Clinton: "God bless you. Thank you very much. And tell Mrs. Clinton we respect her and we're pulling for her."

Pulling for her? What does that mean?

"If we could be one-one-hundredth as great as you and Hillary Rodham Clinton have been together in the White House, we'd take it right now and walk away winners," Rather explained. Incredibly, the Clintons had been in the White House only four months.

WHETHER THEY SUPPORTED THEIR EX-GOVERNOR for president or not, the folks back home in Arkansas finally found their state on the map. Tourists, no doubt, would soon be calling to learn more about this great leader from Hope.

There's an old saying in Arkansas, says *Washington Times* editor-in-chief Wesley Pruden, that "one tourist is better than two bales of cotton—and he's easier to pick."

Pruden, who pens the liveliest, feistiest, most honest political column in Washington, grew up in Little Rock, his next door neighbor none other than baseball great Brooks Robinson. The newspaperman and the Hall of Fame third baseman remain best of friends today, routinely seated side by side at the annual White House Correspondents' Dinner.

When Pruden took his first newspaper job as a copy boy in Little Rock—Bill Clinton was just five years old—nobody ever called them anything as grand as "journalists" or "the media." They were just "newspapermen," the sons and daughters of plumbers, farmers, schoolteachers, fertilizer salesmen, railway clerks, bookies, or in Pruden's case, the son of a preacher man.

"It's important to remember who we are, and to remember that it's what we do, and not who we may think we are, that's important," he's said. "William Randolph Hearst, the king of an earlier era of swashbuckling newspaper publishers, observed that a good newspaper editor has no friends. An editor should be a friendly fellow, but an honest newspaper cannot tailor its coverage of the news to the interests of its editor's friends, or its editor's partisan prejudices, or even to its editor's cultural predilections."

Besides his politically incorrect columns, I always look forward to reading Pruden's periodic "stylebook" reminders posted on the newsroom bulletin board. Take this memo from 2002: "ALL DESKS, STAFF: It has become fashionable even in the *Times*, Lord help us, to describe reporters as 'media members,' and to describe newspapers as 'the media.' We're all better than that. So cut it out.

"Nobody talks to 'media members.' They talk to 'reporters,' and sometimes to 'reporters and editors,' all of whom are God's ladies and gentlemen. We need not seek perfumed words, or use terms we think make us seem grander than we are. Nobody writes letters to 'the media.' They write letters to 'newspapers,' or sometimes even to 'television networks.' Newspapers are the aristocracy of what was once called 'the press,' and what McLuhan called 'the media,' and we should not demean ourselves by lumping newspapers with undeserving other organs. McLuhan is paying in purgatory, or worse, for having coined that miserable word, which is often misused. Let him writhe in peace. If you mean 'reporters,' write 'reporters.' 'Newspapers' are 'newspapers.'"

Pruden came right to the point in this 2003 posting: "ALL DESKS: A reminder that the term 'birth mother' is a redundancy and should not be used. All mothers are 'birth mothers.' A mother is a mother is a mother, to be identified and honored regardless of how she got that way."

———————

DOWN IN HOPE, ARKANSAS, where Clinton got his first spanking, the only visitors they were accustomed to seeing would drift off Interstate 30 in search of gasoline.

"Our industry's basically poultry, wood products, a little cotton," Hope chamber of commerce volunteer June Downs told me over the telephone. But with a native son now securely in the White House, Hope hoped for the best. Like what happened in 1953 to Petit Jean Mountain, northwest of Little Rock, which was literally transformed overnight when transplant Winthrop Rockefeller turned some of the sorriest land ever cultivated into one of the fanciest farms in the world. Now, a hundred and fifty thousand tourists each year visit the estate with its unique glass-and-stone mansion.

Clinton's old digs surely weren't built of Rockefeller material, but that didn't preclude the grand opening of the Hope "tourist bureau." There was just one hitch.

"The James Burton family lives there now, and they're not too well off," Downs said of the new presidential landmark. "The house is pretty run down—it hasn't been kept up. But right now they aren't financially able to do anything about it."

In fact, she was worried what Burton might do if tourists began poking their heads through his dirty windows.

"They're likely to sit on the property and get a lot of money out of it one day," she guessed.

All of which goes to show, whether a person is fed with a plastic fork or a silver spoon, they can grow up to be president. Clinton, to his credit, made it a goal as a teenager to one day live in the White House, and by golly, he found a way to move in.

———

LATCHING SECURELY ONTO the president-elect's coattails was Clinton's half-brother Roger, best known as lead singer of the band Politics. As quickly as the last presidential vote was tallied, Roger bagged the two biggest gigs of his life: playing an inaugural ball and becoming his brother's unofficial spokesman.

Within days he hit the talk-show circuit, telling Maury Povich how Bill got his nickname (one that Clinton's critics have never forgotten).

"I called him 'Bubba,'" Roger gushed. "He was my Bubba."

Bill became Bubba after his mother Virginia married Roger's father. After Roger Sr. died in 1968, Roger said Bubba became his "father, best friend, guardian, and protector." (Unfortunately, Bubba couldn't be guardian enough to keep Roger's nose clean—or out of jail.)

Following Roger into the national spotlight was Clinton's stepsister, ex-con Diane Dwire Welch. After he won the 1992 election, Welch said Clinton "should be ashamed" for trying to keep her silent during the campaign.

Pleading guilty in 1985 to armed robbery (she allegedly held up a bank and doughnut shop), and later nabbed for drug dealing (she served six years in a Texas maximum-security prison), Welch told the TV program *A Current Affair* that two days before Election Day members of the Democratic party spirited her away to a Holiday Inn and told her to keep her mouth shut.

The next relative to step out of the Clinton family closet was Welch's son, Jefferson, the president's stepnephew. No sooner did Uncle Bubba get elected president than Jefferson went off and joined the Ku Klux Klan.

Thomas A. Robb, the Arkansas-based leader of the Knights of the KKK, said in an interview with Alabama's *Huntsville Times* that when the twenty-four-year-old Welch signed up he told Klan leaders, "You can't blame me because of Bill Clinton."

Jefferson went so far as to tell the hooded figures what they didn't want to hear: his uncle would turn the nation over to illegal aliens. In retrospect, Jefferson wasn't so dumb. A racist, sure, but not dumb.

Another relative waiting patiently in the wings for her fifteen minutes of fame—and it found her—was Clinton's cousin, Catherine Cornelius. Cornelius, among others, recommended that the White House Travel Office be reorganized and the size of its staff reduced. The thinking was she could instead run the office and farm some of the work to her Arkansas-based travel company, which had found steady work during the Clinton campaign.

But like cousins Bill and Hillary (the first lady, members of Congress charged, played a significant role in firing seven White House Travel Office employees, including its longtime director Billy Ray Dale who'd worked under eight presidents), Cornelius quickly learned that Washington didn't operate like Little Rock. A subsequent House Government Reform and Oversight Committee investigative report determined that the firings were "unnecessary," lacked "sufficient cause," and Cornelius "had a personal stake in the outcome."

Whether the fall gal or not, Cornelius as penance was removed from her White House post. A short time later, however, I received a tip that she'd filled an empty seat in the White House Agency Liaison Office. I called the

White House Press Office for confirmation but got nowhere. So I called the liaison office directly, and guess who answered the phone?

"Have things settled down for you?" I asked.

"Well, I'm not on the front page anymore," reasoned Cornelius, who was actually very pleasant over the phone. I recall telling her that I'd look her up next time I needed to book a flight.

Roger, meanwhile, continued to bask in his newfound celebrity (two months into the Clinton presidency, the Secret Service leaked out its code name for the president's brother: "Headache"). He went so far as to tell Povich that his relationship with sister-in-law Hillary had been difficult in the past because "she had this hard exterior."

The late Sarah McClendon, the true "dean" of the White House press corps after peppering presidents with questions for fifty-two years, recalled in her memoirs the memorable day when Bill brought Hillary Rodham home to meet their mother, Virginia.

"When the couple walked through the door, [Roger] and his mother were very surprised," McClendon wrote.

"This girl from Yale was not the kind of woman Bill had dated in his high school and undergraduate years. She was really different. No makeup. Thick glasses. Rather shapeless brown hair. After a few awkward moments, Bill excused himself and took his mother and brother into the tiny kitchen.

"There he said: 'Look, I want you to know that I've had it up to here with beauty queens. I have to have somebody I can talk with. Do you understand that?'"

As Hillary quickly learned, Clinton didn't "have it up to here" with beauty queens for long.

A former TV news reporter (I found it somewhat telling that TV reporters during the 1992 presidential campaign went out of their way to ignore that fact) and Arkansas state employee, Gennifer Flowers said her romance with Clinton lasted twelve years. After going public with her story, I was delighted when she granted me a one-on-one interview.

"Arkansas is a very small state, and it's very easy for a good BS'er like Bill to manipulate in a small state," Flowers told me. "He didn't have the powerful Republicans watching his every move and then giving the facts to the people. He didn't have that in Arkansas."

One of the Republican watchdogs, a Texas lawmaker on Capitol Hill whom Flowers wouldn't identify, actually invited the president's former mistress to be his guest at Clinton's inaugural ball. But she declined the invitation, and others like it, explaining that she was embarrassed enough by her just-published *Penthouse* magazine expose, which after editing was "85 percent BS" (not that posing nude helped her credibility any).

A week or so after the interview, I was surprised when a manila envelope arrived on my desk, its return address: "G. Flowers, 3883 Turtle Creek, Dallas, Texas." Above my name she'd written, "Personal."

In a note inside, Flowers thanked me for "accurately" presenting her side of the sordid story. Better yet, the note was attached to the December 1992 issue of *Penthouse:* "Gennifer Flowers Tells All, Shows All." I opened the glossy magazine to the first page where Flowers "shows all," and was amazed to find written across her flesh: "To my friend, John. My very best, always. Love Ya'—Gen."

I must admit I have been tempted to peddle this rare, if not historic piece of presidential memorabilia over eBay.

IT HAD BEEN A SOUL-SEARCHING WEEK for President George H.W. Bush and his wife Barbara. His approval rating was 91 percent following the Gulf War, and now the nation's forty-first president had been denied a second term in the White House.

Just before midnight on the first Tuesday following the election, Bush telephoned White House spokesman Marlin Fitzwater at home to say he and the first lady were going out for a midnight stroll.

Oh, and one more thing, Bush added. "I'm not taking anyone with us."

It's extremely rare that a White House press corps is kept in the dark when the president steps foot outside 1600 Pennsylvania Avenue, particularly at such a late hour and during dangerous times.

But off into the night they went, the president and first lady arriving a short time later at the Vietnam Veterans Memorial. There, volunteers at that unlikely hour were taking turns reading the names of all 58,183 souls inscribed on "the Wall." Soon, Bush stepped in, picking up where the last reader left off. Then, in a moving gesture the world never got to see, Bush thanked the two hundred or so veterans on hand for their wartime sacrifices.

In 1971, President Richard M. Nixon made a similar "unscheduled" late-night visit to the Lincoln Memorial, which now overlooks the Vietnam Memorial. Ironically, during Nixon's midnight stroll, he confronted protesters of the same war Bush was now honoring. But Bush, more than most of his predecessors, knew about war and sacrifice. In World War II, his first war, he piloted bombing raids, getting shot down and plucked from the ocean seconds before Japanese capture. He was commander in chief for his last war.

Looking back on the 1992 election, Bush said what he felt: "I simply was not articulate enough to override a well-run opposition campaign and an often cynical and ugly press—an unaccountable press, the likes of which I've never encountered in thirty years in and out of public life.

"No more politics," he vowed. "I've had it up to here with that."

SATURDAY, JANUARY 2, 1993, dawned warm and sunny in San Juan, Puerto Rico, ideal conditions for the outdoor inaugural of Pedro Rossello as governor of the biggest overseas U.S. territory.

Bill and Hillary Clinton, preparing to assume power in Washington, couldn't be on hand for the festivities in the seaside capitol, but Mrs. Clinton's younger brothers, Hugh and Tony Rodham, happily agreed to be stand-ins. Transportation Secretary Andrew Card was on hand representing outgoing President Bush, as were several foreign heads of state. The ceremonies culminated with a formal state dinner at Fortaleza, Puerto Rico's equivalent of the White House.

"It was real first class," said a member of the U.S. delegation, describing how, in the absence of fighter jets, Puerto Rican National Guard helicopters, trailing a rainbow of colored smoke, flew over in tribute to the governor.

A beaming Rossello acknowledged the presence of the many dignitaries and guests, including Mrs. Clinton's brothers, realizing perhaps that Puerto Rico's chances for statehood had brightened with the incoming administration. He pledged to fight for a new star on the U.S. flag.

During the previous months of campaigning, the Rodham brothers had made numerous appearances on behalf of the Clintons. Once it was pointed out that the siblings were so close to their sister that they joined her and Bill on their honeymoon.

Yet on the island of Puerto Rico, something happened to Hillary's brothers on the way to the state dinner. They were a no-show.

"They told one of their hosts who was taking care of them that they wanted to golf and go shopping," one member of the U.S. delegation told me. "The state dinner was a pretty critical thing to miss."

As it was, another couple was quickly invited to fill the high-powered seats near the disgraced governor.

A week later the Rodhams were in the news again. The *Wall Street Journal* reported that an attorney representing the brothers was calling executives of some of the nation's top corporations to solicit donations to cover their inaugural expenses in Washington. Those approached for handouts included the Ford Motor Co., Mobil Corp., and the Chevron Corp., who all declined to donate ten thousand dollars each to Hillary's brothers.

Hugh Rodham was quoted as saying he saw nothing wrong with the personal fundraising. "We obviously need to pay for it somehow," he reasoned. "We're just small fries, that's all we are."

Whoever ended up footing the bill, the Rodham inaugural celebration at the Mayflower Hotel in Washington was a big splash, or so I reported. While bouncers guarded the door, partygoers were treated to an open bar and presented with snazzy lapel pins inscribed with the Rodham family crest.

Even Roger Clinton and his band were on hand to play through the early morning hours.

"It's Billy Carter all over again," one guest told me. (It wasn't clear whether he was referring to Roger, the Rodham brothers, or the entire clan.)

The icing on the cake, as far as column writing goes, came five months after the inaugural when California Senator Barbara Boxer made the surprise announcement that her twenty-five-year-old daughter Nicole had become engaged to Tony Rodham, now gainfully employed by the Democratic National Committee.

Better yet, the ceremony would be held in the White House Rose Garden, the first such wedding at the presidential mansion since Tricia Nixon wed Harvard law student Ed Cox in 1971.

(I was still writing about the Rodhams in 2001 when, at the close of Clinton's last term in office, Hugh Rodham was forced to return almost four hundred thousand dollars he pocketed by helping to win presidential pardons for alleged cocaine dealer Carlos Vignali and money-launderer Almon Glenn Braswell.)

WHAT'S THE FIRST THING YOU DO when learning one day beforehand that Vice President-elect Al Gore is coming to spend the weekend with you in West Virginia?

Sam Ashelman, co-owner of the Coolfont Resort in Berkeley Springs, quickly telephoned the New York publishing house of Gore's green tome, *Earth in the Balance,* and ordered twenty-five copies for the resort's gift shop.

The Gore family had vacationed at the Coolfont before but never with so many Secret Service agents tagging along for what would be two days of hiking and rubdowns. Thank goodness the agents were there, I reported, because Al and Tipper got lost.

"So they had to use the Secret Service . . . to find their way back down again," Ashelman confirmed by telephone, although he stressed the couple was never in any danger.

As for the books, Gore kindly autographed them all, and they sold out immediately. In the book, Gore writes about saving the spotted owl, yet he did nothing to save the endangered snail darter (a little snail-eating perch) when it threatened completion of the Tellico Dam in his home state of Tennessee.

"I am glad that Congress has now ended this controversy once and for all," he wrote to one constituent. But my favorite Gore "endangered species" story was told in two letters I reprinted in my column.

Joe and Dolores Delgadillo, an elderly couple from Dallas, explained to the vice president how much they relied on federally-operated Amtrak train service to visit their children and grandchildren, who lived on both coasts and in Chicago.

"The train has been our main-stay," the couple wrote. "Yet your administration is killing our Texas Eagle. This makes us sick."

The Texas Eagle the elderly couple referred to was the Amtrak train running between St. Louis and San Antonio. Facing a several-hundred-million-dollar budget shortfall, the Texas Eagle was one of four Amtrak routes targeted for elimination.

"What can you do to save our Eagle?" Gore was asked.

"Dear Mr. and Mrs. Delgadillo," the vice president wrote back. "Thank you for your letter regarding the protection of the Texas eagle. I appreciate hearing from you.

"I share your view that the urgent problem of species extinction and the conservation of biological diversity should be addressed. The first step in saving any plant or animal from extinction is to become aware of and respect the fragile ecosystems that make up our environment. . . .

"Again, thank you for sharing your thoughts with me. I look forward to working with you for the future of our planet."

(In 1998, all of Capitol Hill was laughing when Gore accidentally sent seventy-one-year-old Senator Daniel Patrick Moynihan, now deceased, a letter congratulating him and his wife, Elizabeth, on the birth of twins. Moynihan politely wrote back that Elizabeth hadn't given birth in forty years. That same year, instead of sending birthday greetings to Senator Orrin G. Hatch, Gore told the Utah Republican that he was pleased "to learn about the recent birth of your twins. As the proud parents of four children, we understand the joy you are feeling at this special time." Writing back to Gore, the sixty-three-year-old Hatch observed: "I was very pleased to learn about the recent birth of my twins, but my dear wife wasn't!")

FEW IN THE COUNTRY KNEW MUCH about Hillary Rodham Clinton—except that she stood by her man. Beset with problems on the campaign trail, she let it be known that she turned to Eleanor Roosevelt for advice:

"How did you put up with this? How did you go on day to day with all that would happen, with the kinds of attacks, criticisms that would be hurled your way?" Mrs. Clinton asked Eleanor's ghost.

According to Mrs. Clinton, Roosevelt replied in no uncertain terms: "Get out and do it, and don't make any excuses about it!"

When it came time to unpack her belongings in the White House, the first lady reportedly had her eyes on a highly coveted, strategically situated office in the West Wing, just down the hall from the Oval Office. There was just one problem: the office was reserved for the vice president.

Vice President Dan Quayle spent most of his time working out of the same office, Quayle communications director Jeffrey Nesbit told me. For ceremonial functions—greeting visiting heads of state and the like—he used his more formal office in the Old Executive Office Building.

After vigorous debate, according to my source, Mrs. Clinton gave in and allowed Gore to hang his pictures on the wall. Nevertheless, one thing became clear: Mrs. Clinton, unlike previous first ladies, was a force to be reckoned with. And she wouldn't be satisfied hosting teas and cutting ribbons.

"Staff in the past would fight over being as close to the Oval Office as possible," Mr. Nesbit said. "If she lobbied for a West Wing office on the first floor and got one, it would have been quite a victory for her."

Mrs. Clinton settled into another office, albeit a floor away from the president (she worked out of the traditional first lady's office in the East Wing as well). In retrospect, had she gotten her choice in offices, she could have kept better tabs on what was wiggling past her in the hallway leading to the Oval Office, and history, as we know it, might have been written differently.

A few weeks after the Clintons arrived in town, a former Bush staff member visited the White House Federal Credit Union and was astonished to see two large portraits on the wall: one of Bill, the other Hillary.

In fact, portraits of the president and first lady hanging happily next to each other were popping up all over Washington.

(I'll never forget Housing and Urban Development Secretary Henry Cisneros dropping into a New York HUD office, taking one look at the color photograph of him on the wall, and ordering it removed. He didn't stop there, ordering hundreds of identical portraits taken down in HUD offices nationwide. "This is absolutely not a vanity thing," Cisneros told the *Baltimore Sun.* "I looked like I had just woken up five minutes earlier and had a five o'clock shadow.")

"It's not right," said a White House mailroom veteran of twenty-five years, referring to Bill and Hillary gazing down on him. "The vice president is supposed to be up there next to the president."

Look again, I wrote. The vice president is up there.

Chapter 6

The King and I

FOR NOCTURNAL LISTENERS, KOFI Radio in Kalispell aired three hours of the *Larry King Show* beginning at midnight. The king of talk radio hosted the all-night program out of the old Mutual Broadcasting Network atop Crystal City, Virginia, overlooking the runways of Ronald Reagan Washington National Airport.

King did me a huge favor my first year in the news business by taping several promotional reels, one of which went: "Hi, this is Larry King in Washington. Join my good friend John McCaslin for KOFI (pronounced "coffee") breakfast news each weekday morning, and then join me every night starting at midnight, right here on KOFI."

On those occasional nights when I couldn't sleep (or else made last call at Moose's), I'd lie in bed listening to King's gravelly voice and think how difficult it must be to host an all-night show when the rest of the country was sleeping. In fact, on more than one occasion I could have sworn I heard King snoring. Once I distinctly heard a loud "thump," imagining in my mind that King had dozed off and struck his noggin on the microphone.

Nevertheless, I idolized King. He might have stayed up past his bedtime, but what young person in radio wouldn't want to be in his slippers?

During the late 1990s, former White House aide and GOP operative Mary Matalin, otherwise known for being the better half of Clinton creator James Carville, hosted her own radio show over at CBS. After first broadcasting from Capitol Hill, she moved across the Potomac River to the old Mutual studios where King spent his nights before permanently switching to television.

Kindhearted woman that she is (growing up she was often called Mary Magdalene), Matalin would frequently ask me to be her guest-host whenever she was delivering a speech or a baby. One of her engineers in Crystal City, I came to learn, had worked with King during the four years I spent in Montana.

During a commercial break, the engineer casually mentioned that I was sitting in King's old chair, working his same control board, and speaking through his old microphone. But what intrigued me most was his saying he always knew when King had nodded off because his forehead would strike the microphone with a loud "thump."

No wonder during a Ritz-Carlton Hotel opening in Washington in 2000, J.W. Marriott Jr., chairman and chief executive officer of Marriott International Inc., reminded King that some fifteen years earlier he stayed up to be a guest on the show—sometime "between the hours of 11:00 P.M. and 4:00 A.M."

Marriott remembered asking King, "Who listens to this thing?" To which the host shot back, "The postal workers in the New York City post office."

IN TRUTH, KING HAD MILLIONS of listeners. Which is why companies selling sleep products were among the show's biggest advertisers. Not everybody in Washington, though, was a fan of the host, particularly some Republicans who thought him biased. That never bothered King. Not once during his career, he's told critics, has he ever tried to pass himself off as a journalist.

Instead, he prefers the title "interviewer," or simply "a guy who asks questions." He'll even settle for "entertainer," in the mold of the late Arthur Godfrey. And why not, given his cameo appearances in no less than eighteen Hollywood films, from *Ghostbusters* to *Primary Colors*.

Which, getting back to politics, isn't to say King hasn't sucked up to his favorite politicians, including "old friend" Al Gore. The vice president was barely settled into the White House when he was a guest on CNN's *Larry King Live,* and was the host ever giddy.

King: And it's a great pleasure to have Vice President Gore. You looked great last night, Al. Good applause.

Gore: Thank you, Larry.

King: What is it like to sit there like that? I should say "Mr. Vice President," but it's hard to say to somebody you've been calling "Al" for years.

Gore: Well . . .

King: So, forgive me if I goof.

Gore: Well, we know each other well enough.

King: Okay, what was that like?

Gore: Well, first of all, congratulations on your new time slot.

King: Thank you.

Gore: I think it's fantastic.

King: A little sleep.

Gore: Yeah, yeah, for a change.

King: And congratulations, your book is number one in Germany right now.

Gore: Oh, well, thank you very much.

King: Number one, *Earth in the Balance.*

Gore: Number two here.

King: Yeah.

Gore: I'm real pleased. But we're not talking about that today.

King: Okay.

If that's not obsequious enough banter, a mere two weeks later King interviewed Gore all over again (CNN should have replayed the first interview).

> *King:* In the past, Al—if I may call you that?
> *Gore:* Sure, of course.
> *King:* It's hard not to call you "Al" because I've known you too long.

King once moderated a televised debate among four high-profile candidates, including former Iran-Contra figure Oliver North, seeking a Virginia Senate seat. The next morning, the *Richmond Times-Dispatch* described King as astute, incisive, and well informed, although it was difficult for the moderator not to be informed, the newspaper added, given his questions were being whispered into his ear.

In a scene reminiscent of the movie *Broadcast News,* Washington media darling Larry Sabato, a University of Virginia political professor who gets more airtime than Dick Cheney, monitored the entire ninety-minute debate from his Charlottesville home while hooked up by telephone with King's senior executive producer.

After the candidates would finish giving their answers, Sabato, from the comfort of his La-Z-Boy, would suggest follow-up questions, which the producer then relayed into King's earpiece.

"I was an unpaid consultant to Larry King and CNN," Sabato tried explaining. "I was there to catch misrepresentations and suggest follow-up questions."

Bert L. Rohrer, campaign communications director for Senator Charles S. Robb, son-in-law to President Lyndon B. Johnson, rightfully blasted Sabato's surreptitious involvement.

"He hates Robb," Rohrer said, before delivering the most descriptive line about those in higher education I've ever heard: "If it weren't for the media, Larry Sabato would be nothing more than a college professor with an old Volvo and two pair of Hush Puppies."

KING AROUND THAT TIME was one of Washington's more notable womanizers. Alicia Mundy, Washington bureau chief of *Media Week* and a neighbor of mine in Alexandria, once told me of the memorable date she had with the TV host.

"It was Ash Wednesday, and I'd gone and gotten ashes in the morning," Mundy said. "And I have to admit I probably added to them right before the date so by the time I got to the restaurant I had a cross the size of a coaster on my forehead.

"And Larry spends half the evening saying to me, 'Do you want to go and wash that off? Huh? Huh? Do you want to get rid of that?'"

Soon, King "took out photographs of himself with [former Soviet President Mikhail] Gorbachev and photographs of himself with the first lady and put them on the table and propped them on this stainless steel bowl. I felt like saying, 'Larry, I know who you are, I know who you've interviewed.'

"So anyway, we've got the pictures there and he wondered if I like the 'old songs.' By this time we've ordered dinner, and he's ordered, because of his heart problems, basically water and a tiny piece of fish that has been broiled to the point where you don't recognize it as a carbon life form.

"And I ordered the crab cakes with hollandaise sauce, major cholesterol, with a double vodka on the rocks. And he keeps commenting: 'You're going to eat that? You're going to drink that? You're going to eat that? You're going to drink that? Do you know what that's going to do to you?'

"Then, after asking me about the music, he starts singing a cappella—crooning! And he began singing, 'Sometimes I wonder why I fell in love with you.' It's 'Stardust'!"

At that point, Mundy said, "He takes hold of my right hand—my right hand has the fork in it, thank you, and I'm trying to eat! I'm hungry—I haven't had dinner, OK? So he continues to sing, I think he went into 'St. Louis Blues' next, and he wouldn't let go of the fork.

"I'm holding the fork, and his left hand is holding my right hand. We've got two hands and a fork going over to my mouth with the crab cake on it!"

Mundy, to this day, thinks the world of King.

"Bless his little heart, he's got two lines that he's used on apparently every woman he's ever dated. The first line is, 'There's chemistry here! Can you feel the chemistry? There's lots of chemistry, can you feel it? Huh? Huh?'

"And the second line is always, 'Do you believe in love at first sight?'"

In 1996, King was on the campaign trail of Republican presidential candidate Bob Dole in Nashua, New Hampshire, when he spotted a large contingent of reporters, singling out Rita Cosby of the Fox News Channel.

"Who are you?" King shouted.

Cosby, taken aback, identified herself.

King asked: "How come I don't know you?"

Fellow reporters, amused by the lame pickup line, encouraged King to book Cosby on his show.

"If I did, it would be a private booking!" King replied.

Cosby said she was "mortified."

"Well," said one Dole official who'd witnessed the exchange, "he certainly lives up to his reputation."

SOON, IT WAS LOVE AT FIRST SIGHT. In 1997, King married singer Shawn Southwick, his seventh marriage, and the union signaled several changes in his life. In September 2001, the same month terrorists attacked the United States, King wasn't surprised when *USA Today* dropped his column after more than twenty years. The newspaper said it was looking for "trendier" features and celebrity interviews, although nobody conducted the latter as well as King.

A father of one- and two-year-old sons, Cannon and Chance, King was actually becoming more conservative in his older age.

"I hope your years will not be a time where anything goes," King wrote to his sons in dedicating his book, *Anything Goes.*

When asked to expand on those words during an interview with *World,* a magazine combining current events with the Bible's perspective, King replied: "It's such a world in which things change so fast and fads come in and fads go out."

"I never thought I'd hear cursing on television, now I do," he said. "So this 'anything goes' aspect is an error that I'm glad I missed. Even though I was able to observe it, it didn't affect me as much as it might affect my kids."

"There's a lot of innocence in an 'anything goes' society," King concluded. "There's a lot to be said for some old values."

Chapter 7

Fisticuffs and Fruitcakes

P ENNING INSIDE THE BELTWAY day-in and day-out for over a dozen years—three thousand columns and eighteen thousand anecdotes—you inevitably bump into every player in town. And most, if not all, wind up in print—whether they intend to or not.

"Inside the Beltway" is an expression we Americans hear all the time, yet routinely I'm asked what it means. Geographically, it's everything within the capital Beltway, a sixty-six-mile loop of deadly asphalt that, when not at its customary standstill, carries speeding motorists around Washington.

But more often it refers to a mindset, or malady. A person Inside the Beltway can be devoid of common sense, on the take, out of touch with reality—out of touch with America.

Inside the Beltway symptoms lead to scandals—some serious, some silly: over-priced haircuts on airport tarmacs, consultations with astrologers, commiserating with ghosts. The bigger scandals often lead to "gates," like the granddaddy of them all, "Watergate."

Eagle Scout he's become in mid-stride, President George W. Bush, unlike his predecessor, has opened zero "personal" gates for pundits to pontificate through. Democrats, particularly those vying for the 2004 presidential nomination, kept busy pushing "Missing Weapons of Mass Destructiongate," and "Could Bush Have Prevented 911gate?" But one had to tread carefully when criticizing a patriotic president whose unintended legacy has been keeping terrorists out of our cockpits and condominiums.

As for Iraq, the biggest mistake Bush made was marching on Baghdad in the name of these weapons called WMDs. The war, instead, was about tyranny and oppression and liberating the Iraqi people from the iron clutch of Saddam Hussein and his deranged sons. Furthermore, Hussein's regime has posed a threat to the security of the United States and the world. He did pursue, he did possess, and he did use WMDs on his own people.

"He had links to terror, twice invaded other nations, defied the international community and seventeen United Nations resolutions for twelve years, and gave every indication that he would never disarm and never comply with the just demands of the world," White House National Security Advisor Condoleezza Rice is quick to remind today.

"That threat could not be allowed to remain unaddressed. Now that Saddam's regime is gone, the people of Iraq are more free, and people everywhere need no longer fear his weapons, his aggression, and his cruelty."

Back to the "gates," librarian-turned-First Lady Laura Bush has certainly been "gate free." So unlike her predecessor, there's no point scouring the East Wing for scandals.

Which wasn't the case with the previous administration, when President and Mrs. Clinton opened up so many gates they flooded every political column in town with ink. The Capitalist Conservatives came up with this eye-opening list of Clinton scandals, by no means complete: *Whitewatergate, Cattlegate, Nannygate, Helicoptergate, Haircutgate, Travelgate, Gennifer Flowersgate, Filegate, Vince Fostergate, I Wonder Where Those Whitewater Billing Records Came Fromgate, Joycelyn Elders Masturbategate, Paula Jonesgate, Lincoln Bedroomgate, Eleanor Roosevelt's Ghostgate, White House Coffeegate, Drug Dealer Donationsgate, Buddhist Templegate, Web Hubbellgate, Lippogate, Chinesegate, Blame Kenneth Starrgate, Rightwing Conspiracygate, Zippergate (Monica), Monica Jobgate, Perjurygate, Kathleen*

Fisticuffs and Fruitcakes

Willeygate, Los Alamosgate, Wag the Doggate, Juanita Broaddrickgate, PBSgate, Bomb the Aspirin Factorygate, Pardon My Felonsgate, Load Up the Vangate.

"BELTWAY FEVER!" warns Senator Rod Grams of Minnesota, describing presidents and other elected officials who fall victim to "the unreal atmosphere of this place and eventually forget what it was that first propelled them into public office."

Says Senator Ben Nighthorse Campbell of Colorado: "If you stay here too long you become part of the problem, you become a Beltway animal."

Former Democratic strategist-turned-*Crossfire* host Paul Begala, burrowed in the White House "war room" with Clinton's other believers, once shouted into the telephone: "Bob Dole is so mean he would hand out sticks to people so they could beat little seals."

"Not true," Begala told me later. "I didn't say that. But I said something like that. What I said was it looked to me like Bob Dole couldn't wait to finish giving his speech so he could go club some baby seals." (Glad I didn't misquote him.)

Not that Republicans are kinder and gentler. Visitors strolling through the Capitol Hill suite of House Majority Leader Tom DeLay of Texas couldn't help but read the screen-saver message trailing across computer screens: "Down with booger-eatin' Democrats."

"There has been a tendency in recent years in this town to try to tear things down, to tear people up," says Senator Byron L. Dorgan of North Dakota, who was once handed a memorandum encouraging senators to recite certain adjectives and nouns while campaigning for reelection: "When you are running against somebody, use the word 'traitor' to define your opponent. Call your opponent 'pathetic.' Use the word 'lie.' Use the word 'sick.' Again, use the word 'traitor.'"

One Democratic congresswoman's tirade in 2001 was unlike any witnessed in recent decades, resulting in a most ungracious welcome for the unwitting target: newly-installed Housing and Urban Development Secretary Mel Martinez. When all was said and done, the Cuban-born HUD secretary never got to explain why President Bush proposed eliminating an "ineffective" $309 million public-housing drug program.

Rather than describing the furious assault by Congresswoman Stephanie Tubbs Jones of Ohio, a member of the housing subcommittee of the House Financial Services Committee, let's allow excerpts of the proceedings to speak for themselves:

> *Jones:* Secretary Martinez, it's nice to see you again. I enjoyed seeing you at the Wild Program for the Congressional Black Caucus, but I'm troubled. And I'm a former prosecutor, so I'm going to cross-examine you a little bit. I'd like short answers to my questions, please. Now I want to talk about the Drug Elimination Program. In Cuyahoga County, Ohio, which is my congressional district, the . . . program has been significant in reducing crime and activity in public housing. In fact, I think it was created in the Reagan administration, the purpose was because there was concentrated living in public housing. You'll agree with that, right? Concentrated, densely populated?
>
> *Martinez:* It was begun as an eight million dollar program to a few targeted housing authorities.
>
> *Jones:* No, answer my question. It's densely populated living, is that correct? Public housing?
>
> *Martinez:* Well—
>
> *Jones:* Yes or no? Yes or no?
>
> *Martinez:* I'm telling you that public—in some places public housing has densely populated areas.
>
> *Jones:* High crime rate, yes or no?
>
> *Martinez:* In some places yes and in some places no—
>
> *Jones:* . . .What country have you been in the last ten years? My next question—

Martinez: May I ask—

Jones: No, no, no. You can't, I'm going to keep going, no.

Martinez: I don't get to answer? I don't get to answer? Do you want me to answer all the questions or just the ones you choose for me to answer?

Jones: No. . . . I'm running the questioning, you're answering. You answer my questions and don't get smart with me because I'm not getting smart with you, sir.

Subcommittee Chairwoman Representative Marge Roukema, New Jersey Republican: I'm sorry, I'm sorry. I have never, ever, in my twenty years on this committee, heard this kind of response to members of the panel.

Jones: I've never heard this kind of response to members of Congress. I asked him a question.

Roukema: Excuse me?

Jones: He's trying to make jokes out of my questions, and I don't appreciate it.

Roukema: I beg your pardon. I did not hear any jokes.

Jones: Look at his face.

Roukema: If you want an answer, let him answer.

Jones: I'll tell him when I want an answer, Madame Chairwoman. You can't run my questioning.

Roukema: All right.

Jones: Out of all respect to you, I'm asking the questions, and I'm getting the questions I want answered. Now, when you want to do your questions, then you do yours, but you can't run mine. Now my question is, the purpose of police officers on the beat was so that the neighborhood people get to know the law enforcement folks. Is that a fair statement?

Martinez: Yes ma'am.

Jones: And so for you to terminate the Drug Elimination Program across the country . . . is irresponsible and . . . I wanted you to take back to the administration our frustration. . . . Could you do that for us, please, Mr. Martinez?

Martinez: I will do so. . . . And if you felt that I was, in my facial expressions, meaning some disrespect to you, I sincerely apologize. I did not mean to leave that impression.

Jones: Thank you. And I accept the apology.

After publishing the explosive exchange, one of the congresswoman's constituents in Cuyahoga Falls, Ohio, wrote: "I have mixed emotions about your article about Representative Tubbs Jones. On one hand, America has once again read about one of our congressional buffoons. Conversely, you are a lone soul with the nerve to print the idiocy which passes for the thoughts of America's Democratic elected officials."

Later that week, Jones wrote me a three-page letter, following it up with a phone call. "You may call such dedication a 'tirade.' Others call it passion. I simply call it my job," she said.

Capitol Hill is no place for thin-skinned people, concurs Congressman Steven LaTourette of Ohio, who after one particularly grueling week of partisan mudslinging says he was heartened only after boarding an airplane for Cleveland and "the flight attendant did not tell me to sit down and shut up."

"This place is dysfunctional," says Congressman David R. Obey of Wisconsin. "How many more good people will be destroyed?"

"I think . . . we need to learn how to disagree with each other without disliking each other," suggests Congressman Jay Dickey of Arkansas.

To which Democrat-turned-Republican W.J. "Billy" Tauzin of Louisiana replies, "I recall once we were debating [and] one of the oldest gentlemen in the House stood up and said, 'Now, Billy, you know you can't take politics out of politics any more than you can take kissing out of loving.'"

Very few kiss. I'll never forget when Mark Neumann of Wisconsin stood up to announce that four members of his freshman class of congressmen had "recently filed for divorce" and three others are "in serious trouble" due to the job-related stress they carry home to their families.

South Carolina Senator Ernest F. Hollings remembers the late Richard Russell of Georgia saying: "They give you a six-year-term in this U.S. Senate—two years to be a statesman, the next two years to be a politician, and the last two years to be a demagogue."

"Regretably," Hollings says, "we are no longer afforded even two years as statesmen. We go straight to politics and demagoguery right after the election."

As a result, partisan bullies disguised in business suits and high heels roam the hallowed halls of Congress as warring gangs: Democrats against Republicans, Liberals fighting Conservatives, Yellow Dogs biting Blue Dogs, Pro-Choice Left in a most unholy crusade against Pro-Life Right.

Yet if judged alone, contrary to popular belief, the great majority of Washington's elected officials are decent, honest, ordinary folks like you and me. When not toiling on the Hill they are parents and grandparents, den mothers and soccer coaches, cat lovers and dog walkers. Their logic at times might be hard to swallow, but the rhetoric, the legislation, the amendments they introduce genuinely reflect what in their hearts and minds is best for their country.

It's when they open their mouths to express these "conservative ideals," these "liberal notions," that the fun—and the hollering—begins.

Emotions were running high, for instance, when senators grappled with the almost unspeakable procedure of late-term abortions.

"President Clinton, you were an unborn child once," Senator Robert C. Smith of New Hampshire digressed at one point. (I couldn't wait to hear where this bizarre observation was going.)

"The president's father died, you know, while his mother was pregnant. Is that not interesting?" Smith asked fellow senators. "She faced a very tough decision. Do I raise a child alone without a father? Bill Clinton's mother chose life."

"Regardless of party, regardless of ideology, I think we could say we were thankful," Smith said. "He became president of the United States. He could have been a victim. Bill Clinton could have been a partial-birth abortion."

Wow! Any ladies in the Senate care to speak up?

"I find it a little amusing [that] most of this debate takes place with people who themselves have never been pregnant," said Senator Carol Moseley-Braun of Illinois, a former ambassador and Democratic candidate for president in 2004. "Quite frankly, having been there . . . I can tell you I gained forty pounds, my teeth started to rot."

After describing her pregnancy symptoms to the entire world, the senator concluded it was "very important that those who cannot be pregnant really should think twice before they talk about this issue."

Does her logic make sense?

"I guess the thing that I have found most frustrating about Washington in the . . . years I have been in the U.S. Senate is that we say things that confuse people," admits Senator Kent Conrad of North Dakota. "We use words in a way that are not accurate, that do not really reveal what is actually happening."

Ted Kennedy seconds that, or at least he did in my column in 2002.

> "In the United States Senate, one of the things I observed in the early days—and it's still used—and that is that you take someone's argument and then you misrepresent it and misstate it and disagree with it," he says. "And it's very effective. I've done it myself a number of times. But eventually, eventually people catch on."

Seldom is God's name evoked on Capitol Hill, what with ACLU sentries behind every marble column. But it's difficult not to let the Creator into the argument when grappling over federal funding for abortions.

"I do not believe that it is a human being at the moment of conception," Senator Robert Kerrey opined.

"If it is not a human being, what is it?" asked Senator Bob Smith. "Could the senator from Nebraska answer that question on my time for me?"

"It may surprise the senator from New Hampshire to know," Kerrey replied, "that he is not my God. As I indicated earlier, I make the decision."

The offended Smith replied, "The senator from Nebraska went well over the line with the statement regarding God, and I refuse to yield any more time to him."

Ladies, do you wish to weigh in again?

"Let me answer your first question," said Senator Barbara Boxer of California. "If you want a second question, I will answer your second question. Let me answer your first question."

"You let me ask the question," said Senator Kay Bailey Hutchison of Texas.

"You asked me a question," Boxer reminded her. "I am delighted to yield as long as you want, but I do not want to forget your first question. I am answering your question."

"Will the senator yield?" Hutchison requested.

"I need to finish my answer and then I will be happy to yield," Boxer said.

"Will—"

"If we could have some order!" pleaded the presiding officer.

"You know what I think, having been around a lot of teenagers?" says Congressman Jack Kingston of Georgia. "I know a lot of teenagers who individually are fine folks, but when you get a pack of them in your living room or a pack of them in your kitchen, strange things happen and all those individual good people turn out to do some pretty stupid things as a pack. That is what happens in Washington. These folks . . . when they get together the association causes some real inefficient and irresponsible results."

Not that lawmakers aren't sometimes mistaken for children. Montana Senator Conrad Burns equates Congress to Romper Room—"staking out our corner of the playground."

Bidding farewell to Washington to return home to Massachusetts, Congressman Joseph P. Kennedy II, eldest son of Robert, stated: "I would suggest that having spent enough time around these so-called hallowed halls of justice in Washington, D.C., that we see every bit as much immorality take place on this floor or around this city as we do any place else in America."

I remember when the late Congressman Sonny Bono of California took to the House floor to explain "the reason I am a Republican. My father is a Democrat, my mom was a Democrat, I was raised a Democrat—the reason I am a Republican is because I like the idea that your word is important. I like that. That is how our party operates. So I know that if I shake hands with [a Republican] I have got a deal on whatever we shook hands on."

What happens when you shake hands with a Democrat?

"I feel like I have been kicked in the head," said Bono.

At which point Democrat Melvin Watt of North Carolina stepped up to the lectern: "I just want the gentleman to know that there are a lot of people on this side who agree that you have been kicked in the head."

"Thank you. Thank you," Bono replied. "I suppose I am supposed to be insulted. But by the gentleman from North Carolina I am not."

In the summer of 2002, House Rules Committee Chairman David Dreier was challenged repeatedly by elder Congressman Charlie Rangel of New York to "Ask the old folks! Ask the old folks!" about the impact that proposed legislation would have on senior citizens.

"Okay, Charlie, I'll ask you, because you're one of them," Dreir spat.

Several years ago, two Democrats stormed onto the House floor to warn the world that "a bunch of kooks" and "lunatics" had assumed control of Congress. Aware that school children filled the House visitors' gallery—to observe how this great government of ours functions—the speaker pro tempore cautioned the pair "not to use words that might be taken down. 'Lunacy' and 'lunatics,' in addressing any members on the floor of the House, are not permissible words," he scolded.

If you didn't guess, House Speaker Newt Gingrich was the "lunatic" the Democrats referred to, although they knew better than to call him a kook to his face.

"I prefer respect," Gingrich once said in my column. "If you ever get a chance watch 'Sands of Iwo Jima,' because it was the formative movie of my childhood. My father was an infantryman in Korea when I saw it. I saw it four times in one day. I was about ten or eleven years old. It's about a Marine platoon sergeant who is essentially disliked by his men while he trains them—and does a series of things to them necessary for them to survive the battle—and who is killed in the last part of the movie just as his troops begin to understand why he has been so tough.

"Now, I would say that in a sense the Founding Fathers might prefer the word 'virtue.' It is the perfect example. Your job is to do what is right, to hope the people will respect you for doing what is right," he said.

Former Republican Senator William S. Cohen, tapped by President Clinton to head the Pentagon, never liked being a "politician." He preferred "generalist."

"It seems that the word 'politician' over the years has always been taken in a negative fashion. We hear radio commentators, for example, talk about 'the politicians.' It is not said in a complimentary sense, but rather a negative one.

"Of course," Cohen acknowledged, "we are all familiar with the expression that a 'generalist' is someone who reads less and less about more and more until he knows absolutely nothing about everything."

Which leads to my favorite description of Congress: "A place where someone takes the floor to speak, says nothing, nobody listens, and then everybody disagrees."

OFTEN IT'S DIFFICULT to keep Republicans and Democrats in the same room, which makes it difficult to approve legislation. Longtime Congressman William Goodling of Pennsylvania once had to resort to some slick maneuvering to shepherd a Republican welfare-reform bill through committee. He had heard through the grapevine that Democrats planned to "stall" movement of the bill by introducing thirty amendments, a strategy called "hunkering down" until the opponent grows weary and calls it a day.

So, at the beginning of the session, Goodling outlined unprecedented ground rules that included when exactly recesses would be called. Otherwise, under no circumstances would anybody be allowed to leave the committee room until the fate of the bill was decided.

"What if we have to go to the bathroom?" inquired disgruntled Democrat George Miller of California.

"Well, just put up one finger or two," Goodling replied.

RING ANNOUNCER: Standing in the left corner, weighing in at 175 pounds and representing the minority, Senator Frank Lautenberg of New Jersey. Standing in the right corner, weighing 155 pounds and representing the majority, Senator John McCain of Arizona.

"Mr. President," Lautenberg complained, "the chair has an obligation to recognize the senator who stood up first."

"The Senate is out of order," ruled the presiding officer. "Both senators were standing. The senator from Arizona has been standing."

"I have been standing!" Lautenberg shot back. "With all due respect, I have been here—was here before the senator from Arizona, and I called for recognition from the chair. And the chair, I guess, has that right. But that is not the way this body is to operate."

"The senator from Arizona has the floor," ruled the presiding officer.

"Mr. President, my friend from New Jersey is obviously upset," McCain said. "May I state that I believe it is a very close call. I believe the rule of the Senate is who is on their feet and speaks first is who seeks recognition. I believe we were both on our feet. I do not believe that the rule of the Senate is who has been standing the longest."

The moral of the story: Stand, but by all means speak.

Unless you speak of the president by only his given name—as in "George," or "Dubya," rather than "George Bush" or "President Bush." Although, as I pointed out, who in Washington, Republican and Democrat, didn't refer to our previous presidential pair as "Bill and Hillary?"

Longtime Senator Wendell H. Ford, Kentucky Democrat, for one. In fact, Ford found first-name references of presidents "degrading."

"Never . . . have I heard Gerald Ford called 'Jerry,' Jimmy Carter called 'Jimmy,' Ronald Reagan called 'Ron,' George Bush called 'George,' and I have never heard a [former] first lady called by her first name," he told senators. "I think it is time we have some respect for the office if we do not have respect for the individual who holds it."

I recall when Senator Bob Kerrey ripped into then-freshman Senator Rick Santorum of Pennsylvania for referring to Clinton as "Bill."

"I am fifty-one years old, fifty-one years old," Kerrey lectured. "And I was taught when I was in the Navy [that] the commander in chief, the president of the United States, deserved respect, and I never called the president . . . by his first name in public, let alone on the floor of the Senate. I just ask my colleague, do you feel this is disrespectful? You can disagree with the president, say you have something you do not like about what he is doing, but, for God sakes, 'Where is Bill?'"

Santorum said nothing—for ten days.

"I did a little looking back," the Republican came back and informed Democrats. "Frankly, you did not have to do extensive research to quickly find references to presidents which were, in my opinion, a heck of a lot more pejorative in nature than mentioning the president's first name in a chart."

He cited 119 references by members of Congress to the term "Reaganomics," which is "not a flattering term. That is not a very nice thing to say," the senator said.

He then held up some old issues of the Congressional Record, highlighting where Senator Hollings referred to President Reagan as "Ronnie." And he presented additional stacks of Records showing that Ted Kennedy, over a period of months, repeated the phrase "waiting for George."

I always get a kick out of congressmen who honor and insult in the same breath:

"The *gentleman* from Pennsylvania does not understand the new basic structure," opined Howard L. Berman of California.

"The *gentleman* does not have to tell me what I understand. I understand," replied George Gekas of Pennsylvania.

"Will the gentleman yield?" asked Martin Meehan of Massachusetts.

"No, not at this particular time," replied Steve Buyer of Indiana. "If you became sensitive, that is your particular problem."

Some congressmen prefer to display their manners in writing, like when health subcommittee chairman Pete Stark, a Democrat from California, scrawled a message across the top of a page and handed it to ranking Republican Congressman Bill Archer of Texas: "Dear Bill: This is pure, unadulterated [expletive]. You don't want health reform and you know it! Regards, Pete."

I had to laugh when the National Legal and Policy Center asked Llewellyn H. Rockwell Jr., president of free-market-minded Ludwig von Mises Institute, if he'd be interested in signing a coalition letter to Congress calling for the elimination of funding for the Legal Services Corporation.

Rockwell replied: "Thanks for asking, but I am only interested in signing letters that begin: 'Dear Mr. Majority Leader and Mr. Speaker: You lying bastards.' Best, Lew Rockwell."

Senate Minority Leader Tom Daschle of South Dakota experiences a wide range of emotions in his difficult and stressful post: "I'm prepared to be very disappointed and shocked. Shocked and disappointed. Dismayed. Frustrated. Alienated. Minimized," he rattled off before one vote.

I myself was placed in an uncomfortable position not long ago when Florida Senator Bob Graham, the first Democratic candidate to bow out of the 2004 presidential contest, climbed aboard a "press" elevator that lifts scribes from the basement of the U.S. Capitol to the Senate Press Gallery.

Not until the elevator opened onto the third floor—a level above where the senator wanted to climb off to cast his vote—did Graham realize the button for his floor never got pushed.

"Sorry about that," I apologized to the senator. "I obviously knew you weren't a reporter."

"Why?" Graham asked. "Because of my incoherent speech and stuttering?" I kept my mouth shut.

OFTEN IT'S EVERYDAY CONSTITUENTS who are sensitive, if not down-right ornery. Congressman Vic Fazio was walking down a House corridor reading aloud to aides on either side of him a letter he'd just opened from one California constituent.

"'[Expletive],' 'amoral,' '[expletive],' 'traitor,' and the worst stuff is on the inside!" the lawmaker said, shaking his head.

Senator Campbell of Colorado, a Democrat-turned-Republican, knows how it feels to be labeled a traitor. He now keeps his distance from people he knows he'll never please.

"It's not that I'm avoiding the public, or avoiding questions," the senator told me in an interview. "It's just that once they knife you, why the hell should you help 'em keep knifing you?"

Speaking of being stabbed in the back, Senator Ford of Kentucky once observed: "I've got all of the problems in my state—beautiful women, fast horses, bourbon, cigarettes, and coal, so I am up here on the defensive all the time."

Even reporters get assaulted by constituents. House Speaker Newt Gingrich had just finished telling a crowd in Nashua, New Hampshire, that the liberal media often distorts his views. Using a cellular phone to file his story, Ralph Z. Hallow, political reporter for the *Washington Times*, was suddenly confronted by a well-dressed man who grabbed the phone from the reporter's ear, shouting, "I'm going to put this where it belongs!"

To Mr. Hallow's astonishment, the man then opened the door of a nearby portable toilet and dropped the phone down the chute.

If only more constituents could be like the UPS deliveryman on Florida's Gulf Coast who left his two-cents worth at the door of Congressman Porter J. Goss: "He scribbled his message right on the little yellow delivery ticket," the amused lawmaker observed. "The sentiment was very clear. It said: 'Today's tax system is unfair and needs to be changed.'"

IOWA CONGRESSMAN JIM LIGHTFOOT, assigned the unpopular task of downsizing government, opened a congressional hearing by announcing to colleagues: "Since there's a lot of cuts in this bill, and you all had a lot of time to look at it, I thought I'd come prepared."

The subcommittee chairman then stood up and removed his suit jacket, revealing a bulletproof vest strapped across his chest. Thankfully, the hearing room erupted in laughter and not gunfire.

ONCE WAS THE TIME congressmen settled their disputes by galloping up Bladensburg Road for a good old-fashioned duel. This fine tradition was banned by Congress in 1839, but not before William Graves, a Kentucky Whig, blasted the last breath from Maine Democrat Jonathan Cilley. It took three shots at a distance of a hundred paces "to kill that damned Yankee," remarked one lawmaker who'd witnessed the duel. All told, the "dark and bloody" dueling ground was venue for twenty-five duels, and lawmakers weren't the only targets. The most notorious showdown was in 1820 when, at a mere eight paces, Commodore Stephen A. Decatur, hero of the War of 1812, was mortally wounded by James Barron.

Today, lawmakers prefer fisticuffs. My own Virginia congressman, Democrat James Moran, is a self-described "bully." The lanky Irish American and former amateur boxer has chased, grabbed, shoved, even threatened to punch people he finds disrespectful, including California Republican Randy "Duke" Cunningham, a former combat fighter pilot who by no means is a weakling.

But the size of his opponents has never stopped Moran, who during the middle of one congressional debate pushed Cunningham through the House chamber door, shouting at the top of his lungs, "You pull that again and I'll break your nose!" More than a dozen U.S. Capitol Police officers had to be called to restore order.

Capitol cops were summoned again in the summer of 2003, this time to restrain California Democrat Pete Stark during a heated hearing of the

House Ways and Means Committee. Tempers flared after Congressman Scott McInnis of Colorado told Stark to "shut up!"

"Oh, you think you are big enough to make me, you little wimp? Come on. Come over here and make me. I dare you," Stark shouted. "You little fruitcake. You little fruitcake. I said, you are a fruitcake!"

"Recess is over," Chairman Bill Thomas of California announced. "The classroom has been resumed."

All in all, being packaged a fruitcake ain't so bad.

"That goes with the territory," says former Senator Alan Simpson of Wyoming, one of the nicest guys ever to come out of Laramie. Or so we thought.

"The Al Simpson who was on federal probation at the age of eighteen is not the same Al Simpson standing here," the senator confessed in my column. "The Al Simpson who was thrown in the clink at age twenty for clubbing a guy around the streets of Laramie is not the same Al Simpson standing here, although sometimes the feelings are still burning down there."

But, he reasoned, "That is politics. It was always a little rough and tumble, and it still will be, and ever shall be, world without end." Amen.

Chapter 8

Coconut and Other Homeless

WELCOME TO THE NATION'S CAPITAL—always in the hunt as murder capital of the world. And it's not getting any safer. If the constant terrorist threat isn't enough to fret over, Washington's chief of police in the summer of 2003 declared a "Crime Emergency."

It would only get worse in 2004. On the last day of April, Supreme Court Justice David Souter, one of the top judges in the land, was attacked and beaten by an angry, if not ignorant, group of young thugs while jogging around the streets of Washington. Which makes Supreme Court Justice Ruth Bader Ginsburg's prior purse-snatching outside the infamous Watergate Hotel petty in comparison.

"Outside of the killings, [Washington] has one of the lowest crime rates in the country," once boasted former D.C. Mayor Marion Barry, twisted logic from a man whose greatest legacy was putting Columbia back in the District—and his nose.

"I wish I were back in Indiana," said Congressman Ed Pease of Indiana, robbed at gunpoint while delivering Christmas presents. In town for historic House Judiciary Committee impeachment proceedings against you-know-who, the lawmaker asked the robber to leave him with enough change to ride the subway back to Capitol Hill. The bandit showed the congressman the sidewalk, which he eventually took back to Indiana.

Three months later, President Clinton's health and human services secretary Donna E. Shalala, one of the kindest cabinet members you could ever meet, was retrieving her hard-earned dollars from an automated teller machine in one of Washington's upscale neighborhoods.

"Give it up! Give it up!" a pair of bandits warned the pint-size secretary, who must have hiked in Montana because she quickly dropped to the fetal position and began screaming at the top of her lungs.

Shalala once played shortstop in Cleveland's Pigtail League, coached by none other than New York Yankees owner George Steinbrenner. He once said he wished he had eight other players like Shalala on the team. She didn't give her assailants a penny—and lived to tell about it.

Kansas Senator Sam Brownback, who assumed the seat of retiring Senator Bob Dole, took issue with Barry's insistence that Washington was as safe as Topeka, Kansas.

"I have some statistics, and they show the District has a long way to go," said Brownback, who that very week announced "my fourth staff member had a burglary on Capitol Hill."

What was stolen?

"The guy stole a 1984 Caprice Classic with 184,000 miles on it," the senator said. "My staffer said the bumper stickers were worth more than the car." So many car thieves patrol the nation's capital they can't afford to be choosy.

Hoping to glorify living in the shadow of the Capitol Dome, the Capitol Hill Restoration Society once hosted a house tour. Just before the doors opened, the vehicle carrying the tour's kiosks, signs, and tickets was stolen and later found stripped.

Driving along Interstate 295 near RFK Stadium, where the Redskins played in their glory days, I was surprised to come upon a broken down and abandoned car in the fast lane. Believe it or not, the car's owner clamped an anti-theft device across the steering wheel, just in case any car thieves stuck in the ensuing traffic happened to be good mechanics.

Vanity Fair contributing editor Christopher Hitchens once painted an hysterically accurate, albeit bleak portrait of life in the nation's capital. Afterwards, D.C. government spokeswoman Linda Wharton Boyd fired off a letter to the magazine charging that Hitchens grossly exaggerated everything from the depth of the city's potholes (one smart-aleck suggested to cops they might search for Chandra Levy in one) to the deplorable conditions at the D.C. morgue, where bodies were stacked at room temperature.

"Outright lies," Boyd called them.

Hitchens, when I called him to follow up, not only stood by his story, he said he framed the city's rebuttal—"a last squeak from the dying planet of Marion Barry."

"In my article I said that the mayor [Barry] was a crook and a friend of crooks, that the [former] police chief was a lout who protected officers on the take, that the prison system was a hellhole, that the schools didn't open on schedule and spent most of their time dealing with crowd control when they did, that the infant mortality figures were worse than for some Third World nations, that diseases such as AIDS and TB were stalking the city largely uncontested, that the fire trucks and patrol cars and ambulances and snowplows were out of commission as often as not, that garbage pickup and recycling had been abandoned, that the water supply had been subject to emergency advisories [in 2004, lead contaminants in the water became a serious problem], that the morgue was a disgrace and the potholes a standing joke, and that federal money to the alleviation of all this was going unspent because of a mixture of incompetence and venality.

"Now comes a painfully written letter—dated March 31 but not received by our office until a month later—which says the water is now fit to drink! Nice work!" Hitchens said. "It's good to know that the morgue now has a working fridge."

The refrigerator didn't cool everything. In September 2003, the city's chief medical examiner, Jonathan L. Arden, resigned over numerous operational problems. For example, city health inspectors said formaldehyde fumes from uncovered containers were so noxious in the morgue's unventilated laboratory that, for those still breathing, it was "immediately danger-ous to life and health." In addition, unclaimed bodies decomposing in stor-age rooms were found to have been stored there for three years; the morgue's records were kept in unsecured paper case files, not on computer; and the good doctor himself was fingered by five deputy medical examiners for alleged sexual harassment.

One day Frank Bell of Bell Builders called me to say he thought it news-worthy that the D.C. government—more incredibly, the D.C. treasurer—was delinquent in paying rent for the post office box used to collect taxes. That's right, Washington residents couldn't pay their taxes even if they wanted to.

"BOX CLOSED FOR NONPAYMENT OF RENT—WASHINGTON, D.C.," the post office stamped on Bell's returned letter.

ONE WOULD HAVE THOUGHT Congressman Jerry Lewis, California Republican, would have moved back to Redlands after twenty-seven frus-trating years on Capitol Hill, or at least found a safer neighborhood. He and his wife Arlene just finished dinner at a Capitol Hill restaurant and were walking back to their 1984 Olds (he doesn't dare buy a newer model) when the congressman noticed a man sitting in the driver's seat.

Lewis, who had his 1977 Olds stolen from the backyard of his Capitol Hill home four years earlier "never to be seen again," wasn't about to part easily with this newer model. When the thief started driving off, the con-gressman darted out onto Pennsylvania Avenue, caught up with his beloved ride, and started banging on the window.

A police officer on routine patrol spotted the commotion and joined in the chase. Being pursued on foot and by siren, the thief hit the gas, spun around Folger Park, then slammed into two vehicles, a parking meter, and finally a tree. He tried running but was chased down by the cop. As for the Olds, it sustained substantial front-end damage, "and the guy screwed up the ignition system, so I need a screwdriver to start the car," the congress-man told me.

But get this: because the car was stolen in Washington, the thief escaped conviction. It's no different, actually, than stealing a bicycle.

One year later, Lewis awoke on a Sunday morning and looked out his window. The same 1984 Olds—now repaired—was gone. It was the third car heist from the congressman in four years.

"The first time this happened, I just said, 'Oh well, these things are bound to happen in Washington.' The second time, I chased the guy down and counted myself lucky not to get shot. After the third time, I'm just shaking my head and wondering whether I should start walking to work," he said.

And it's not just car problems.

"My house has been broken into three times," the congressman revealed.

WITH HIS ADVANCED MILITARY TRAINING, retired General Norman Schwarzkopf knows better than most leaders when Washington is under siege.

"Every time I've been there it's worse than before," said the general, who was posted in the nation's capital on five separate occasions. Washington, he quipped, "is the only place you can run ten miles in a straight line and still be at the scene of the crime."

LIFE'S NOT ANY BETTER FOR THE DOGS. I broke the story when D.C. animal control officials received an emergency call from a Secret Service officer guarding the entrance to the vice president's mansion along Massachusetts Avenue. The officer reported that a sick dog was lingering around the heavily secured property and he requested somebody come rescue the pooch. Given the VIP address, the dogcatcher responded right away and determined the dog, a poodle, required immediate emergency veterinary care.

According to my veterinary source at D.C. animal control, the dog was suffering from "maggot infestation of the muscles, resulting from an open, untreated wound."

Sadder yet, the vet whispered to me, the maggot-riddled poodle—named "Coconut"—belonged to Al Gore.

You don't say?

The suffering animal was immediately transported to Friendship Animal Hospital, a twenty-four-hour Washington facility that provided emergency care under its director, Dr. Peter Glassman.

"No, I have no comment," Glassman said when I called to inquire about Coconut's condition. When I told the good doctor that my source at the hospital had told me the staff there was under "strict order" not to discuss Coconut's condition, he huffed: "I told my staff not to comment on anything that goes on here!"

Going above Glassman's head, I learned that anybody that had anything to do with dogs in Washington was "under a gag order" when it came to Coconut. Any official comment, I was told, would have to come from Mary Healey, executive director of the Washington Humane Society.

"We had received a call to pick up a dog in the vicinity of the vice presidential property, and we responded to the call. We located the dog; I believe it was a poodle," Healey told me, "named Coconut."

I immediately called the Gore mansion, to make certain the family was aware that Coconut was safe, rescued at their front gate, and was now being treated for maggot infestation. Although nobody picked up the phone, Tipper Gore later issued a statement: "What happened is we've been having construction on the house and Coconut got out and was missing for a couple of days." (No, Coconut was not wearing a nametag, as required by city ordinance.)

Mrs. Gore did not say whether the family ever reported the dog as missing. "It's an amazing dog," she said. "She's sixteen years old. It had been outside the grounds and found its way home, and that's when it was discovered."

I was told, however, that the Secret Service officer knew the entire time whose dog it was and he "was just trying to get the suffering animal some help without jeopardizing his job."

TRY FINDING A PARKING SPACE in Washington. With her young son in tow, Susan Au Allen, a partner in the law firm Paul Shearman Allen & Associates, left her home at 7:00 P.M. to pick up Mr. Allen at his law office.

Pulling out of the family's garage, the lawyer encountered a black Volvo parked illegally in the alley entrance. She tried, but couldn't squeeze past the car. "I couldn't back out of the alley. I blew my horn, tried to squeeze through, and touched the car. But I didn't damage it," she said.

Figuring correctly that the car's owner was dining at the restaurant next door, Allen approached the establishment's parking valet and, getting nowhere, the restaurant manager. The latter refused to disturb his patrons while they were eating and told the woman if she didn't like it to call the police.

"I said, 'Okay, I'll call the police.' I waited forty-five minutes for the police to arrive," she said. "While waiting, the valet came back three times and cursed at me. When the police finally came, I told them what happened, and the valet did the same thing in front of them. The police had to pull him away.

"Meanwhile, the valet went in and found the [Volvo] owner. A gentleman came out . . . his name was John Richardson," she said. "But his registration, I told him, said 'Margaret Richardson.'

"'That's my wife,' he said, 'and she's the IRS commissioner, and I hope you paid your taxes!'

"I said, 'What?'

"And he repeated, 'My wife is the commissioner of the IRS, and I hope you paid your taxes!'

"I couldn't believe he was telling me that," Allen said.

Nor could readers of my column. In fact, Margaret Milner Richardson, a personal friend of Hillary Rodham Clinton, was appointed by President Clinton to head the Internal Revenue Service. Needless to say, Mrs. Richardson's husband, if not Allen, was obviously impressed with his wife's clout.

SPEAKING OF PARKING PROBLEMS, let's drop into the U.S. Information Agency, more commonly known as USIA. If you haven't already gathered, most of official Washington communicates via memorandum. Without the back-and-forth shuffle of white and yellow slips of paper, it is estimated that the U.S. government would self-destruct in sixty seconds.

Most memos are boring. The few that aren't find their way to unofficial eyes: mine.

Take the outrageous chain of memos exchanged by then-USIA Inspector General Marian C. Bennett and her two top deputies.

"As you know," Bennett wrote to executive assistant Louis J. Leporatti, "I have assigned Parking Space No. 71 . . . to Anne T. Young, my assistant inspector general for Management and Authorization."

Leporatti had previously parked in Space 71, and Bennett ordered him to turn over his garage access card "by today" or else his car "may be subject to being towed."

An outraged Leporatti responded with his own memo, which wasn't his first: "As I advised you last week, I had already given the card to your deputy, Brian Dowling, at his request. Therefore, your request that I provide the card to Ms. Young puzzles me."

The inspector general wasn't satisfied, firing a memo back to Leporatti.

"As the person assigned the access card, you are not authorized to give the card to someone else on your own," she wrote. "I assign the parking spaces for the Office of Inspector General. Furthermore, to give Brian the card knowing I intended to assign the space to Anne is insubordination. I will file copies of the correspondence on this matter in your personnel file. Again, I am requesting that you return the access card to me by Tuesday."

Leporatti couldn't believe his eyes.

"At this point," he wrote back to the inspector general, "there is no purpose in your continuing a dialogue with me on this matter. As I have previously advised you, the person you should be talking to is your deputy. By copy of this memorandum, I am formally requesting that the director intercede on this matter to avoid aggravating what has become an embarrassing and stressful situation."

Embarrassing, in part, because I was being leaked each and every piece of correspondence. Soon, all of Washington was anxious to learn whose car would wind up in Parking Space No. 71. Five days later, Bennett sent a memo to Deputy Inspector General Dowling.

"As you know," she wrote, "I have assigned Parking Space No. 71 to Anne Young. I understand that you have the access card to the garage. Please provide it to me by COB [close of business]. Anne is authorized to use that space, and any other use is unauthorized."

Dowling now was forced to write a follow-up memo, which wasn't his first either.

"I have difficulty responding to your request when you have not furnished me with any rationale for this unorthodox behavior despite my request for the same outlined in my [earlier] letter," he said.

"I will be happy to return the garage access card as soon as I receive from you an explanation as to why a female junior GS-15 is receiving favored treatment over a senior male in personal rank (SES-5) and in office position (deputy inspector general). By copy of this memorandum, I am also asking your supervisor, the [USIA] director, Dr. Joseph Duffy, to be the decision maker in the resolution of this conflict."

Weeks passed, and I was concerned my covert USIA pipeline had dried up. Readers were getting antsy, writing to ask who came out on top. Rumor had it the president of the United States wanted to know who found parking in Space No. 71.

Finally, another memo, sent by the inspector general to the deputy inspector general.

"I am citing you for insubordination," Bennett wrote. "Your conduct was disruptive, inappropriate, and demoralizing for other senior staff."

Fighting words. Relying on Webster's dictionary, Dowling fired yet another memo back to Bennett.

"'Insubordination' is defined as 'not submissive to authority; disobedient,'" he wrote. "I expressed my opinion, which is my right, concerning serious problems affecting this office . . . [and] I concluded by suggesting that the time had come for you, the inspector general, to give some serious thought to resigning because of the damage you have caused to this office."

All of this, ladies and gentleman, over a parking space.

UNDER THE HEADLINE "BLIND FOR A DAY," I pointed out that Washington's residents try to steer clear of the D.C. Department of Motor Vehicles. But having read that the DMV, under a new and improved Mayor Anthony Williams, had been transformed and modernized, D.C. resident Mary Ann Novak decided it safe to renew her driver's license—for once "with some optimism."

Sure enough, the woman's assigned number indicated she would be processed in record time: four minutes. Barely enough time to fill out the required forms. That is, until a highly observant DMV officer spotted a small bandage on Novak's foot.

And "anyone with a bandage has to be cleared by D.C. Medical Services," the officer told Novak.

You're kidding, right?

"When I protested that I had just put on that bandage before coming down to renew my license, and I could just as quickly take it off, they sternly dismissed me and firmly directed me to Room 1033," Novak told me.

Arriving in Room 1033, the Band-Aided woman pulled a paper number like you do in the bakery. The number indicated there were roughly forty people in front of her.

"I noted that I was definitely the youngest person around, until I was joined by a man who I learned had an artificial leg and was there for his annual handicap parking renewal," she said.

After nearly two hours, Novak was called into a cubicle ruled by "a sullen young woman whom I had watched deny licenses to a steady stream of senior citizens, including many for failing the vision test. To my surprise, instead of being questioned on my foot bandage, I was tersely directed to take the vision test.

"So, I shrugged and bent my head to the vision machine, crisply reading off the numbers to the clerk. To my further surprise, she stated that I couldn't get my license because I was legally blind and unable to see the correct row of numbers. I responded that there was no other row of numbers and that I wasn't blind, and when she asserted that there were lines above where I was reading, I told her it was too dark to read anything. She then handed me a form for my ophthalmologist to fill out, denied my license renewal, and dismissed me sternly."

This is surreal, I remarked, like the Twilight Zone. Are you certain Candid Camera wasn't it town?

"From being too lame to drive and now too blind to see, this was beginning to feel almost Biblical to me," Novak agreed, getting to the most shocking part of her story. "As I turned to go back into the clerk's cubicle, I saw her lean over and look into the vision machine. Suddenly, she called out that her machine was broken!"

All's well that ends well—for Novak, if not the dozens of drivers the DMV proclaimed "blind." As new light bulbs were being installed into the machine, the clerk calmly and, without apology, took Novak's thirty dollars and directed her to the next room for her photo and license.

"Don't cry for me," Novak said, "cry for the many others who failed the eye test, especially the senior citizens."

"PROBLEMS ON THE POTOMAC" was the title of a report by Princeton Survey Research Associates, conducted on behalf of the Brookings Institution. It found potential presidential appointees couldn't embrace the idea of living in Washington.

"The prospect of relocating to Washington emerged from the survey as one of the most statistically significant barriers to serving as a presidential appointee," the report stated. "Most respondents viewed Washington as a somewhat less favorable place to live than their current residences."

Why? Because of crime, high mortality numbers, searing heat, and enervating humidity?

"Almost half said relocating their 'spouse' to Washington would be somewhat or very difficult, and more than two-thirds said a presidential appointment would create much or some disruption in their personal lives."

Whatever the reason, the report concluded that "fears of moving to Washington increase the likelihood that presidents will appoint cabinet and sub-cabinet officials who already live in the Washington area, thereby biasing their administrations toward people who can already afford the cost of living, while giving up the diversity of experience and insight that might come with more talent drawn from outside the Washington Beltway. No matter how much they promise an administration that looks like America, recent presidents have had increasing difficulty actually appointing administrations that come from across America."

Brookings suggested several incentives to lure presidential appointees and their families, including congressionally authorized reimbursement for travel and relocation, helping spouses find jobs, securing schools and childcare, and home-buying assistance.

Which isn't to say everybody in Washington wants to live in a house. The city has a large and proud army of homeless people, many bunking down within sight of the White House. Yes, there are plenty of available shelter beds, but homeless people prefer the fresh air and great outdoors. The only time you get them to budge is when a more efficient steam-grate becomes available. Of course, you wouldn't know this watching the local television news stations as they tag along behind city officials to distribute blankets on cold nights.

I'll never forget the *Washington Post* dishing up a warm and fuzzy piece about a "homeless" person President Clinton encountered when leaving the Bombay Club near the White House.

Restaurant owner Ashok Bajaj told the newspaper that it was Clinton who'd approached the disheveled man, not the other way around. The restaurant owner described the man as "a street person like you might see on the steam-grates—and he was obviously drunk."

The president, the *Post* reported, actually placed his arm around the bum and the two proceeded to take a stroll through Lafayette Park—the first lady, daughter Chelsea, and select dinner guests following in the limousine.

"You could see the president with his arm around this quite disreputable-looking fellow walking off into the night," the restaurant owner told the *Post,* painting a rather surreal picture that piqued the curiosity of Frank Murray, White House correspondent for the *Washington Times.*

For an entire week, Murray sought the homeless man's identity, then kindly allowed me to publish the results of his search. It turned out the homeless man was P.F. Bentley, who doesn't sleep on a steam-grate but rather on a feather bed overlooking a Pacific lagoon in Stinson Beach, California.

Bentley was a photographer for *Time* magazine. He'd been granted an entire year of private access to Clinton during the 1992 presidential campaign. In talking to Murray, the photographer was reluctant to appear to be seeking publicity over the encounter, but he confirmed that he was the bearded man and had been outside the restaurant by arrangement to see a friend on the White House staff.

"Clinton saw me and we say 'Hi' and we're walking and talking and he puts his arm around me," Bentley explained. "I am extremely distressed that the *Post* said I looked homeless. I believe I had clean clothes that weren't that tattered and torn. I left my shopping cart at the hotel."

IT WAS WELL PAST MIDNIGHT, around 2:30 A.M. when an unkempt man stumbled up to the entrance gate of the White House. It was the latter half of the Clinton presidency, and security was tighter than usual. A Secret Service officer confronted the man, asking him where he thought he was going.

"I need to get into the White House," answered the man, who was described by the officer as looking "disheveled."

"Sure you do. Get out of here," the officer warned the man, who instead proceeded to pull a White House badge out of his pocket. It was Roger Clinton. The gates were opened.

Chapter 9

No Ifs, Ands, or Buts

Yes, it happens all the time, said Dave LesStrang, press secretary to Congressman Jerry Lewis, referring to California constituents and similar misinformed Americans who somehow confuse Jerry Lewis "the congressman" with Jerry Lewis "the comedian." Visitors to Capitol Hill will even poke their heads into the congressman's office and ask, "It's not really Jerry Lewis, is it?"

Once when I was in the office, a Lewis staff member happened to be responding to a letter mailed by a man in Lake Villa, Illinois.

"I am a big fan of your work," he wrote. "My favorite movie is the *Disorderly Orderly* and I like what you are doing with the fight against Muscular Dystrophy, keep it up. My mother really loves you. Can you also send her a picture? Her name is Gale. Again, thank you in advance. God Bless, and long life to you."

Not everybody is a member of the Jerry Lewis fan club, like the disgruntled constituent who wrote, "I hate your movies. I hate you on TV. I wouldn't vote for you if you were running for dogcatcher."

Stacks of hilarious letters like these are opened every day, whether on

Capitol Hill or at the White House, where one of our more recent presidents got an earful from six hopping mad citizens of Silver Spring, Maryland:

"Dear President Clinton and Family: Today we went to the Easter Egg Roll. We got there around 9:50 A.M. and got into a very long line. After we got onto the White House lawn it was after 2:00 P.M. and then found out you had run out of eggs. The Turnhams' cousin, Miranda Todd, came all the way from Tennessee for Easter and your Easter Egg Roll. She didn't get an egg. We are really angry.

"P.S.: We think we should get an egg or an apology. Our parents voted for you and we are disappointed!"

Talk about creative writing at a young age. I once republished a letter to the editor of the rightwing newspaper *Heterodoxy,* written by Washington student Sam Munson: "I am eleven years old and I cannot thank you enough for publishing this wonderful paper. I go to public school in D.C., and to a lifelong conservative, that is hell. My schoolmates are a bunch of feminist, liberal, PC, vegetarian multiculturalists. *Heterodoxy* is just the thing for recovering from a six-and-a-half-hour school day surrounded by them."

WITHOUT A DOUBT, the most valuable tool for a political columnist in this town is a Rolodex containing the names of reliable sources planted in the bowels of bureaucracy. As for what type of leaks to publish, my rule is that if something tickles my funny bone, or else gets my blood boiling, then chances are readers will giggle or get irritated, too.

And there's never a shortage of intriguing anecdotes given so many Washington bureaucrats manning the BATF, CIA, DEA, DOD, DOE, DOI, DOJ, DOL, DOS, DOT, EEOC, EPA, FAA, FBI, FCC, FDA, FDIC, FEC, FEMA, FHA, FRS, FTA, FTC, FWS, GAO, GSA, GPO, HHS, HUD, IMF, INS, IRS, ITC, NASA, NEA, NHTSA, NIH, NPS, NSA, NSF, NTSB, OMB, OPM, OSHA, SBA, SEC, SSA, USPS, and, last but never least, Congress—where 535 lawmakers are always up to something. (I once asked political satirist/pianist Mark Russell, who also lives in Washington, how he comes up with so much hilarious material, and he replied he had 435 writers in the House and 100 in the Senate.)

Take the lawmaker who when finished grilling a congressional witness rose from his chair to leave the room. Instead of walking out the door, however, he accidentally stepped into a closet. Like Inspector Clouseau's "Old Closet Ploy" from *Shot in the Dark.* The embarrassed member of Congress actually remained in the closet for several seconds, then casually strolled out as if he had intended all along to pay homage to the mops and brooms.

Other items I publish leave readers astonished. Like when Congresswoman Sheila Jackson Lee, a Texas Democrat and member of the Science, Space, and Aeronautics Subcommittee, participated in a fact-finding tour of the Mars Pathfinder Mission Control Center in Pasadena, California. During the tour, she reportedly asked in so many words: Did the Pathfinder mission succeed in taking pictures of the American flag planted by astronaut Neil Armstrong in 1969?

"We just don't teach enough science," lamented fellow committee member Vernon J. Ehlers, Michigan Republican, a former physics professor.

Believe it or not, the same congresswoman in 2003 alleged racial discrimination when it came to the government's naming hurricanes. Jackson Lee said hurricane names like David and Mike are too white and "all racial groups should be represented" when storms wreak havoc on our lives, limbs, and property, particularly "African-American names."

I once wrote about a very high-ranking member of Congress who made it his practice to stash silverware and food items in a duffel bag placed under his airplane seat. He regularly ordered two breakfasts—one to eat, one to forage.

"What was incredible was that in between the meals he ordered multiple bagels and muffins," said my reliable source. "When he got the bagels, he'd take out Ziploc bags and start putting them away. He ordered at least four bagels and two or three muffins."

Some stories bring tears to the eyes of readers, like when Congressman Floyd D. Spence of South Carolina approached the lectern and asked to be excused from floor debate: "I ask the House if I might apologize for making a personal comment at this time, but I would not be able to take part in these discussions—indeed, I would not be alive—if it were not for the fact, as many of you know, I received a double lung transplant a few years ago. And the mother of the young man whose lungs I have is presently in my office visiting with me for the first time, and I just wanted to pay respect to her."

It wasn't too long afterwards that Spence's lungs stopped pumping.

Others cried tears for a different reason when Senator Howell Heflin of Alabama, hosting a lunch in the Senate cafeteria, reached into his pocket for a handkerchief and pulled out a pair of women's panties. Everybody at his table burst out laughing, including Heflin. The slow-talking, now red-faced chairman of the Senate Ethics Committee explained that his wife, Elizabeth Ann, stacked the couple's laundry into a single pile and leaving the house in a hurry that morning he'd obviously scooped up her undies by mistake.

The always entertaining Heflin used to tell the story I called "Grey Poupon," describing people too sophisticated to be from Alabama as "Gucci-wearing, Mercedes-driving, Perrier-drinking, Aspen-skiing, richy-rich Republicans who eat broccoli."

Like Robert Byrd of West Virginia, the senator always put his Alabama constituents first. Once the Senate was drafting drought aid and considering a long list of impacted commodities. When they finally finished, Heflin raised his hand and asked, "Mr. Chairman, what about peaches?"

Nobody had thought about peaches, but after Heflin reminded senators how juicy a ripe peach tastes in the summer they ended up inserting peaches into the package. Heflin plugged more than peaches. Bob Dole said he learned a great deal from the Alabama senator "about issues ranging from peanuts to the boll weevil."

Readers tell me they enjoy Inside the Beltway because they never know what—or who—will appear in the column next. Nor do I, until stumbling upon it—or them—along Pennsylvania Avenue. Following are some chance encounters I turned into stories.

RIDING A PADDED ELEVATOR at the headquarters of the U.S. Nuclear Regulatory Commission, two bureaucrats, Glenn and Pete, noticed the cleaning lady had "stacks and stacks" of Scott's "low-cost" toilet paper she was delivering to the agency's restrooms.

"I also noticed a separate container with 'Charmin Big Squeeze' tissue, the ultimate in softness," one of the bureaucrats said. "I asked what the Charmin was for? The lady answered that was for the . . . chairman's private bathroom."

The NRC chairman being Shirley Ann Jackson, a Washington native who earned a doctorate in theoretical elementary particle physics from the Massachusetts Institute of Technology in 1973.

"This is clearly an improper use of power," the bureaucrat observed.

Glenn and Pete felt so strongly about the softness afforded the chairman but nobody else, they wrote a memo to the NRCs Office of Administration demanding "soft tush paper, too."

The men were happy to report a short time later that, "in the spirit of partnership," NRC administrators solved the problem with a pledge that "all NRC employees at headquarters should be noting the results soon."

WHEN FIRST ELECTED TO CONGRESS, Mark Sanford of South Carolina (he's now the state's governor) promised not to be drawn into the Capitol Hill lifestyle, which is "part of the problem in Washington."

So, instead of moving into a townhouse or apartment, the former real estate investor, who pledged to serve no more than three terms in Congress, blew up an air mattress and slept on the floor of his congressional office. Six years later, I wrote, he was still waking up there.

"Last night was a little tough," he told me. "We were voting until about 1:00 A.M. and the cleaning lady came in around 2:00. It can be an exercise in sleep deprivation, exacerbated with a vacuum cleaner about five feet from your head."

Anybody who's been on Capitol Hill knows congressional quarters are cramped enough without somebody bedding down there. So when Sanford's staff required additional working space, the congressman agreed to vacate his more private space in exchange for a section of floor "sandwiched" between two other offices.

"That's the whole reason I wanted a door," he said.

Sanford approached architect of the Capitol Alan M. Hantman about installing a door at the entrance to the office where he was now sleeping. A door, he explained, would provide him—and future office holders of Room 1233 of the Longworth House Office Building—needed privacy. Sanford even offered to hang the door himself.

It took seven months for a reply, and when it came the congressman was . . . well, floored.

Hantman and his team of door-project coordinators—assistant project estimator Sandra K. Turman, senior project estimator Curtis P. Dyer, and assistant architect of the Capitol Michael G. Turnbull—together estimated the cost of one congressional door at $2,753. Taxpayer dollars, of course.

In addition, as Hantman informed the congressman in writing, the price of the door does *not* include costs for demolition, preparation, finishing, and labor, plus fees for construction branch field supervision, and architect of the Capitol construction management.

Oh, and there's one more thing: "Door stops are not contemplated in this estimate." How much can a door stop run?

"It took seven months just to get a reply to say that not only can you not hang a door yourself, we will have to do it at a cost of $2,753," said Sanford, who had actually spotted several "spare" doors unhinged in the hallways of Longworth.

"My simple thought was to grab one of those doors," he said. "Seven bucks of hinges at Lowe's or Home Depot and I could have hung it myself. I've hung plenty of doors in my life."

With all due respect, sir, are you adept at demolition?

"There is no demolition required. Preparation maybe, but no demolition."

The bottom line?

"Needless to say, I'm not doing the door."

REPRESENTATIVE JOE KNOLLENBERG, Michigan Republican, tells the story of Jean English who, while reading through the mail of her recently departed brother, discovered a bill for his final hospital stay. It should be pointed out that her brother, suffering from a terminal illness, died only a few days after being admitted.

Incredibly, the bill for his four-day stay in the hospital came to $368,511.09—the entire amount forwarded to Medicare for payment. Shocked at the expense, English called the hospital for an explanation. What she got was a fourteen-page itemized statement, with the greatest cost being a seven-hour stay in the emergency room requiring $347,982.01 worth of supplies.

"Well, after much hemming and hawing," said the congressman, "the hospital admitted that it had made a mistake. Oops! Instead of $347,982.01, the actual charge should have been $61.30. That is right, $61.30. An overcharge of $347,920.71. The problem was found."

End of story? Hardly.

"The errant bill had been sent to Medicare and paid by Medicare. That is right," the congressman said, "they paid the bill!"

THE DEPARTMENT OF LABOR's much-heralded "Glass Ceiling Commission" urges government and private business to open opportunities to women and minorities, with the hope that the "glass ceiling" will one day be shattered.

Yet some folks in this great democracy of ours remain confused about the exact function of the Glass Ceiling Commission, as evidenced in this memo from Rene A. Redwood, executive director of the commission, to her fellow Glass Ceiling commissioners:

"Many of us take for granted that the words we use connote the meaning we intend. The term 'glass ceiling' is still quite new to the lexicon and is routinely literally interpreted as an architectural feature. I share this citizen's correspondence with you for awareness that we must constantly define the phenomena of 'glass ceiling' and not assume others know what we are talking about. The good news is that our fellow American heard of the commission and knew where to inquire."

She attached a letter (I took it to be a hoax, but the director obviously didn't) written by a gentleman from Maplewood, New Jersey. It reads: "I am glad to have recently learned that the government has finally opened a task force to help me and others out on the type of project I am planning for spring. I am planning to install a glass skylight in my extension, but I am hoping to avoid the problems my friend Larry faced when he installed a partial glass ceiling in his kitchen, went out one day when it was raining, and came back to almost $13,000 worth of damage to his house and a lawsuit against his contractor. In addition, my brother-in-law enclosed an area with a glass ceiling up in his country home, but now he has wound up with really ugly condensation between the panes, which sort of defeated the purpose of trying to make the house look real spiffy. I certainly would appreciate you sending any brochures you have which could help me avoid these problems and wind up with a job I will be happy with."

MEMBERS OF THE U.S. INTELLIGENCE COMMUNITY won't forget the winter's day in 1994 when FBI agents swooped down on one of their own— fifty-two-year old Aldrich Ames, a thirty-one-year-veteran of the CIA, arrested on charges of spying for the Soviet Union and Russia.

For much of his career, Ames was responsible for CIA clandestine operations around the globe. His espionage activities, which consisted of feeding secrets to Moscow from 1985 to 1994, not only resulted in severe, wide-ranging, and continuing damage to the security of the United States, but the death and/or imprisonment of men and women who were CIA and FBI contacts.

It obviously was no laughing matter.

Well, actually, there was a grain of humor following Ames's conviction, which I stuck beneath the headline, "Those Wacky Spooks."

A well-placed source revealed to me that several CIA agents had been victimized by upper-level CIA "pranksters" who had actually crept into their offices during the night and jotted down Ames's name and telephone number into their Rolodexes.

The innocent targets of the prank didn't find anything funny about it, for Ames's ability to acquire intelligence he wasn't authorized to see had prompted widespread questioning of anyone within the agency who knew or even talked to him. Imagine trying to explain why Ames's name and phone number appeared in your Rolodex.

———

TWO EMPLOYEES at the National Oceanic and Atmospheric Administration were cautioned about "racial insensitivity" after labeling various recycling containers in their office.

One container they labeled "white paper," the other "colored paper."

"They were told that was insensitive and sent for some sensitivity training," said an NOAA official. "Since then the trash cans have been relabeled 'white paper' and 'non-white paper.'"

———

IF YOU, DURING A MORE DIFFICULT TIME in the Clinton administration, were to have called 202-565-9161, a Labor Department phone number, you would have heard this actual recording: "You have reached the Office of Workers Compensation Programs, Ruth Wilson speaking. I will be in the office between the hours of ten and three. We are affected by the [government] shutdown. Most of the agency is on a furlough; however, we will continue to try to assist you to the best of our ability, considering we are not receiving our full pay. This is a travesty! But we continue to do what we were hired to do. Thank you."

———

IT WAS DECEMBER 1995, and the Senate was embroiled in debate on what constitutes physical desecration of the U.S. flag. Then, Senator Joseph Biden of Delaware, whose small state boasts several popular beaches—Rehoboth, Dewey, Bethany, Fenwick Island, and Lewes—posed a question that, for once, stumped the entire Senate body.

"How about the woman who buys the revealing thong bikini that is made in a flag?" Biden wondered. "Is that profaning the flag? Is she to be arrested?"

Complete silence.

Biden solved the problem by offering an amendment that would make it "unlawful to do the flag harm: no ifs, ands, or buts."

AS FAR AS THE NOW-RETIRED SENATOR Jesse Helms is concerned, a rodent can do a heck of a lot worse than live out its lifespan in a medical-research laboratory. Like having its head snapped off by an owl, suffocating in the chute of a snake, or succumbing to painful death administered by the neighborhood exterminator. (Where's People for the Ethical Treatment of Animals when you need it?)

So in 2002, Helms offered an amendment that would exclude mice, rats, and birds from the definition of "animal" under the Animal Welfare Act. That way, lifesaving medical research would not be delayed, made more expensive, or otherwise compromised by what Helms called regulatory "shenanigans" at the Agriculture Department.

"The medical-research community was astonished the U.S. Department of Agriculture—weary and browbeat into submission by numerous lawsuits and petitions by the so-called 'animal rights' crowd—gave notice of its intent to add rats, mice, and birds under the regulatory umbrella," Helms noted.

Which meant, among other burdens, additional reporting requirements and paperwork that could cost medical researchers up to $280 million annually. Instead of searching for cures for breast cancer, cystic fibrosis, heart disease, and diabetes, the USDA would force researchers out of the laboratory so they could fill out myriad forms and questionnaires.

"I was surprised to learn," Helms said, "that ten times as many rodents are raised and sold as food for reptiles as are used by the medical-research community. But nobody raises a point about that. I wonder if anyone in this chamber has seen a hungry python eat a mouse? If you have, then you know it is not a pretty picture for the mouse.

"Isn't it far better for the mouse," Helms reasoned, "to be fed and watered in a clean laboratory than to end up as a tiny bulge being digested inside an enormous snake?"

And, the senator asked, what about millions of mice that take up residence—many pregnant and anxious to start families—in the basements, bedrooms, and boardrooms across America, only to be labeled "pests" worthy of extinction by the Orkin man?

"Alas," Helms concluded, "extermination remains the fate every year of hundreds of thousands of rodents that have not found the relative safety of a research facility."

———————

THE CONTROVERSY BEGAN when a disgruntled employee of the Social Security Administration wrote a letter to his boss.

"For about a year I have been dodging pigeons when they take flight from the building," the employee wrote. "I have been bombed while mailing letters at the mailbox and when walking to my car at lunchtime and after work. At least one [bureaucrat] feeds these birds every day, thereby attracting even more pigeons. Can anything be done to get rid of these pigeons?"

The Office of Facilities Management agreed the pigeons "are a nuisance—not only for people but for mechanical equipment." They spied on the pigeon-loving bureaucrat, then issued a written warning to stop feeding the birds: "If the problem persists, OFM plans other methods to discourage the pigeons, such as the application of a nontoxic chemical irritant on places the birds perch."

The pigeon-feeder ignored the warning. So the original complainant went a step further, sending letters to Congressman Kweisi Mfume (now head of the NAACP), who in turn contacted SSA associate commissioner Barbara Sledge, requesting that something be done to rid the complex of these "nuisances."

With the higher-ups involved, nests were soon removed and new trees and shrubs were planted. But this only attracted more pigeons. Additional complaints were lodged, leaving the SSA no choice but to take "special steps" to remove the birds. Soon, dead pigeons began to appear on the SSA grounds. As for the pigeon-feeder, he was issued one last warning: "Feeding any animals on SSA property is prohibited; doing so is considered insubordinate, and will result in suspension or termination."

And they were just talking about the pigeons.

The entire time the SSA and Congress was doing all in their power to eradicate pigeons, Congressman George P. Radanovich of California was shocked to discover that another federal agency—to justify its existence—was spending huge sums of money studying what pigeons eat. (Why they didn't just ask the SSA pigeon-feeder is beyond me.)

"There is a million dollars spent on discussing the eating disorders of pigeons," the congressman said. "I will tell you, if I was a pigeon and had . . . a person following me around all day, watching everything I did, I would have an eating disorder, too."

THE WALCOTT-TAYLOR COMPANY of Bethesda, Maryland, supplies furniture to the U.S. government. An invoice shows where the General Services Administration ordered a walnut study desk with bookrack and medium-size blue chair. The cost was $6,594.00, less a GSA contract discount of $2,868.39, plus $370.55 in transportation charges, for a grand total of $4,096.16.

A short time later, the GSA spent 29 cents in postage to send Walcott-Taylor an Administrative Difference Statement showing that the furniture supplier overcharged the government by 21 cents.

No Ifs, Ands, or Buts

SENATOR ORRIN G. HATCH OF UTAH offered a bill aimed at eliminating burdensome government regulations. Take Hatch's "silly regulation No. 10," which requires a company to alert the U.S. Coast Guard in Washington if it spills just one pint of antifreeze.

"That is silly," Hatch said.

Or "silly regulation No. 8," requiring a person who is atop a six-foot scaffold to be tethered to a "fall-protection device" also measuring six feet.

"I cannot help laughing at some of these," the senator said. "If you think about it, the person with the six-foot tether would already hit the ground before the device could save him."

SO, SENATOR BYRON DORGAN, North Dakota Democrat, you have a way with words. What is the stereotypical notion of a welfare recipient in this country?

"It is some bloated, overweight, lazy, slovenly, indolent, good-for-nothing person laying in a La-Z-Boy recliner with a quart of beer on one hand, a Jack Daniel's in another hand, with his hand on the television changer watching a 27-inch color television set and unwilling to get up and get out and get a job and go to work, munching nachos all day long watching *Oprah, Geraldo,* and *Montel.*"

ONE OF THE SENATE'S BIGGEST HISTORY BUFFS ever is Mark O. Hatfield, Oregon Republican. His favorite historical subject: Abraham Lincoln.

In fact, he's an avid collector of Lincoln memorabilia.

Shortly before their boss was presented with the annual Silvio O. Conte Joy of Politics award, Hatfield's staff had experts at the National Archives reproduce Lincoln's 1865 appointment of Ulysses S. Grant to major general. Hatfield had been told to expect a gift from the Archives some time that year, but exactly what and when he didn't know.

The co-chairman of the Conte dinner was former Louisiana Congressman Robert Livingston, who announced he was privileged to present

Hatfield with a special gift—a priceless Lincoln document, compliments of the National Archives.

As the congressman held up the document, a beaming Hatfield rose from his seat to claim the priceless piece of history.

"No, Mark, stay in your seat," Livingston insisted. "I want to make a toast to you."

At which time Livingston raised his full glass and "accidentally" spilled its entire contents onto the document.

As Livingston shouted, "What have I done?" a horrified Hatfield rushed forward almost in tears. It was only after he picked up the soggy, dripping document that he was finally let in on the prank.

HALEY BARBOUR, FORMER CHAIRMAN of the Republican National Committee who has now been elected governor of Mississippi, was helping kick off the American Conservative Union conference and recalled his days as director of the Mississippi census.

"One day a bunch of us were sitting around the office in Jackson looking at some business census forms," Barbour said. "I'll never forget we got this one response from a little mom-and-pop operation up in Iuka, Mississippi. And as they went down the questionnaire they came to the question, 'Number of employees broken down by sex?'

"And they answered that question, 'None broken down by sex, but we do have two with a drinking problem!'"

EMBATTLED ENERGY SECRETARY Hazel O'Leary, as if she didn't have enough problems during her tenure with the Clinton administration, acknowledged publicly in 1996 that she was married to two men at the same time.

Back in 1979, O'Leary was being considered for administrator of the Energy Department's Economic Regulatory Commission. It was in a letter to Senator Henry "Scoop" Jackson, chairman of the Energy and Natural Resources Committee, that she first explained her "matrimonial history."

In 1969, began O'Leary, she and husband Dr. Carl G. Rollins decided to end their ten-year marriage. They opted to go to Alabama to get the divorce because of New Jersey's "restrictive divorce laws." The divorce was granted March 20, 1970, by Circuit Judge Bob Moore Jr.

Four months later, on July 31, O'Leary married Washington newscaster Max Robinson. But in November 1970, "I learned through a newspaper of a fraudulent scheme involving attorneys and a judge in Alabama who issued invalid divorce decrees," she wrote.

O'Leary, in fact, soon found out that she was one of twenty-seven hundred couples for whom divorce decrees had not, in fact, been filed. "Upon learning of the invalidity of my Alabama divorce, I informed Max Robinson, and we separated," she wrote to Jackson.

The marriage was officially annulled in D.C. Superior Court on June 23, 1971. Her divorce from Dr. Rollins had become official May 13, 1971, in Essex County, New Jersey.

Surprisingly, O'Leary never remarried Robinson.

Later, at the Department of Energy, she met John F. O'Leary, a deputy energy secretary. They were married in April 1981. O'Leary died of cancer in 1987. Meanwhile, Robinson went on to become the first black co-anchor of ABC News, his desk in Chicago. He died in 1988 of complications from AIDS.

ONE OF THE MOST HILARIOUS MEMOS I ever intercepted was sent by President Clinton's National Security Council Executive Secretary Glyn T. Davies to the State Department's executive secretary William J. Burns:

"Late submissions of reports to Congress may reflect unfavorably on the administration and the president personally, particularly when, as here, the late report is a report on why reports are late."

UNTIL MONICA LEWINSKY CAME ALONG, a menu item was the punch line for every Clinton joke. Not that Bubba didn't ask for it.

"I read in your column that President Clinton was influenced by the values of Roy Rogers," reader Stephen Lewis wrote. "I think Clinton meant to say that he was influenced by the value meals at Roy Rogers."

During his final years in office, Clinton issued a memorandum to executive department heads, asking them to use plain language when communicating. The first bureaucrat to make more sense, he said, would win a prize.

"We are determined to make the government more . . . understandable," Clinton wrote. "The federal government's writing must be in plain language. To ensure the use of plain language, I direct you to do the following: By October 1, 1998, use plain language on all new documents. By January 1, 2002, all such documents created prior to October 1, 1998, must also be in plain language."

When it came time to announce the winner, whom did Clinton choose? A Food and Drug Administration official who rewrote the recipe for turkey:

> Before: *"Turkey Basics: Stuffing. Thermometer Essential when Stuffing a Turkey. If stuffing a turkey, use a meat thermometer (Note: Vice President Gore was wondering why you wouldn't use a spoon to stuff the turkey). Cooking a home stuffed turkey can be somewhat riskier than cooking one not stuffed. Bacteria can survive in stuffing which has not reached the safe temperature 165° F possibly resulting in foodborne illness. Even if the turkey itself has reached the proper internal temperature in all parts of the stuffing sufficient to destroy foodborne bacteria . . . during the added cooking necessary to bring the stuffing up to a safe temperature, the meat may become overcooked. For optimal safety and uniform doneness, cook stuffing separately."*
>
> After: *"Make sure you cook both your turkey and your stuffing completely. If you don't, bacteria that can make you sick may still be alive."*

My favorite rewrite was accomplished by the Interior Department's Mineral Management Services, which was presented with a Hammer Award by Vice President Al Gore for explaining the proper way to pay a bill:

> Before: " . . . *Insufficient estimates also result in interest charges. These exceptions are generated when the actual royalties reported for a given sales month exceed the previously paid royalty estimates on file for that lease. In the 'Dear Pryor' letter, dated July 8, 1991, and the Federal Register, 57 FR 3435 (January 29, 1992) MMS informed you of the procedures for calculating interest for insufficient estimates. If the enclosed invoice(s) include charges for insufficient estimates, a detailed insufficient estimate used to calculate these charges is also enclosed.*"
>
> After: "*How to pay your bill: To avoid penalties as well as further interest, you must pay this bill by its due date.*"

I've come to learn that behind everyone in Washington is a story. American history had forgotten Olah Gabor, and I set out to right that wrong. After all, it was the longtime general manager of the Watergate who was roused from sleep one dreary night thirty-plus years ago and told: "There's been a break-in!"

"I lived at the Watergate in an apartment and went immediately there and found the whole situation with the police," Gabor told me. "Then the police ordered the arrest of these five guys."

How did you manage to stay out of the newspapers?

"There were many reporters, and I didn't talk to them," Gabor explained. "I tried to avoid them. I did my utmost to avoid involvement, as a person and hotel. The hotel didn't want any kind of scandal surrounding it."

Which proved impossible. As quickly as President Richard M. Nixon resigned from office on August 9, 1974, the Watergate complex, which Gabor cut the ribbon for in 1967, was an historic landmark.

"I wrote my mother a letter at the time," he said. "I became an American citizen in 1973, having been a political refugee from Hungary. 'So you should be proud of your son,' I wrote to her. 'I have become an American citizen and already I've destroyed a president of the United States.'"

SPEAKING ON THE FLOOR OF THE HOUSE of Representatives is a privilege reserved solely for members of Congress. Recently, an exception was made when a distinguished service award was presented to Chaplain Emeritus James D. Ford.

"Chaplain Ford will finally have his opportunity, which he has long sought, to speak," observed House Speaker J. Dennis Hastert of Illinois.

Ford began by saying that he never imagined that a Minnesota "country pastor" from a town of seven hundred, who followed his father and grandfather into the pulpit, would inherit the title of congressional chaplain. Then, the soft-spoken minister, who for twenty-one years opened Congress with prayer, disclosed a past that left lawmakers in awe.

"I went to West Point . . . in my twenties," he revealed, "and met General Eisenhower who came to church one Sunday. Omar Bradley—I discussed D-Day with him. I knew MacArthur.

"In fact, I was there when MacArthur gave a famous speech. He gave one here, but he gave a more famous one called, 'Duty, Honor, Country' at West Point in the early 1960s. All he had on the podium was a crumpled piece of paper. He said he worked on that speech for forty years, and his little piece of paper only said the word: 'Doorman.'

"He began his speech this way. He said, 'As I left the Waldorf this morning, the doorman said to me, 'General, where are you going today?' And MacArthur replied, 'I'm going to West Point.' And the doorman said, 'Nice place. Have you been there before?'

"Over the years, I got to know these men," Ford said. "Norman Schwarzkopf, whom you know as a general, I remember as a captain and the meanest player in the noontime basketball league. Wes Clark, who just retired as NATO commander, was one of my cadets. U.S. Southern Command General-turned-White House drug czar Barry McCaffrey . . . was one of my cadets."

On Capitol Hill, where the chaplain never removed his clerical collar, he recalled how the Catholic House Speaker Thomas "Tip" O'Neill always greeted him as "Monsignor."

"He thought I was an Irish priest from South Boston," the chaplain laughed.

Ford wasn't finished. He celebrated "democracy" with Czechoslovakia President Vaclav Havel and a former electrician named Lech Walesa from Poland. He huddled with Nelson Mandela—"twenty-seven years in prison, who stood up here and spoke about reconciliation."

He concluded by paying members of Congress the kindest compliment a man of the cloth could ever bestow, quoting Martin Luther from 1530.

"'Send your good men into the ministry, but send your best into politics.' I grew up that way," Ford said. "I believe it."

FEW WASHINGTONIANS ARE ADMIRED as much as Brian Lamb, founder and CEO of C-SPAN. Unlike other TV hosts in town, Lamb rarely if ever has revealed his political stripes.

In 1998 I wrote about the time Lamb was scheduled to address a feisty group of Republican congressmen on Capitol Hill. In a memo the GOP chairman sent to each congressman beforehand, he wrote of Lamb: "We will NOT be accusing the guest speaker of liberal media bias. However, our usual policy will apply in future meetings."

In a *New Yorker* magazine story about C-SPAN, portions of which I republished, James Lardner wrote that no other network has done so little to call attention to itself. Lamb, he said, is no different—"a measured smile the only expression of on-air emotion he permits himself."

Unlike media stars of the other television networks, Lamb "practices an austere brand of reporting and interviewing. He doesn't chat. He doesn't philosophize. Just when everyone in journalism has agreed that objectivity is a snare and a delusion, Lamb refuses to convey even the slightest hint of his own views, or even whether he has any. . . . As a TV journalist covering Washington, he has never spoken his own name on the air."

But there was a time, during the 1992 Republican National Convention in Houston, when a woman complained to Lamb that she was hearing too many Republicans on C-SPAN.

"She really teed off at me, and I teed right back at her," admitted Lamb, who ultimately told the woman to switch channels.

"Lamb was so disgusted with himself over this outburst," Lardner wrote, "that he left Houston that day, assigning others to fulfill his remaining interview commitments, and took himself off the air for the next two weeks."

Rest assured, the nation can trust Lamb to be fair and balanced. But can Lamb trust the nation—particularly its senior citizens?

In the summer of 1998, I'd written, a caller telephoned Lamb while he was on air to accuse a group of elderly ladies in Florida of clogging the phone lines during *Washington Journal,* C-SPAN's daily viewer call-in program.

Caller: There's a group of ladies sitting down in central Florida right now who watch your show, and they have hospital rooms where they live. They run all the telephone lines into one room. They get on C-SPAN more than anybody I know of, simply because they created their own phone bank.

Lamb: Where is this?

Caller: Central Florida, Orlando area.

Lamb: How do you know this?

Caller: Because I watched them do it last Tuesday.

Lamb: Last Tuesday?

Caller: They do this often. It's incredible. First time they did it was about '92, they were doing it with telephones. Now they do it with a computer that automatically dials. This happens to be a Democratic group. One of my old schoolteachers is in this group.

Boy, am I going to get it. When they call in, they don't say we're calling from Orlando or Winter Garden, Florida, they say we're calling
from their place of birth—Flint, Michigan; Ohio, whatever.

Lamb: How did you happen on this little operation?

Caller: My dad was in the retirement home, and he told me
about it. And I went down the hall and looked in on it.

Lamb: How many women do this?

Caller: There were about twenty chairs there and about eleven
people sitting there last Tuesday morning. So, if they really horse it
up, they can get twenty in there working full time.

Lamb permits himself to laugh. And he did.

Chapter 10

God, Nuns, and Guns

THE WHITE HOUSE OUGHT TO MIX church and state more often. A cleric, after all, is less likely to color the truth. The Reverend Imagene B. Stewart, an inner-city pastor in Washington, was enlisted during President Clinton's final term in office to work on national race relations. When "Reverend Imagene," as she calls herself, called to inform me that the White House Conference Against Hate Crimes "is turning out to be a White House Conference Against White People," I was all ears.

"I don't know if I'll ever be invited back to the White House after I opened my mouth on Wednesday," said the pastor of Pearly Gate Baptist Missions. "During the meeting, I stated there are a lot of blacks who promote hate, and I feel that black racists should be included in the agenda."

"At that point," she continued, "I was immediately denounced by two or three persons of the NAACP [National Association for the Advancement of Colored People]. They were aghast. Their mouths dropped open. One member of the NAACP came up to me later and said I was not helping our cause as a race."

The pastor reminded her brothers and sisters that racism breeds in all classes and colors.

"I don't believe until we admit there are problems on both sides we will ever solve the problem," she told the NAACP officials. "There are black racists out there."

Did her message get through?

"I think they were listening," she said. "And Clinton, bless his heart, he didn't mean for this working group to wind up like this."

WHETHER TENDING TO FLOCKS in the ecclesiastical pawnshops of Anacostia or gargoyle-laden cathedrals along Embassy Row, men and women of the cloth in Washington speak their religious and political minds. You can't help to in this city.

I wrote in 1999, for instance, when President Clinton's pastor and spiritual advisor, J. Philip Wogaman of Foundry Methodist Church, extended his hand of charity to souls swayed by Marxism.

"Marxism can speak to the conscience of Christians," said the pastor, who moonlighted as a professor of Christian social ethics at Wesley Theological Seminary, "precisely because it expresses some basic human values which are very close to Christian ones. . . ."

"How could Christians support any other economic ideology?" Wogaman wondered.

Washington has its share of ex-priests, former altar boys, and even guardian angels, too.

Syndicated columnist Cal Thomas, a close friend and neighbor of mine, mentioned one December morning that he'd attended President Clinton's White House Christmas party the previous night. After shaking hands with the embattled commander in chief, Thomas had an unexpected yet wonderfully revealing encounter with a heavily-armed guardian angel watching over the president.

"I ran into this Secret Service guy standing off to the side, and he whispered real low some nice things about me and my column," said Thomas, this country's most widely syndicated columnist. "Then the agent said, 'You know, I'm a Christian, and I honestly feel that I've been strategically placed here to pray for the president. And I do, every day.'"

In 1985, I married the former Catharine Gohn of Baltimore, who at the time was working for Washington TV host and interviewer John McLaughlin. An ex-Jesuit priest, McLaughlin had a reputation in his early days of television for terrorizing his staff, particularly women. My wife escaped the former priest's wrath, although she was instructed on more than one occasion to eat her lunch at her desk.

Which meant the one noon hour I sneaked away from the White House beat, I ended up getting carryout and eating at her desk, too. It was like serving Catholic school detention all over again. You could even hear the bellowing voice of the "dean" down the hall.

Fortunately, I was covering Ronald Reagan and didn't have to interview McLaughlin when three other women in the office targeted him for sexual harassment. But fifteen years later I was sent an advance copy of former McLaughlin panelist Jack Germond's memoir, *Fat Man in a Middle Seat*, which I reviewed under the headline, "Bye bye!"

The no-nonsense scribe from the *Baltimore Sun* dared suggest that McLaughlin's viewers "obviously took the show more seriously than it deserved." Consider the popular "predictions" segment at the close of each program.

"I would wing it," Germond admitted, "secure in the knowledge that if I couldn't think of anything on the air I could manage by nodding sagely and saying, 'Two more members of the . . . cabinet will be gone by June 1'—a safe bet at any time in any administration. If McLaughlin demanded to know which two, I would simply look smug and tell him to buy my newspaper. . . .'"

"If the viewers and politicians took the show too seriously, so did McLaughlin," Germond continued. "He began to believe we were performing some educational function for the great unwashed . . . as if our viewers had been on the moon all week. And he became increasingly testy . . . always irked when I would be quoted as saying that it was 'just television' and that my 'serious job' was writing a newspaper column five days a week for the *Sun*."

Germond drew his final straw with McLaughlin in San Diego, where reporters and columnists were gathered for the 1996 Republican National Convention. McLaughlin announced at a luncheon of General Electric executives that the program GE helped underwrite would soon be distributed internationally. When the host called on each panelist to say a few words, Germond—rather than shouting hip-hip-hooray!—said now "we could take credit for dumbing down the whole world."

Everybody except McLaughlin laughed.

Pat Buchanan, a close friend of McLaughlin's, is one of Washington's many former altar boys. Despite what you periodically read and hear about Buchanan, he's actually one of the nicest people in Washington politics. Even People for the Ethical Treatment of Animals was impressed when the former presidential candidate, driving home late one night from a campaign appearance, spotted a turtle in the middle of the road and ordered his top aide out of the car to "put him in the woods."

Buchanan, nevertheless, fell victim to character assassination. After winning the Louisiana caucus and a strong second-place finish in the Iowa caucus, conspiratorial rumors began swirling that he used "code words" when speaking unkindly of his enemies.

Yes, Buchanan later conceded, if the code words were "Bill Clinton" and "liberal Democrat."

During his last presidential bid, I was the only one to write when Buchanan pledged to John Snyder, dean of Washington gun lobbyists, that "when I get to that White House, I'm gonna take that medallion you gave me—the patron saint of hand-gunners, Gabriel Possenti—and I'm gonna hang that in the Oval Office right along with Robert E. Lee's pistol!"

You can imagine the ensuing uproar among my more liberal readers (I tried pointing out that worse things had been hung of late in the Oval Office), and it had nothing to do with Saint Possenti. A Catholic seminarian, Possenti rescued the Italian village of Isola in 1859 from a band of terrorists with, as Snyder tells it, a striking, one-shot, lizard-slaying demonstration of handgun marksmanship. For his excellent aim, Possenti was canonized by Pope Benedict XV in 1920.

No, it was mere mention of the Confederate general and his pistol—a double-edged sword—that had the leftwing establishment complaining, regardless of the fact that historians regard Lee as the "greatest military genius" of his time. Truth said, any pistol fired or even held by Lee would be the prize possession of any gun collector, and Washington has more than its share, many of them Democrats.

Take Senator John D. Rockefeller IV of West Virginia, who was told through my column that he'd better store his Colt AR-15 semiautomatic assault rifle across the Potomac River in Virginia because it is classified a "machine gun" under D.C. law. Rockefeller no doubt would cherish a Lee pistol.

Former Clinton Attorney General Janet Reno also knows a good gun when she fires one. When Reno was a little girl, her mother taught her how to shoot by setting cans up on a box. When she came to Washington to work for Clinton, Reno boasted that she test-fired police weapons and the officers "were impressed that I could do as well as I did."

It is very important that Washington VIPs remember to store their firearms before setting off for work. Randy Sheunemann, national security advisor to former Senate majority leaders Trent Lott of Mississippi and Bob Dole of Kansas, was duck hunting and forgot that he'd left his shotgun in the back of his SUV. Although well known by U.S. Capitol Police, a cop peered into Sheunemann's vehicle, and before he knew it the senior aide was arrested, fingerprinted, and charged with possession of an unloaded 12-guage and two rounds of ammunition. Then again, Washington is a city where hunting people—not ducks—is the preferred sport.

If Vice President Gore invented the Internet, then Bill Clinton was a member of the National Rifle Association. At a private fund-raising dinner in 1999, Clinton surprised guests—and this columnist—by insisting that he was once a card-carrying member of the NRA he now decried. He said he even owned an NRA jacket. Come to think of it, I published in my column an NRA poster from 1996 showing Clinton clutching a Beretta semiautomatic shotgun during a duck hunt. (That same weapon, while not specifically banned under Clinton's signature, is identical in function to semiautomatic firearms that the president worked to outlaw.)

All of which helps explain why the much-hyped Million-Mom March against guns marched little past its National Mall starting point. Democrats on Capitol Hill tried to help the mothers' cause by rattling off the names of gunshot victims each morning Congress was in session. But Republicans soon took the hint and began reciting names of Americans who, because of their beloved guns, are alive today.

"We can come up with 2.5 million crimes thwarted every year when someone used a gun in defense of themselves or their property," says Republican Senator Larry E. Craig of Idaho. "In many cases, armed citizens not only thwarted crime, but they held the suspect until the authorities arrived. Yet Americans using their Second Amendment rights to save lives isn't news in America. It isn't hot."

Which is why Senate Democratic leader Tom Daschle, having just paid tribute to gunshot victims "James Allen, 27, Houston, Texas; Ladred A. Austin, 21, Chicago; Carimo Ali Deremy, 23, Detroit; Rufus Denuel, 50, Charlotte," purposely skipped over "Jason McCulley."

Mr. and Mrs. Stanley Horn were going about their peaceful, law-abiding lives in Cumberland, Tennessee, when the knife-wielding McCulley broke into the couple's home, tied them up, and demanded money. While Mrs. Horn directed the robber to a jar of spare change, her husband wriggled free from his hand restraints, retrieved his gun, shot McCulley dead, then called police.

As Craig put it: "If some senators on the other side of the aisle had their way, perhaps the Horns would have been killed and Jason McCulley would have walked away."

Contrary to popular belief, not all liberals view the Second Amendment—which guarantees Americans their right to keep and bear arms—as outdated. Especially the dean of House Democrats, every liberal's liberal, Congressman John D. Dingell of Michigan.

"Like Martin Luther, who said he didn't think the devil ought to have all the good music, I say that criminals ought not to have all the guns," Dingell observes.

In fact, when a Republican of all politicians—the distinguished Henry Hyde of Illinois—tried in 1999 to impose a seventy-two-hour criminal background check at gun shows, it was the liberal Dingell who cried foul. The Democrat not only argued that twenty-four hours was sufficient time to sniff out a criminal, he enlisted other leading Democrats—Robert E. "Bud" Cramer of Alabama, Charlie Stenholm of Texas, Chris John of Louisiana, James Oberstar of Minnesota, and John Tanner of Tennessee— to sign a letter stating that the three-day waiting period proposed by the Republican side violated law-abiding citizens' "Second Amendment Rights."

So the mothers can thank Dingell and other gun-toting Democrats in this town for helping to kill whatever chances the Clinton White House had at passing broader gun control.

Which came as no surprise to the president. He never forgot the bitterly cold morning in 1993 when, barely settled into the White House, a pair of Democrats handed him a hunting license, earplugs, and a semi-automatic shotgun and took him duck hunting on Maryland's Slaughter Creek. One of the Democrats was Congressman Bill Brewster of Oklahoma, who after leaving Congress became an NRA board member. The other hunter was Dingell.

The NRA's executive vice president, Wayne R. LaPierre Jr., told me that Clinton was "lying," that he never, ever was a member of the rifle association.

"You know, if he's that delusional maybe he did inhale," LaPierre said in an interview. "He never had a lifetime membership, he never had a jacket. He made it up."

I called White House spokesman Barry Toiv, and at my urging the presidential aide all but rifled through Clinton's wallet searching for an NRA membership card.

"Perhaps he is an honorary member," Toiv called back to say.

BACK TO BUCHANAN and his periodic campaigning for higher office, law enforcement officers from Virginia to Arizona enthusiastically endorsed the rightwing candidate because of his tough stance against crime. I'll never forget writing about the time radio talk-show host Oliver North was conducting a live interview with Buchanan as the candidate sat in the backseat of a speeding campaign car steered by a local Iowa volunteer. When who should pull into the interview but an Iowa state trooper.

As the trooper carefully approached the car, his hand on his holstered gun, Buchanan rolled down his window and asked the lawman if he'd like to speak to Ollie North?

"I'm fine, Mr. North, how are you?" the trooper was soon heard saying coast-to-coast over the Radio America Network.

"I sure hope you're going to be kind to my friend, Pat," North encouraged.

"I will be very kind. We have to help the cause, don't we?" the trooper announced.

Not only did the officer let the driver go with just a warning ticket, he gave Buchanan directions to his next campaign event and congratulated the candidate on his Iowa straw poll victory.

In his book, *Right from the Beginning*, Buchanan wrote affectionately of a Holy Cross nun named Sister Marie de Carmel, who groomed him as an altar boy. Several years later, the same nun taught me the belfry ropes and, even better, was the best writing instructor an eighth-grader could ask for. I don't bump into Buchanan today without the sister's name and the influence she had on our two lives coming up. She died of cancer not long ago at Holy Cross Convent in Notre Dame, Indiana, where she lived in retirement.

Several months before he passed away, former House Speaker Thomas

"Tip" O'Neill similarly paid tribute to a Dominican nun at St. John's School in North Cambridge, Massachusetts. O'Neill's mother had passed away when he was a young boy, and the sisters of the convent took over caring for O'Neill and his siblings. His favorite was Sister Agatha.

"Sister Agatha was the one who put me next to Mildred Miller at those Friday afternoon dances," O'Neill said, "and now Millie and I have been married fifty-two years."

FEW PEOPLE HAVE EVER HAD THE PRIVILEGE of a private sitting with Pope John Paul II, the "Man of the Century." Tim Russert, Washington bureau chief of NBC News and moderator of *Meet the Press* (Russert was an altar boy in Buffalo) is one so fortunate.

In an interview with the *St. Anthony Messenger*, portions of which I reprinted, Russert recalled: "I'll never forget it. The door opened—and there was the pope dressed in white. He walked solemnly into the room. I was there to convince His Holiness it was in his interest to appear on the *Today* show. But my thoughts soon turned away from . . . NBC's ratings toward the idea of salvation. As I stood there with the Vicar of Christ, I simply blurted, 'Bless me, Father!'

"He put his arm around my shoulder and whispered, 'You are the one called Timothy, the man from NBC?'

"I said, 'Yes, yes, that's me.'

"'They tell me you're a very important man.'

"Somewhat taken aback, I said, 'Your Holiness, with all due respect, there are only two of us in this room, and I am certainly a distant second.'

"He looked at me and said, 'That's right.'"

No offense to Russert, but I had to laugh (and do some soul-searching of my own) after publishing a Trends Research Institute study finding that Sunday morning news shows like his *Meet the Press*, CBS's *Face the Nation*, and ABC's *This Week*, featured "a predictable cast of dozens endlessly circling the Beltway."

"New faces and new voices expressing new or unwelcome opinions are rare," the study said. "At best, they present in-depth discussion of already familiar material; they feature the 'usual suspects' spinning the news in their favor, defending their well-known sociopolitical views, promoting their own agendas or lofting trial balloons. Viewers . . . would be better served by spending their time with any of the major Sunday national or regional newspapers and a generous portion of lox and bagels."

A few days later a letter arrived on my desk.

"I read with interest the Inside the Beltway item . . . about how to spend one's time on Sunday morning. While I have no quarrel with the suggestion that watching television just might not be the best use of those hours, I think that just a little bit of thought might have produced an even better suggestion than newspapers and bagels."

The letter was signed: "Father Randolph M. Bragg, Rector, Saint Andrew's Episcopal Church, Arlington, Virginia."

I KNEW I'D GET AL GORE INTO HOT WATER one Christmas Eve after he had just launched a Clinton administration initiative to end homelessness. In typical "Gore-speak," the vice president called for a "reinvention" of homeless programs, then couldn't help but add: "And speaking from my own religious tradition in this Christmas season, two thousand years ago a 'homeless' woman gave birth to a 'homeless' child in a manger because the inn was full."

I thought the Mary and Jesus being "homeless" persons so unusual that it led my December 24 column, beneath the headline: "The Homeless."

Sure enough, Gore succeeded in opening the floodgates so wide that Noah's Ark would have sunk. Instead of wrapping Christmas presents, irate readers jammed the telephone lines. One Christian layman charged that the vice president's religious education was about as faulty as his political viewpoints. But David Powell of Washington was the most clever of the critics, noting that Joseph and Mary weren't really homeless, they were just fleeing the same government taxes that today drive other married couples from similar shelter. To support his argument, he cited Luke, Chapter 2, Verses 1-7:

"And it came to pass in those days that there went out a decree from Caesar Augustus, that all the world should be taxed. . . . And Joseph also went up from Galilee, out of the city of Nazareth, into Judaea, unto the city of David, which is called Bethlehem. To be taxed with Mary, his espoused wife, being great with child. And so it was . . . she brought forth her firstborn son, and wrapped him in swaddling clothes, and laid him in a manger; because there was no room for them in the inn."

But there was another unexpected message left on my phone—from a "sheltered" woman, as she referred to herself. She said for the first time in her life she "gathered strength" from something a politician said, in this case the vice president's analogy.

"I just read your article about the homeless and I have to say you have lifted my spirits beyond the beyond, only because your article overrides the popular opinion that the homeless today are all mentally ill," she explained.

"I thank you for that because as a woman who is a teacher and because of a violent crime against me, I lost my profession and I have been in a shelter over the last six years and am trying to recoup my profession. Perhaps your article has let me know this very minute that what has happened to me is a blessing from the Lord and there is some reason that this has happened."

The woman closed by saying, "I pray that your Christmas is very, very holy and blessed, and I'm going to pray that the rays from that Christmas star reach all the hearts of the people that have closed minds, and that the educational teaching doors for me will be opened this new year and I will be able to do my greatest joy, working with children again."

Her message, which I published the next day, made for a wonderful Christmas story.

––––––––––––

UNLIKE PUBLIC SCHOOL STUDENTS, public servants are permitted to bow their heads and pray on Capitol Hill. And, in the course of their daily routines, they occasionally cite Scripture (or try to) without fear of getting sent to the principal's office.

Take Senator Frank Lautenberg of New Jersey, who during debate surrounding the nomination of a Clinton surgeon general had everybody thinking twice when offering, "If you have the first sin, then pass the stone."

Which if uttered crisply—"Let him who is without sin cast the first stone"—would have been a fitting piece of Biblical wisdom.

"I like the senator's version," wrote New Orleans reader John Schenken. "It confirms my suspicion that people with kidney stones are a bad lot, a very bad lot."

During debate on highway safety and the need for passive restraints, the late Daniel Patrick Moynihan of New York cited Deuteronomy, Chapter 22, Verse 8: "When thou buildest a new house, thou shalt make a battlement for thy roof, that thou bring not blood upon thine house, if any man fall from thence."

"It's a simple idea," Moynihan reasoned. "Have a railing, so in the dark you do not step off and land forty feet below."

During heated discussion on whether Whitewater fit into the "scandal" category, I happened to be standing in the Senate press gallery above the presiding officer, Senator Hank Brown of Colorado. To my surprise, he was refereeing the warring sides while at the same time reading a book. I peered over the railing for closer inspection and was amazed to see it was the Holy Bible, opened to the book of Psalms: "Deliver me from mine enemies, O my God: defend me from them that rise up against me."

During his years on Capitol Hill, I greatly admired Democratic Senator Sam Nunn of Georgia, who was keynote speaker at one of the more recent annual National Prayer Breakfasts. He got things off to an honest start by greeting several thousand attendees, including President and Mrs. Clinton, as "fellow sinners."

"Have I left anybody out?" he asked.

God, Nuns, and Guns

WHEN VICE PRESIDENT AL GORE'S YOUNG SON, Albert III, was on death's doorstep after being struck by a car in 1989, one of his consulting physicians was Dr. Ben Carson, chief of pediatric neurosurgery at Johns Hopkins in Baltimore.

Carson similarly was guest speaker for the 1997 National Prayer Breakfast, and in the overflow crowd of four thousand sat Al and Tipper Gore. In a very moving gesture, the couple publicly thanked Carson for helping save their son's life. After which the distinguished surgeon told an amazing story.

Growing up fatherless in inner-city Detroit, he informed the hushed audience, he once tore open the forehead of a fellow classmate while clutching a metal lock in his fist, tried to stab a youngster in the abdomen with a knife, and went after his own mother wielding a hammer.

His temper out of control, Carson remembered running into the bathroom of his house, where "I got on my knees and prayed."

Three hours later, when he unlocked the bathroom door, his mood—and outlook on life—had drastically changed. "I never had a problem with my temper again," the doctor said.

Determined from that day forward to give her son the education she never had, Carson's mother forced the floundering student to read two to three books every week. And to make certain he read every page, she had him write book reports for each volume, then submit them to her, as if she was his teacher.

"And she couldn't read!" the doctor recalled with amazement. "But I didn't know that!"

Within a year's time, the boy went from the bottom of his class to the top, later becoming one of the leading neurosurgeons in the country. In 1987, he led the team of doctors at Johns Hopkins that successfully separated German Siamese twin boys, Patrick and Benjamin Binder. And in 1994, he traveled to South Africa to assist in the separation of Siamese twin girls, Mahlatse and Nthabiseng Makwaeba.

Carson credited his incredible turnaround to his mother and God, whom he calls his "heavenly" and "earthly" Father. As for his mother, she eventually learned to read and in 1994 was awarded an honorary doctorate.

———————————

T.C. WILLIAMS HIGH SCHOOL, in my hometown of Alexandria, was made famous by the movie, *Remember the Titans*. Somebody should have made a movie about T.C. Williams, instead, the longtime superintendent of Alexandria's public schools. Fifty-five years ago he set in place unprecedented standards that would behoove students today—public and private—to adhere to.

I somehow came across a report card from Alexandria's 1947-48 academic year, issued to Jefferson School seventh-grader Dawn Motley. It contained an outline of attitudes and habits that the school was trying to help the children practice. The teacher's comments were based upon this list of attitudes and habits, while the grading was also based on these qualities:

> a. Sits, stands, and walks correctly
> b. Carries and uses a handkerchief
> c. Covers mouth and nose when coughing or sneezing
> d. Respects the opinion and property of others
> e. Obeys pleasantly and politely, all teachers, the patrolmen, etc.
> f. Takes and follows directions
> g. Shows interest in ideals of conduct

Uncle Sam certainly could do more today to steer students down the right path. Instead, "sexual-behavior surveys" are being distributed to public high school students across the land, including in Indiana to the children of Congressman Mark Souder. The lawmaker was so furious he walked onto the House floor and read the survey out loud:

"Are you a virgin? What age were you when you lost your virginity? Do you use contraceptives? Have you had sex with more than five people? Do you have sex more than three times a week? Have you ever had an HIV test?

Have you ever performed or received oral sex? Have you ever performed or received anal sex? Have you ever had an orgasm? Have you ever had a homosexual experience?"

What really upset Souder was that these surveys "imply that it is normal to have as a freshman in high school multiple sex partners," the Republican said. Not to mention "this type of questionnaire is reprehensible and extremely inappropriate . . . to be passed out in English classes."

Anybody else care to comment?

"I see a society where we have twelve-year-olds having babies, a society where we have fourteen-year-olds selling drugs and fifteen-year-olds killing each other, a society where our eighteen-year-olds who have diplomas cannot even read their diplomas," said Congressman Christopher Shays of Connecticut. "That is the society I see in our country, and I believe a society like that cannot endure."

If the nation's capital is any example, it's not enduring. Hundreds of students in the city don't live long enough to receive their diplomas. Discussing education funding on Capitol Hill, senators introduced a statement by Susie Kay, a twelfth grade teacher at H.D. Woodson Senior High School. (Woodson's student population is 100 percent black, and Kay was one of four non-minorities on the faculty.)

"There is an unwritten creed that making it to graduation day alive is, in itself, a victory," Kay wrote. "Death is a culture in the inner city, and one that is prevalent. One of the most incredible aspects in these children's lives is the amount of death that they must constantly deal with, and the accompanying complacency and acceptance of it. This year alone, I have attended the funerals of three of my graduating . . . seniors. This is not a sane way to grow up."

———————————

ONE DAY I WAS SITTING IN THE HOUSE PRESS GALLERY when excerpts of a prayer delivered in the Kansas legislature by Joe Wright of Central Christian Church were read aloud by a U.S. congressman. I thought it so accurate a reflection of today's American society that I reprinted it in my column and for weeks on end was inundated with republishing requests.

We have ridiculed the absolute truth of God's word and called it pluralism.

We have worshiped false gods and called it multiculturalism.

We have endorsed perversion and called it alternative lifestyle or diversity.

We have exploited the poor and called it the lottery.

We have rewarded laziness and called it welfare.

We have killed the pre-born and called it choice.

We have neglected to discipline our children and have called it building self-esteem.

We have polluted the airwaves with profanity and pornography and called it freedom of expression.

We have ridiculed the time-honored values of our forefathers and called it enlightenment.

We have censored God from our public life and called it religious freedom.

We have abused power and called it political savvy.

Representative Dave Weldon of Florida says his most memorable conversation while campaigning for Congress was with a hospital administrator. The administrator once participated in a program where he'd visit inner-city housing projects and read books aloud to young children.

"Those children were, by and large, children of single parents on welfare," Weldon recounted, "and he would ask, many of them five-, six-, and seven-year-old children, 'What do you want to be when you grow up?'

"And yes, some of them would say I want to be a fireman or a nurse, but some of them would say, 'I don't want to work, I want to collect a check.'"

———————

God, Nuns, and Guns

SEEING THE TROUBLESOME PATH the nation was headed down, Congresswoman Helen Chenoweth of Idaho introduced a resolution calling for several days of national prayer, fasting, and repentance. She explained that the resolution was patterned after a once-common practice by national and state elected leaders—"from the Revolutionary War to the Civil War, ending with President Abraham Lincoln's great proclamation of March 1863, calling for a national day of humiliation, fasting, and prayer."

"I don't know of any member of this House who opposes God or prayer," reacted Congressman Henry A. Waxman, California Democrat. "But what we should discuss is whether we are seeing a continuing trend of inching closer to mixing politics and religion, government and religion, which we have traditionally separated."

Not so, chimed in Republican Congressman John Kasich of Ohio, who was campaigning for president at the time.

"I do not know how many know this," he said, "but the state of Massachusetts actually had a state-supported church well into the 1800s. It was only when the other churches objected that state funding was cut off."

Furthermore, he revealed, "the Congress of the United States actually at one time engaged in the printing of Bibles. The resolution urges a prayer. It is consistent with our founders, our Constitution, and it is unbelievable that we are even having this debate today."

Hold on, said Congressman Chet Edwards, Texas Democrat: "Under our Constitution does this Congress have the right to tell any citizen that it is his duty to pray? The answer is, we have no right to do so."

When a vote on the measure was taken, 275 members were in favor of enacting national prayer, 140 were opposed. If you don't remember publicly praying, it's because the measure lacked the two-thirds required majority.

"I would not want the world or the nation to believe that the defeat of the prayer bill had anything to do with the personal beliefs of members of the United States Congress," Congresswoman Sheila Jackson Lee, Texas Democrat, said afterwards.

"For us to go and solicit on the floor of the House, urging all Americans to unite in seeking the face of God through humble prayer, is not respecting and not tolerating those who are different from us."

SECRETARY OF STATE COLIN L. POWELL, who was supposed to be concentrating on foreign affairs, not domestic, actually told his staff by memo that the State Department, until they hear otherwise, shall remain "under God."

Powell's memo read: "SUBJECT: PLEDGE OF ALLEGIANCE RECITATION—Wednesday's decision by a U.S. Court of Appeals found that the teacher-led recitation of the Pledge of Allegiance in public schools violated the Constitution because it includes the words 'under God.' This decision has not yet taken effect, and has been placed on hold indefinitely while the other judges decide whether to reconsider the case. Furthermore, this was a specific court opinion applicable to that particular situation and location. Consequently, the State Department's legal advisor assures me that employees at post may publicly recite the pledge at any appropriate event."

Before the 108th Congress adjourned in 2003, senators reaffirmed the reference to "one nation under God" in the Pledge of Allegiance, citing numerous findings related to the historical intersection of government and religious expression: the Mayflower Compact in 1620, the Declaration of Independence, the Constitutional Convention, the Gettysburg Address— each cited in addition to numerous Supreme Court rulings upholding religious expression in government activities.

And lest we forget the motto of our country, In God We Trust.

DON'T TRY TELLING Senator Robert C. Byrd of West Virginia that God isn't present no matter what roof you're standing under.

"I ask doctors, when I go to the office of a physician, I say, 'Doctor, do you believe that there is a Creator?' And I have yet to come across a doctor who has not answered without hesitation, 'I do. I believe in a Creator.' I had one doctor less than one week ago talk with me in his office. I asked him the same question. And I sat, open-mouthed and open-eyed, listing to him talk about the audacity of men who would say there is no God."

Days after George W. Bush assumed Bill Clinton's seat in the Oval Office, he and his wife Laura invited Byrd and his wife, Erma, to the White House for dinner. Just the four of them. It was quite the gesture on the part of the Republican president. What impressed the Democrat the most?

"I like the fact that he said Grace. He asked God's blessing upon the food," Byrd replied. "In many circles in this town and across this land, the word 'God,' except in a profane use, is taboo. Don't mention God."

Particularly, he said, in school, although F.R. Duplantier, the great political limerist, wrote in my column that no matter what barriers are put in place, God always finds his way into the classroom:

> No religious beliefs were expressed
> In his valedictorian address
> But he feigned an "achoo!"
> And his classmates on cue
> In unison shouted "God bless!"

Still, children of America today are growing up in a culture where anything goes but God. And, once again, it's Byrd who is speaking most loudly against this anti-religious culture that is eroding America's foundation.

"Political correctness gets in the way of all too many things in this country of ours," Byrd says. "I am not a subscriber of political correctness by any means, shape, or form. . . . The pendulum has swung too far. The Framers [of the Constitution] did not intend surely for a totally secular society to be forced on the populace by government policy."

It's the "new sort of intolerance about religion that I find most disturbing," he continues. "It has become the thing we don't talk about, because it is not politically correct. So many of us are driven into a closet."

In fact, the trend in recent years has been to strip every religious overtone from the American calendar and its schools, to rename the Christmas holiday a "winter break," and the Easter holiday a "spring break."

"I am not sure that the result—a nation more interested in consumption, department store sales, junk television, and professional sports performances than in church, community, and family—is a happy one," Byrd wonders.

The great English novelist Charles Dickens began his epic novel, *A Tale of Two Cities,* with the words: "It was the best of times, it was the worst of times." That passage, says Byrd, best describes the plight of America today.

"The United States has never been more affluent in terms of material wealth and creature comforts, or more impoverished in terms of spiritual well-being. It is the best of times materially. It is the worst of times spiritually."

Chapter 11

'Splaining the Canoodling

I T WAS THE PERIOD IN HIS PRESIDENCY when Bill Clinton was compiling a list of convicted felons to grant presidential pardons. William Arthur Burchett was hoping the president would feel his pain.

"I admit I lied and was dishonest to myself," federal prisoner No. 03655032 wrote halfway through his fifteen-year sentence at the federal penitentiary in Petersburg, Virginia. His petition for commutation of sentence was forwarded by the Bureau of Prisons to the White House on October 5, 1998.

"I'm requesting a pardon," Burchett said. "My motive for my crime of bank robbery was lust. I had an uncontrollable sex drive."

After such a promising start, this is what the Clinton presidency had been reduced to: one sex maniac writing to another. The one behind bars hoping the one who escaped could break him out.

"American people are by nature neither cynical nor angry, but who can blame them for their distrust of politicians in Washington, D.C., when they are forever being disappointed?" grumbled one retiring U.S. senator who, given the Oval Office escapades of late, recalled T.S. Eliot's poem, "The Hollow Man":

Between the idea
And the reality
Between the motion
And the act
Falls the shadow

Burchett, who had no brain for spelling, told the president that his wife had left him and "I thought if I could get some money out of the bank robbery I could get her back. You asked for forgiveness from America. I want you to know that I forgive you for your dishonest ways. Where [*sic*] both in the same boat. Our personal lust got us into trouble. The Bible tells us to do unto others as we would have others do unto us. With that in mine [*sic*], I prayerfully await your positive respond [*sic*]."

THREE-THOUSAND MILES AWAY in Silicon Valley, California, Todd Giles's wife assembled with fellow jurors in a Santa Clara County courtroom to decide the fate of a man accused of his third armed robbery in as many years. Before entering the courtroom, though, the jury's hot topic of conversation had been President Clinton's just-concluded grand jury testimony. When the judge asked the jurors to recite, "I swear to tell the truth, the whole truth, and nothing but the truth, under penalty of perjury," Mrs. Giles couldn't help but laugh—out loud—at the irony.

"And the entire courtroom, as if on cue, busted out in rollicking laughter at the idea that citizens should be held to a standard that half the country does not hold the president of the United States to himself," wrote Giles, a reader of my column.

"I swear, I have respect for a court of law," Mrs. Giles said when she returned home and recounted the day's events. "But it was just so strange to hear those same words that the president heard and ignored, and it was so strange to realize that this judge really expected that I would speak truthfully in her courtroom after the public precedent has been set that lying under oath is okay."

According to Mrs. Giles, the judge held back any laughter, but "she did have a wry, resigned smile on her face, as if she realized that her job had suddenly gotten twice as difficult."

I headlined the item, "The Fallout."

"I wish I had a nickel for every time I've heard it in court," said Kate Untiedt, a criminal defense lawyer in Fairfax, Virginia.

Heard what?

"The Clinton defense," she said. "Anyone who invokes the name of the president in connection with a case is setting a dangerous precedent for the entire country. And if this is happening in Fairfax, Virginia, I guarantee you it is happening in courtrooms all across America."

Are you saying that Bill Clinton's case will forever be cited in the nation's courtrooms?

"Exactly," the lawyer said. "It's just disgusting."

———————

THE PRESIDENT, MEANWHILE, continued opening his mail. In one stack was a three-page memorandum from Marine Corps Sgt. Charles W. Little, who was requesting a presidential pardon for a finding of "misconduct for adultery and fraternization."

"You explained that your private life is no one else's business. I wholeheartedly agree," the sergeant wrote. "However, I feel it is a travesty that I am being discharged while you remain in office."

The Marine had a point. A congressman on Capitol Hill handed me correspondence he received from a lawyer within the Pentagon's Judge Advocate General's (JAG) Office.

"For your information," the JAG lawyer wrote to the lawmaker, "here is a list of offenses from the Uniform Code of Military Justice that President Clinton seems to have violated. Although there is no court-martial jurisdiction over the commander in chief, he is the one who authors the Manual for Courts-Martial and sets the maximum punishment for the offenses Congress has enacted. The amount of jail time authorized by Mr. Clinton himself for each occurrence of these offenses is also listed."

- Perjury: five years
- Subordination of Perjury: five years
- Obstruction of Justice: five years
- Oral Sodomy: five years
- Adultery: one year

I telephoned Little, a well-spoken man, who while awaiting his discharge was assigned to the Marine Corps detachment of the Naval Education and Training Center in Newport, Rhode Island.

"Mine was a one-night stand" with a junior Marine not in his chain of command, Little told me, and as with Clinton and White House intern Monica Lewinsky, it was "a consensual relationship" and "there was no criminal intent."

According to the Marine manual, Little should have received a discharge within fifty days of notice. Rare exceptions allow fifty-five days.

"Today I'm going on 101 days," he said. "I'm still waiting for the general to sign off, but they're not quite sure what to do. My case and the president's parallel each other so much. Apparently the general doesn't want to be the one [to make the final decision]. It's not a good thing for the troops."

Nor was it good for civilians.

Much of America rolled their collective eyes long before Lewinsky flashed her thong in the president's direction. All told, by one Republican count, the Clinton White House in two terms attracted 61 indictments or misdemeanor charges, 33 convictions, 14 imprisonments, 7 independent counsel investigations, 72 congressional witnesses pleading the Fifth Amendment, 19 foreign witnesses who declined interviews by investigative bodies, and 17 witnesses fleeing the country to avoid testifying.

'Splaining the Canoodling

NO WONDER FEDERAL OFFICIALS POKED FUN at the Clinton White House—starting with its inception. G. Wayne "Duke" Smith, associate director of the U.S. Marshals Service, was one of two speakers to address fourteen hundred law enforcement officials in Sioux Falls, South Dakota. (The keynote was delivered by former Bureau of Alcohol, Tobacco, and Firearms Director Steve Higgins, who blamed the Clinton administration for forcing him out of his job in the wake of the botched ATF raid on the Branch Davidian compound outside Waco, Texas.)

During his remarks, Smith joked that he was seated behind Bill and Hillary Clinton at the all-star baseball game when the president suddenly grabbed the first lady by her hair and belt and threw her onto the field. A White House aide accompanying the couple, Smith said, shouted, "No, Mr. President, you're supposed to throw out the first 'pitch!'"

To make sure I gave proper credit where it was due, I telephoned Smith's office. Spokesman Jim Sullivan confirmed that the associate director told a story "that, in retrospect, he feels untimely and insensitive. Certainly, he meant no disrespect to the administration nor the first lady [no, of course not], nor was it meant to be insensitive to women. He deeply regrets any distraction his remark may have caused."

I commiserated with the marshal. Once I passed along a Clinton joke in my column, and to make doubly sure that readers knew I was joking I stuck it under the headline "Just a Joke." I had written that Clinton walked into a press conference with a pair of pink panties stuck to his arm. Reporters observed this phenomenon and wondered what the president was up to this time.

As the afternoon press conference wore on, a reporter finally got up the nerve to ask Clinton why he had a pair of pink panties stuck on his arm.

"It's the patch," the president replied, "I'm trying to quit."

"I did not find the president's joke amusing," a woman named Vicki wrote to tell me. "If he cannot have any respect for the office of the presidency, he could at least have some respect for his wife and daughter."

Another woman named Catherina said: "This will sound like a stupid question, but I just want to clarify. I'm assuming you're kidding about Bill walking into a press conference with a pair of pink panties attached to his sleeve. Am I correct? The reason I ask such an obvious question to which the answer must certainly be, 'Yes, I'm right in assuming you're kidding,' is that it is so easy to picture Bill doing just that."

Finally, "Father Ed," a priest in Plymouth, Massachusetts, apparently was in search of fresh fodder for his Sunday sermon.

"I'm an avid reader of your column," he wrote, "but the bit you mentioned concerning the president coming into his news conference with pink panties stuck to his arm floored me. No one else has even mentioned it. And they wonder why no one respects the president. What an embarrassment. First, the pickup truck with the [Astroturf], now this."

IN JUNE 1996, I WAS LEAKED a transcript of the monthly meeting of the U.S. Commission on Civil Rights, the agenda centering on the propriety of reforming the subpoena practice. President Clinton's newest appointee, Judge Leon Higginbotham, argued that it was necessary that subpoenaed witnesses bring pertinent documents with them to court.

As the distinguished liberal jurist observed: "Documents don't just walk around on their own."

"Oh, really?" fellow commissioner Robert George reportedly piped up. "I hear there's a room in the White House where they do!"

Referring to Hillary Rodham Clinton's insistence (as in four hours' worth before a federal grand jury—unprecedented testimony for a first lady) that she was just as confused as the next guy how missing Whitewater documents suddenly turned up in the White House living quarters.

Pandemonium broke out in the meeting room, and according to my source, Civil Rights Chairwoman Frances Berry, another Clinton appointee, struggled to stifle her own laughter. She stated "for the record" that she "strongly objected" to her fellow commissioner's remarks.

THINGS WERE NO MORE ORDERLY within the White House, where a game of musical chairs was underway. The *National Journal's* White House Notebook revealed: "Halfway through his [first] term, after a spate of changes on his staff, President Clinton is now on his third political director, his third chief spokesman, his second economic coordinator, his third presidential director (or fourth, depending how you count it) and his second secretary to his cabinet, not to mention his third counsel, his third scheduler, his second chief of staff and his fourth deputy chief of staff charged with running the place day by day. . . . It's a wonder, in fact, that a staff that's seen so much churning hasn't screwed up more than it has."

And talk about fresh out of college, when Robert B. Reich abruptly resigned as labor secretary in 1996 he kept mum about his working relationship with the Clinton White House. But a few years later he went on national television and described almost a childlike atmosphere existing at 1600 Pennsylvania Avenue. The staff was so inexperienced, Reich said, that whenever a White House aide dispatched him to an official event he would have his secretary call the White House to find out the age of the person giving the order.

If the White House aide was thirty-two or younger, Reich said he would "ignore" the request. If the aide proved to be thirty-three or older, the cabinet secretary would inquire directly of the president as to the validity of the request.

I RECALL WHEN THE WHITE HOUSE had to extend an apology to Ronald and Lila Wilson of Santa Susana, California, after the couple received an official postcard from the White House signed (albeit by machine) by President Clinton.

"Dear Mr. and Mrs. Wilson: If you have many gay friends and relatives, do you refer to them as 'fags' to their faces? Intolerance is a disease."

"We don't know who the person was who wrote the note," Lorraine Voles, deputy press secretary to the president, told me. The California couple had earlier written to the president about his desire to end the ban on homosexuals in the military.

Another item of mine could easily have been torn from the pages of *National Lampoon*. It surrounded an official presidential appointment and the White House Office of the Press Secretary announcement of same dated Monday, January 31, 1994. I thought it outrageous because the announcement contained not one spelling error, not two, not three, not four, not five, but a record six glaring mistakes in three short paragraphs—something a third grader shouldn't get away with.

President Clinton announced his nomination of Maria Elena Torano to be a member of the U.S. Advisory Commission on Public Diplomacy, which oversees the operations of the United States Information Agency—or, as the White House spelled it, the "Ynited" States.

Torano, or "Tonano" as the White House preferred on second reference, "sered" from 1977 to 1979 in the Carter administration. A native of Cuba, Torano was once a program "manger" for Eastern Airlines, having received her degree at the University of "Havanna." Finally, the presidential wordsmith left the "s" off of a word begging to be plural.

These, mind you, were the same people who wanted to fill the nation's prescriptions.

AS IT TURNED OUT, by the close of 1994 Hillary Rodham Clinton's first ladies' exhibit at the Smithsonian's National Museum of American History was filled with relics of her failed health care reform task force—pins, buttons, even a bumper sticker promoting the federal takeover of the health industry.

I was one of several to obtain early copies of task force records, released amid a lawsuit filed by the Association of American Physicians and Surgeons. The association had argued that the task force illegally operated in secret and was stacked with special-interest groups handpicked by the Clinton White House to help implement government-controlled care.

A review of the records revealed the usual bureaucratic memos and statements about health care. But there also happened to be a collection of jokes that caught my eye, which the White House working group had received from an obviously circumspect public. I was more intrigued to learn that the entire batch of riddles, jokes, and limericks was actually inserted into President Clinton's Presidential Records housed at the National Archives.

My favorite was the patient who went under the knife to have his left leg amputated, only to wake up and find that his right leg was missing.

"Hey, Doc!" he screamed. "What happened?"

"Sorry, I screwed up, but we're going back right now and take the other leg off."

"I'll sue you for everything you have!"

"Forget it," the doctor smiles. "When I get through with you, you won't have a leg to stand on."

Dr. Jack J. Rosenberg, an orthodontist in Burke, Virginia, did not bother to send Mrs. Clinton a joke, but he did object in writing to the policies set forth in the first lady's health care proposal.

"Now a personal note," Dr. Rosenberg told Mrs. Clinton in closing. "I know that you have chosen perhaps the most expensive orthodontist on the East Coast to continue your daughter's orthodontic care. I know this provider personally, and I applaud your choice. I am equally certain you chose this orthodontist after careful consideration of all factors. You passed up many orthodontists closer to your home. Fort Meade would also provide free care for your daughter. Therefore, I assume that when it comes to your own family, freedom of choice, based on the skill and care you will receive, not price or convenience, dictated your decision."

In another letter, Dr. Charles F. Colao, an internist in Marlow Heights, Maryland, noted with interest that a cardiologist would be joining President Clinton's medical staff, which already included practitioners of several medical subspecialties to provide services for the Clintons and Al and Tipper Gore.

"In the Clinton Health Care Plan, care is to be delivered by a gatekeeper or a primary care physician who then will decide whether any specialty care is needed," Dr. Colao noted. "It appears that there is considerable hypocrisy here in that the Clintons and the Gores are not following the recommendations of their own plan."

I knew the first lady's health crusade was in trouble when the White House tried to create an eye-catching "symbol" for government medical care. Somebody suggested a white cross against a bright-red background, and the others seconded the motion. Soon, brochures, fliers, and other materials touting the Clinton plan began to take shape. Each featured the new logo: a white cross over a bright-red background.

Enter the Embassy of Switzerland. After all, the White House had virtually copied the Swiss flag. Not that the Swiss were angry, but they politely reminded Mrs. Clinton's team that its careless duplication of the Swiss banner was "trademark infringement."

I rang Yvana Enzler, the Swiss press attaché in Washington, and she confirmed that the embassy's legal affairs section had asked the White House to "cease and desist" using the Swiss colors to promote its plan.

A few days later, I checked back with the White House to see if any other allied flags were under consideration.

"I've got a couple of different colors here, and I don't want to give you the wrong information," said a White House spokesman. (One administration source told me the subsequent logo consisted of a white cross on a blue background.)

Just for fun, I called Yvana back and asked if a white and blue scheme would suit Switzerland, and she laughed, "Yes, absolutely!" So long as the Finnish don't mind.

Regardless of the logo, the Clintons insisted that health care reform offered "choice." But the National Taxpayers Union Foundation, in a detailed study of the proposal, found it highly restrictive to personal liberties, rolling up scores of new penalties, restrictions, quotas, and prohibitions. In fact, the Clinton plan used the terms "ban," "enforce," "fine," "limit," "obligation," "penalty," "prison," "prohibit," "require," "restrict," and "sanction" a total of 1,494 times.

ONE OF MY BIGGEST SCOOPS during the Clinton administration dealt with four White House aides who, instead of driving for an hour, flew by presidential helicopter (actually, two Marine choppers made the trip) to the Holly Hills Country Club east of Frederick, Maryland. Touching down directly in front of the pro shop, the four White House aides proceeded to survey each and every fairway, making sure the course met the president's high standards of play.

After I was alerted by Lisa Lyons Wright, an aide to Maryland Congressman Roscoe Bartlett, that something was up—as in helicopters—I telephoned Mike McGinnis, head golf pro at Holly Hills.

"Actually, I don't know what they were here for," said the stumped McGinnis.

I immediately called the White House, reaching Deputy Press Secretary Arthur Jones, who getting back to me later insisted that President Clinton didn't know the first thing about any taxpayer-funded round of pasture pool—that is, until we'd alerted him.

Five days later, Congressman Dan Burton of Indiana, who had tangled before with the Clinton White House over using presidential aircraft for personal business, fired off a letter to the president. He demanded answers to nine questions, my favorite, number seven: "What were their scores? This will help determine the actual time they were on the course."

To make this shameful story short, White House administrator (and golf enthusiast) David Watkins, lifelong millionaire friend of Clinton's from Hope, Arkansas, resigned just hours into an investigation as to why he and the three others commandeered two Marine Corps helicopters for a golf outing.

Shortly thereafter, the House of Representatives voted on an amendment to reduce the White House budget by $13,129.66—the minimum cost of Watkins' personal golf outing.

But the story isn't over yet. Two weeks later, several members of the Army-Navy Country Club outside Washington were "indignant" when they spotted Watkins taking a private golf lesson—days after he resigned his White House post. Not that Watkins, a dues-paying member of Army-Navy, wasn't entitled to a lesson. Rather, the military brass couldn't believe he had the nerve to show his face at the mainly military club so soon after he had "abused" military officers and their aircraft.

And the story still needs an ending. Six months later, *Washington Golf Monthly,* a glossy magazine owned by my newspaper, learned that Watkins had landed a most cushy job on the West Coast: senior executive vice president of investor relations for Callaway Golf.

"Had it not happened as it did," Watkins admitted, "I would probably not be here today. And this is terrific."

———————

THE WHITE HOUSE SCHEDULER who typed President Clinton's schedule in November 1998 had everybody in stitches: "11:00 A.M.—The President attends the Presidential Wreath Lying [sic] Ceremony, Tombs of the Unknown, Arlington National Cemetery."

Who in Washington wasn't calling Clinton a liar?

In 1996, Senator Bob Kerrey, Nebraska Democrat, had a lot of explaining to do after he told *Esquire* that Clinton is "an unusually good liar." Kerrey wrote it off by saying he wished he hadn't said it.

Two years later, Judy Woodruff of CNN asked the *Washington Post's* Ben Bradlee if he thought it was proper for Americans to be comparing Bill Clinton with Richard Nixon. The editor made famous by Watergate bluntly replied: "There are some similarities. They're both lying."

"This is a seamy situation, obviously," ABC newsman Sam Donaldson told me. "People say that those of us who are the reporters on this case just love this somehow. I don't love it at all. It's a big story. And it's an important story. The press did not make up Monica Lewinsky. The press did not come up with a dress. The fact that it's a scandal that appears to have sex as the base of it is not anyone's doing but the participants."

"It didn't have to be," former Clinton advisor George Stephanopoulos told me in an interview the same day the House approved and sent to the Senate two articles of impeachment. "The president didn't have to do what he did, and he didn't have to lie about it."

Hoping that Clinton would be reading the *Times* that next morning, I printed a most fitting passage from Fyodor Mikhailovich Dostoyevsky's, *The Brothers Karamazov*:

> The important thing is to stop lying to yourself. A man who lies to himself, and believes his own lies, becomes unable to recognize the truth, either in himself or in anyone else, and he ends up losing respect for himself as well as for others. When he has no respect for anyone, he can no longer love and, in order to divert himself, having no love in him, he yields to his impulses, indulges in the lowest forms of pleasure, and behaves in the end like an animal, in satisfying his vices. And it all comes from lying—lying to others and to yourself.

As Lewinsky recalled it, Clinton thoroughly searched the Bible before finding the loophole he was looking for—happily concluding that oral sex does not constitute adultery. Is there such a waiver in the Sixth Commandment?

"No, I wouldn't defend his interpretation of that," Reverend Rex Horne, pastor of the 2,900-member Immanuel Baptist Church in Little Rock, told me over the telephone. The preacher spent much of the previous day praying for Clinton, who had been a member of his church for seventeen years.

"I'm very burdened about it, honestly, for everybody concerned," Rev. Horne said.

"This is a sexual incident—a twenty-one-year-old!" an unusually feisty Bob Woodward of the *Washington Post* said during an appearance on CNN's *Larry King Live.*

"Well, I happen to have a twenty-one-year-old daughter, and if I found she was at the White House and something even approximating this was going on, I would be mighty disturbed," Woodward said.

Instead of labeling the president a liar like everybody else, Congressman Burton of Indiana took the bait from a reporter and repeated the scribe's observation that Clinton was a "scumbag." Within days, congressional interns opening the congressman's mail had to wear latex gloves because the president's supporters were sending used condoms to Burton's office. Only for the sake of his interns did Burton apologize, saying he wished he'd chosen a different word—"like Mr. Clinton is not a man of 'honor,' he's not a man of 'integrity,' he's not a man you can 'trust,' he's not 'trustworthy.'"

Burton should have just said "liar" in the first place.

Utah Senator Orrin Hatch, a staunch Mormon, appeared on NBC's *Meet the Press* and labeled Clinton "the first presidential 'canoodler' in history."

Huh?

The word dates from 1859, derived from "canoe." There are at least two meanings: (1) to neck or kiss or caress, (2) to cajole or coax by display of affection. Either definition, however, would fit the president.

Which makes one pre-Monica memorandum from White House Deputy Chief of Staff Harold Ickes to Health and Human Services Secretary Donna Shalala all the more hilarious: "The president was somewhat mystified as to why there was no mention of him in the 3 October 1995 article in the *Arkansas Democrat Gazette* entitled 'Sex Can Wait Plan Gets $200,000 Grant: Federal Aid to Benefit 16 School Districts.'

"Apparently the program is called 'Sex Can Wait,'" said Mr. Ickes. "Obviously, not every announcement will specifically refer to the president, but all federal departments are being urged to make sure that announcements of grants and other programs refer to the president."

Before long the president had all the name recognition he could handle. Julianne Ryder of Annandale, Virginia, wrote to my column:

"During a weekend car trip I instructed my six-year-old daughter, Caitlin, to amuse her one-year-old brother as he was growing restless in his car seat. She quickly obliged by setting up the following role-playing exercise: 'I will be the president and Patricia (Caitlin's favorite doll) will be the vice president.'

"I pointed out that she wasn't including her brother. In response, she announced grudgingly: 'Jack can be my lawyer.'"

———————

SPEAKING OF ATTORNEYS, you'd think the Clintons, each graduates of law school, would know not to tangle with the law.

"Remember, I taught Bill and Hillary Clinton when they were at Yale," said Supreme Court nominee Judge Robert Bork. "Let me rephrase that. Bill and Hillary Clinton were in the room when I was teaching at Yale."

Any thoughts on the president's shortcomings, James Carville?

"I love Mrs. Clinton like I love my sisters, and I think the president is—what did Ricky used to say to Lucy?—'You've got some 'splaining to do here.'"

And you, Mary Matalin?

"When the Clinton scandal broke out I said to my husband, 'James, we both understand the rules of marriage—right, James?'"

Even the couple's mirthful two-year-old daughter, Matalin "Matty" Carville, couldn't help but be obsessed with Monica Lewinsky. Accompanying her mother to the airport to pick up her dad, Matty surprised both parents by abruptly asking: "Daddy, do you like Mock-ina Lew-hisky?"

Her father laughed, but said nothing for the record.

Anything for the record from you, Clinton spokesman Joe Lockhart?

"Let me try to be serious for at least one or two moments, before I go back to what it is I do normally," the spokesman said on one particularly miserable day.

So, does anybody think the president should resign?

"I think it's plain that the president should resign and spare the country the agony of this impeachment and removal proceeding. I think the country could be spared a lot of agony, and the government could worry about inflation and a lot of other problems if he'd go on and resign," said Bill Clinton on August 8, 1974, referring to President Richard M. Nixon.

"Impeachment should apply to those offenses which proceed from the misconduct of public men, or, in other words, from the abuse or violation of some public trust. They are of a nature which may with peculiar propriety be denominated political, as they relate chiefly to injuries done immediately to society itself," said Hillary Rodham and fellow Democratic staff of the House Judiciary Committee in 1974, quoting Alexander Hamilton in one of the Federalist Papers.

No, I meant President Clinton.

"The president has pursued a strategy of deceiving the American people and Congress since January 1998, delaying and impeding the criminal investigation for seven months, and deceiving the American people and Congress in 1998," said Independent Counsel Kenneth W. Starr, accusing President Clinton of obstruction of justice, witness tampering, abuse of presidential powers, and perjury—evidence that may constitute grounds for impeachment.

Anybody who still believes Starr, appointed mind you by Attorney General Janet Reno, was part of a "vast rightwing conspiracy," might be interested to learn that while a student at George Washington University, he was a member of the Young Democrats who supported Hubert H. Humphrey in 1968. And while a member of the Young Democrats at Hardin University, Starr campaigned for Lyndon B. Johnson.

And as for the "exorbitant" forty million dollar price tag of Starr's independent counsel investigation, Clinton spent eight times that amount in a matter of seconds when launching overseas missile strikes on the same day Lewinsky testified before a federal grand jury.

His back pinned against the Oval Office wall, the president huddled with his cabinet, the first such meeting in eight months (when these same cabinet members staunchly defended the president as his worst scandal yet was metastasizing). A short time later, Energy Secretary Bill Richardson emerged from the meeting, described it as "emotional," and left. At 6:03 P.M. that same evening, Richardson issued to every bureaucrat in his department a new policy on sexual harassment.

He wrote that he will not tolerate sexual advances; requests for sexual favors; verbal and physical conduct of a sexual nature; unsolicited letters and telephone calls; uninvited and deliberate touching; leaning over, cornering, and pinching; sexually suggestive looks or gestures; sexual teasing and jokes; and pressure for dates or a personal relationship. (I opined it was lucky for Clinton that Richardson wasn't his boss or he'd have been shown the door.)

———————

"I FOUND IT WRY, BUT IN A WAY SAD," said Tom McBride, recalling the exchange he had with his five-year-old son after Clinton's name came out of the car radio.

"Is Bill Clinton that guy who was with Monica Lewinsky?" asked his son.

"Yes," replied the dad, immediately trying to change the subject by asking, "Hey, who is George Washington?"

"America's first president," said the boy.

"Who is Abraham Lincoln?"

"Another president."

"John Wayne?"

"Sergeant Striker."

"Who's that guy who plays for the [Denver] Broncos?"

"The quarterback? He's John Elway."

"Who is Bill Clinton again?" asked the dad.

"That guy who was with Monica Lewinsky."

William M. "Bill" Watson, president of the Cross Keys Bank in St. Joseph, Louisiana, called to say he was buying some groceries and noticed the attractive young store clerk was wearing the name tag, "Monica."

"My natural impulse to be humorous caused me to say, 'Gee, I guess Monica's not a great name to have this year, is it?'

"She never missed a beat, looked up at me, and said, 'Neither is Bill!'"

Kaeilin Emery, a fifth-grader at Stratford Landing Elementary School in Fairfax County, Virginia, received a note from the White House explaining that President Clinton gets too many letters to respond to each one personally. Lucky for him, because Kaelin's letter was a tough one to answer.

"Did you ever think about how you would feel if your wife had a relationship with another man?" wrote the eleven-year-old girl. "Please write back when you have the chance."

IN THE FALL OF 1997, a mysterious Lebanese-American oil financier said in testimony before the Senate Governmental Affairs Committee that he paid three hundred thousand dollars to gain access to President Clinton. But signing the check, he added, only got him through the White House door.

The bigger hurdle followed, Roger Tamraz testified.

"The only reason to make donations is to get access," Tamraz explained to senators. "You think you get into the White House, so you've won. It's only the fight begins when you get into the White House. Then there's a guerrilla fight to get close to the president. First, the president is surrounded by the ladies, because they swoon around him—"

"This one doesn't!" Senator Susan Collins of Maine shot back.

Collins, apparently, is in the minority.

"I don't care what they tell you," ex-football star O.J. Simpson told Matt Labash of the *Weekly Standard*. "A twenty-two-, twenty-three-year-old girl who has her mind set on a fifty-year-old guy is more in control than the fifty-year-old guy. . . . When their minds are set on something, more than not, they're going to get what they want."

CONGRESSMAN PAUL MCHALE of Pennsylvania was the first Democrat to call for President Clinton to resign in the wake of his affair with Lewinsky. And the White House never forgot that fact.

In 1997, and in the previous Congress, McHale introduced the Theodore Roosevelt Medal of Honor bill, urging the U.S. Army to award a medal to honor Colonel Theodore Roosevelt. McHale was assisted by Republican Congressman Rick A. Lazio, who several years later would challenge Hillary Rodham Clinton for a prized New York Senate seat.

While the Democrat McHale was calling on Clinton to spare the country further embarrassment and "immediately resign the office of the president," the Republican Lazio was trying to move the Roosevelt bill through Congress before the close of the session. That chore finally accomplished, the bill went to the White House for the president's signature.

Excited about the long-awaited medal ceremony, Lazio's office called the White House on numerous occasions to learn the date. On November 10, White House aide Matt Bianco assured Lazio's office that nothing was on the calendar yet, but they would be the first to know. When Lazio's office hadn't heard anything by November 12, they again called Bianco. Still, no ceremony scheduled, he assured them.

However, I subsequently learned that the previous evening, November 11, the White House had notified Senator Kent Conrad, North Dakota Democrat, that the ceremonial signing would take place the following afternoon at 12:45 P.M. Senator Strom Thurmond, South Carolina Republican, also was notified by the White House the prior evening. Even Congressman Peter T. King of New York, a Republican who loudly called for the president's impeachment, was invited to attend. Tweed Roosevelt, great-grandson of Theodore, was also given plenty of advance notice about the time of the ceremony so he could be on hand. Plenty of others were also on the invitation list.

As for the two congressmen who made awarding the medal possible?

"Our office was not notified of the 12:45 P.M. signing by the White House until 11:30 A.M. on November 12," Lazio's spokesman told me. "The congressman was at home in his district of Long Island at the time and could never have flown down to D.C. in time."

And as for McHale, who already knew he'd fallen out of favor with Clinton when a bogus charge surrounding his military record was circulated by somebody within the White House—he was notified sixty minutes before the ceremony, when he was at home in Bethlehem, Pennsylvania.

When I called Bianco for comment, he referred me to his boss.

WILLIAM GINSBURG, Monica Lewinsky's lawyer, ducked into Hunan Chinese Gourmet in Washington for a late-afternoon lunch with another attorney. Much of the crowd was dispersed by then, but taking no chances, the two chose a corner table that afforded them some privacy (my fly on the wall was a table away, pretending to be reading a book).

Unfortunately, Ginsburg didn't answer the question of the day: whether he felt Monica would be indicted for trying to cover up her cozy relationship with the commander in briefs. But Ginsburg did bring up the White House intern's infamous blue dress, seized from her closet by Kenneth Starr's "panty-raiders," as the president's supporters called the investigators.

"We're never going to see that again," Ginsburg said. "It will be tied up for years."

THANKS TO BILL CLINTON, Sunday morning television was no longer safe for children to watch. As much of America ate its corn flakes, Sam Donaldson, George Will, and Cokie Roberts drilled Linda R. Tripp about the semen stain on Monica's blue dress.

"You found out about the dress because she told you, is that correct?" asked Donaldson on ABC's *This Week*.

"Was it an ambiguous stain?" wondered Will.

"Well, you did see it eventually?" noted Roberts.

"I did. Yes, of course, I saw it," Tripp replied. "It certainly was not a guacamole stain or a blue cheese stain, as I've read. It was a splatter effect."

As gross as that was, I nearly choked on my TV dinner when Maria Shriver of NBC News dared ask Mrs. Clinton: "Have you ever wanted to put one of those [cots] in the Oval Office?"

Dorothy Welsh of Avon Lake, Ohio, wrote: "I am a mother of four children, ages nine to two years of age. I was reading a book to my seven-year-old daughter on Great American Heroines. The book is old, but I am finding that those are the best ones to read to my children. I was reading to her a short chapter on Dolley Madison. I asked her if she knew what the title 'First Lady' meant? She didn't, so I explained the title and the functions of the first lady's job. I then asked her if she knew who our current first lady is?

"She didn't miss a beat and answered 'Monica Lewinsky.' Unfortunately, she was serious."

It wasn't any easier for Senator Charles E. Schumer, the senior New York Democrat and a juror in Clinton's impeachment trial. I added Schumer to a growing list of lawmakers who didn't know how to explain the actions of a president they once loved to the daughters they loved.

Schumer told a Park Avenue synagogue how his nine-year-old daughter Alison stumped him for an answer when she asked what it meant when Clinton was "aroused" during encounters with Monica Lewinsky.

The senator replied: "Well, Allison, it meant that he was very happy." (I rudely pointed out that if this reflects answers children are getting from their parents, maybe sex education in schools at an early age isn't such a bad idea after all.)

And how do you feel, Miss Lewinsky, about parents all over the world having to explain to their children why some cigars aren't smoked?

"I think that more of the criticism should be heaped on the person who is married since I had not taken a vow before God to protect the relationship," she told reporters in Sydney, Australia.

BANG!

"We have calculated lawlessness which takes us for fools and chips away at our legal system!" shouted House Judiciary Committee Chairman Henry J. Hyde, hammering his wooden gavel on December 11, 1998, an historic day when two articles of impeachment were approved against Clinton.

Bang!

"Perjury is not sex!" the Illinois Republican continued, hammering a gavel again.

Bang!

"Obstruction is not sex!" Hyde reminded his colleagues.

Bang!

"Abuse of power is not sex!" he said, clenching a gavel in his fist.

Bang!

Bang!

Bang!

Whoa, why all the hammering, Mr. Chairman?

"Souvenirs."

Like a dozen ink pens used by a president to sign one treaty, like U.S. flags flown above the U.S. Capitol Dome if only for a brief moment on Inauguration Day, so too are gavels hammered by a presiding chairman during a rare impeachment vote against a sitting president destined to become collectors' items. Hyde acknowledged as much, hammering away the way he was. Some of the gavels, I was told, were sent to him by ordinary Americans who wanted to own a piece of presidential history.

But by the time the banging ended, Bubba wiggled his way out of the twisted maze he'd waltzed into. *Newsweek* reporter Michael Isikoff explained how by saying the president knew that to prove his lies his foes would be forced into the sewer with him until, in the end, they stunk more than he did.

"It was his coldest and most cynical calculation—the mutual assured destruction at the core of his political survival," Isikoff wrote.

'Splaining the Canoodling

I called Stephanopoulos, who reads Clinton better than most. Obviously, he said, the president was relieved it was over. And Clinton said as much in his brief statement to the nation from the Rose Garden after the Senate voted to acquit on the two articles of impeachment.

"He really did at the end finally give the speech that he probably should have given at any of a number of points over the last year," Stephanopoulos said. As for the president purposely separating Americans in Washington from those around the nation, the former Clinton aide said: "That was the one slight tiny edge of bitterness in the president's remarks. I think he feels he's been persecuted a bit inside the Beltway."

He then acknowledged: "I think [Clinton] was doing everything he could not to be accused of gloating."

BILL CLINTON WAS HAVING A DELICIOUS TIME with his guests at his final New Year's Eve gala dinner as president, or so I was informed by one highly reputable source in attendance at the White House dinner (I was delighted when *Washingtonian* editor Diana McLellan called it the "best item of the millennium").

Clinton pulled rank after his table's seating had already been arranged, making sure to stick himself between Sophia Loren—wearing a low-cut black Armani gown—and Elizabeth Taylor.

Taylor, according to my source, simmered toward a boil as the dinner progressed. You see, she thought the president was focusing entirely too much attention on Sophia Loren.

"I hope you are not going to spend the whole evening staring at her boobs!" Taylor finally blurted out for the entire table to hear.

"I don't do that anymore!" Clinton shot back.

"Bulls—!" replied Taylor.

The president turned so red he barely spoke to Taylor—or Loren, for that matter—for the rest of the evening.

Chapter 12

Gipper, Gorby, and Phyrne

URING THE CLOSE OF THE COLD YEARS, they were the most closely watched pair on the planet. Ronald Reagan and Mikhail Gorbachev, painstakingly presenting their demands and, in doing so, showcasing their differences.

When all was said and done, the Iron Curtain was raised and the wall torn down. Certainly among the top historical events of my lifetime.

Which is why I found it so amazing in November 1996 to stumble across Gorbachev well off the beaten path. His visit to Washington was in such contrast to his historic state visits of the past, when he'd jump from his heavily-fortified limousine and press flesh with admiring crowds of Americans.

But on this day, when a most boring U.S. presidential campaign was in its final swing, no one paid Gorbachev attention. Not that he cared. Finally, he was able to experience for himself what this "Land of the Free" talk was all about.

Free to roam, his stomach growling for home, the last-ever president of the Soviet Empire paid a surprise visit to Misha's Deli, a none-too-fancy sandwich shop in the quiet Eastern Market neighborhood of Capitol Hill.

INSIDE THE BELTWAY

Gorbachev showed up at half past seven o'clock on a Saturday morning, before the deli had even opened, and waited patiently outside for Misha Vasilevsky to arrive and light the grill.

It would be an understatement to say the deli owner was in awe to find the great Gorbachev standing at his doorstep.

"I was very surprised," said the native of Odessa, Ukraine, his accent as thick as his delicious "Gorbachev"—$4.25 worth of pastrami, lappi, sauerkraut, lettuce, and tomato, piled high between thick slices of mustard-laced Russian bread.

Gorbachev was tickled pink to see the menu creation in his honor, although he questioned being listed in the same company as "Lenin" and "Stalin," two of Misha's other sandwiches.

"Everybody in America knows their names," Misha explained to his distinguished guest, who stopped dead in his tracks when spotting two large posters of himself above the counter next to a Dole-Kemp campaign sign.

"I don't remember when I looked like that," said the former president, shaking his head.

Relaxed and, for once, unhurried, Gorbachev quietly sat down to a bountiful Russian breakfast. He explained that he came to Washington to pitch his memoirs—doing what Americans do after an accomplished life and career.

"I love America. I love Americans," Gorbachev said. "They are people who understand me."

Misha understood. After all, it was Gorbachev who'd given Ukraine back to her people.

WITH MY SIX-YEAR-OLD DAUGHTER Kerry in tow, I found Ronald Reagan happy, healthy (or so I wrote) and ever charming during our 1994 visit to his thirty-fourth-floor suite in Century City, California.

Wearing a hearing-aide, the eighty-three-year-old former president winked when saying he didn't long for the politics of Washington. Still, he was curious to hear my opinion of President Clinton and any other unusual arrivals in the nation's capital since he bid farewell to the city on January 11, 1989.

"We made a difference," he said the day he left. "All in all, not bad, not bad at all."

After I tried to explain Clinton, Reagan recalled a few highlights of his own two terms in the Oval Office, captured in photographs lining the walls and bookshelves surrounding his desk. The old cowboy's favorite was of him and Queen Elizabeth II on horseback.

He walked to a wall of windows, affording a view west along Avenue of the Stars towards the Pacific Ocean. He wanted to point out the seascape a little girl like Kerry doesn't see in Washington's swamplands. But this day it wasn't there.

"This is usually a beautiful view, but we haven't seen the ocean for two months," said Reagan, a closet environmentalist (Los Angeles so far that year had seen more air-pollution advisories than during the previous two years combined).

Another of his favorite vistas, he said, was looking out from the rear veranda of the Ronald Reagan Presidential Library, an hour's drive north in Simi Valley. But his favorite view of all, he commented, was from the solitude of his California ranch.

He was taken with my daughter's bright red dress, which didn't surprise me. Women of the White House press corps liked to wear red dresses to Reagan's news conferences, knowing the color caught his eye and increased the chances they'd be recognized for a question.

Several days later, I was happy to receive several photographs from our visit. "To a beautiful young lady with a bright future," Reagan wrote to Kerry.

By the time I could get the picture framed, he revealed he had Alzheimer's disease. I had no clue, I told MSNBC the same day as Reagan's announcement.

In an incredibly worded statement I read over and over, Reagan thanked "the American people for giving me the great honor of allowing me to serve as your president.... I now begin the journey that will lead me into the sunset of my life."

Despite what pundits had to say, Reagan biographer Edmund Morris told me during an interview in 1999 that the former president showed no signs of Alzheimer's during his tenure in the White House. The first symptoms, he said, became apparent in 1993, four years after his second term ended.

IRONICALLY, ABOUT THE SAME TIME Gorbachev was devouring his Russian breakfast at Misha's, Reagan was breaking bread with his eldest son. The occasion was the Gipper's eighty-fifth birthday.

"It will be a private lunch, just dad and I," Michael Reagan said by telephone from Los Angeles. "There will be a big birthday dinner out here, but I didn't want to celebrate my dad's birthday with a thousand other people."

It took many years, but Michael, the adopted son of Reagan and his first wife, actress Jane Wyman, and his father were finally close.

"You know," Michael told me in a most personal interview, "I used to wonder about my relationship with my dad. It was so often easy just to sit back and say to myself, 'You know, dad has never once hugged me,' or 'dad has never told me before that he loves me.'

"And all of a sudden one day I woke up and asked myself, 'When was the last time I hugged my dad, told him that I loved him?' I had never hugged my dad, yet here I was mad because he had never hugged me. So when dad got out of office in 1989, I made a promise to myself that every time I saw him I was going to give him a hug hello, or a hug goodbye, or a hug on both ends—just do that and show him how much I care.

"And so I did, the first time when dad came down to San Diego to do my radio show in 1989, just after his book came out. And the first time he was a little startled by it. He obviously wasn't used to it. His generation was not used to men hugging one another. Frankly, he was a little taken aback by it.

"But what's happened over the years is that dad actually now looks forward to these moments. He's always standing at the door, waiting for a hug, when I arrive or when I leave. And especially at this point of his life with Alzheimer's. While he can't carry on normal conversations, and while he may not have the memory to recall certain things about my life . . . what's interesting is that when I get up and get ready to leave the house, he's at that door, with his arms open, waiting for that hug."

He was quiet for a moment.

"Other things he might not be able to remember," Michael said, "but he remembers that."

WITH REAGAN AND BILL CLINTON no longer making waves in Washington, I turned my attention to other newsmakers. I found out I had something else in common with Robert S. Bennett, Clinton's lawyer, besides learning more than I cared to about the president's private parts. The attorney, the brother of former education secretary Bill Bennett, not only owned "a gorgeous piece of property" along the Yellowstone River in Montana's Paradise Valley, he too has a hair-raising grizzly bear tale to tell.

In fact, if the giant beast he encountered was any hungrier, Bennett might not have been around to keep Clinton out of the clink.

Accompanied by Tom Murphy, a renowned wildlife photographer, Bennett hiked deep into the backcountry of Yellowstone National Park, home to some 350 grizzlies and 4,000 bison. Make that 3,999 buffalo.

Suddenly ("suddenly," I've come to learn, is a popular adverb when telling bear stories) the two men came upon a large sow and her three cubs—the mamma bear literally standing on the carcass of a buffalo.

"She stood up on this downed bison," Bennett told me. "They have lousy eyesight, but excellent smell. And she smelled us!"

The next thing you know, he said, the grizzly "charged us!"

For a quick refresher course, if a grizzly charges the last thing on earth you want to do is run. (My good friend Gene Mueller, who writes the award-winning outdoors column for the *Washington Times*, says you needn't worry about outrunning the grizzly, just the guy next to you).

Instead, the best defense is to drop into the fetal position, curling your arms around your head. If the bear is either angry or hungry, this won't save your life. But say it's a sow, whose instinct is to protect her young. In this case, the fetal position could spell the difference between a visit to the emergency room and the undertaker.

"We were down in our crouch, prepared to be mauled," Bennett said. "She charged us, but only to scare us—which I should add she was monumentally successful in doing."

And there's more to this grizzly tale, too.

Seconds before the grizzly charged, Murphy was able to snap what Bennett describes as a "remarkable" photograph of the bear "standing literally on the bison looking right at us."

The prized photo now hangs in Bennett's office.

Back in 1999, Bennett mentioned to me that he'd been trout fishing in Montana with, of all unlikely anglers, Supreme Court Justice Sandra Day O'Connor. I assumed he was joking, but he wasn't.

"Next week, it will be Clarence Thomas," he said. "And then in September, Supreme Court Justice Antonin Scalia."

Bennett, when he wasn't providing legal counsel to the embattled president, was a board member of the University of Montana Law School in Missoula. Also on the board was U.S. District Judge Jack Shanstrom, chief federal judge for Montana.

One day the two men put their legal minds together to try and figure out the best way to lure the top justices of the land to lecture at the remote law school, its campus in the direct shadow of the Rockies.

For his part, Bennett agreed to approach the nation's highest bench (familiar territory in light of the recent escapades of you-know-who). Judge Shanstrom, at the same time, agreed to disclose his favorite fishing holes (unheard of for a Montana fisherman, even when on his deathbed). Soon, Bennett was approaching the justices offering a blue-ribbon trout/lecture package.

"It's pretty remarkable for a small law school to attract that caliber a speaker," Bennett conceded.

BOB BENNETT didn't need concern himself when yet another sex scandal—in the shape of shapely courtesan named "Phyrne"—rocked Washington in 1998. And at the National Press Club, no less.

"Silver Owls," as aging reporters of the club are affectionately called, had been feasting their eyes on Phyrne for decades.

She has "hung in the club for over fifty years," outgoing National Press Club President Richard Sammon told me. "It is a classically-done nude painting."

Not in the eyes of the politically-correct breed of "journalist" that has descended on Washington. They considered Phyrne "inappropriate," and with their noses pointed up, they didn't mind saying so.

"In many ways she has become the Confederate flag of the National Press Club," Sammon explained. "The older members of the club . . . find that the painting is a connection to the past, an identity marker for the club through the years. The painting harks back to a time at the press club when the only woman in the club was a naked one hanging on a wall." (Women were first allowed to join the NPC in 1971.)

In the early 1980s, the dawn of political correctness in Washington, Phyrne was lowered from her hanging place during much-needed renovations to the club. When it came time to put her back up, however, several of the club's new members—men and women alike—"expressed offense at attempts to rehang her," Sammon said.

Complaints about Phyrne persisted for the next fifteen years, finally coming to a boil in 1998 at a raucous meeting of the club's board. As one outraged Silver Owl was overheard conceding to a fellow octogenarian, "I guess we can't have any pictures of that old hooker hanging around here."

"You mean we're going to have to take down the photo of Pamela

Harriman, too?" the aging scribe replied, his heart no doubt skipping beats.

Five months later, voting nine to one, the club's board of governors agreed to expel Phyrne from the club. It didn't matter if she'd been a club member longer than anybody in the room.

"Not only that, the board, in its infinite wisdom, directed the Silver Owls to come up with a plan for disposing of Phyrne by December 1," said David K. Martin, the lone board member who voted to save the elegant lady. "I pointed out that no matter how you flush it, it's censorship. No one agreed with me."

I suggested to Martin that he simply carry Phyrne around the corner to the White House, where Bill Clinton surely would find her a proper place. Martin took my comment as an insult.

"I did warn them I thought this was foolish and it would come back to haunt them," he told me.

"For the board to rule what is art and what is not art, and what should hang and what should not hang—what's next to come down, all the cartoons hanging around the club?" he asked.

Exactly two weeks later, newly elected Press Club President Douglas Harbrecht pleaded that "it's time to end this unremitting debate and move on."

But as I wrote, Silver Owls were still intent on re-hanging their faithful mascot.

"Many longtime members remain offended by your message and have asked me to respond," Don Larrabee, club president way back in 1973, told Harbrecht. "They were bothered by its implications that the club we joined many years ago was nothing but a place to drink and ogle a nude painting. It would not be the institution it is today if this were the case.

"Those who cared enough to spend money on Phyrne's restoration as art that was part of our history are not to be faulted for their love of tradition," Larrabee continued. "They cannot be blamed for feeling that a vocal minority who were active in the Women's National Press Club and the Washington Press Club seem to have driven the board's decision, which had the effect of rubbing salt in a wound that went back many years and was healed, we thought, when women were admitted to membership in 1971.

"I was one of those who felt we were wrong to deny women access to a journalists' club, but I also felt we righted that wrong twenty-five years ago. Many women quickly joined the club without batting an eye or uttering a complaint about the club's historic artwork.

"The question of disposition remains. Many members believe that Phyrne is a 'keeper'—and we want to keep her!" Larrabee said.

Over the next few weeks, Silver Owls had the grand dame appraised. To everybody's surprise, particularly the club's newer members, she came back with a minimum price tag of $75,000. By then, however, the club's board already found Phyrne a new home.

"From my standpoint it would be a happy ending to the story," Harbrecht said. "We're still in negotiations, but Phyrne would have a place where she is revered, the Silver Owls would know Phyrne is in a place where she is honored and respected, and the Press Club is rid of the controversy."

So Clinton didn't take her?

No, Phyrne was eagerly snatched by the Brazilian ambassador, who obviously knows a fine piece of art when he sees her. Around the turn of the century, I came to learn, Phyrne was painted by a famous Brazilian land-scape artist, Antonio Parreiras. She was his one-and-only nude. The delighted ambassador couldn't wait to hang Phyrne in his official residence.

Larrabee, who for his noble effort was crowned "Chairman of the Fine Arts Committee of the Silver Owls," stressed in no uncertain terms that Phyrne was only "on loan" to the Brazilians, "with the hope that the board would one day reconsider and bring her back to the Press Club.

"There's still much to be worked out with the Brazilians. We want it understood that under no circumstances will Phyrne be taken out of the country, that this is strictly a loan," he said.

"Plus, since she's worth so much, we now have to get her insured. Antonio Parreiras is said to be one of the top two or three great artists of Brazil, and you know they'd love to get the painting back."

INSIDE THE BELTWAY

AL GORE HAD HIS EYES SET on the Oval Office. And in his mind, deservedly so. As vice president he accomplished a great deal more than met the eye, as *Baltimore Sun* staff writer Paul West rudely found out.

In fact, I found Gore's reply to the question, "What do you see as your major accomplishments as vice president?" so robotic and long-winded—West clocked it at three-and-a-half minutes—I reprinted it word-for-word:

> Oh, I think stewardship of our environmental policy; the reinventing government [initiative] and beginning a process of transformation in the federal bureaucracy that holds out the promise of helping to redeem the promise of self-government; telecommunications reform and the launching of a program to complete the information superhighway and connect every classroom and library to it, and the beginning of a worldwide effort to construct the global information infrastructure; the launching of and early success of the community empowerment program; the crime prevention council and measures related to community policing that are contributing, along with other factors, to four years of crime reduction in a row and the largest drop in thirty-five years just a few weeks ago; the shepherding of science and technology policy generally; the launching of the national Father-to-Father program and the new focus on family policy with many new developments in addition to the Father-to-Father program; a new approach to giving employees the opportunity to choose, themselves, whether to take more time off instead of overtime, not leaving it in the hands of the employer to choose that; the international space station linkup with Russia; going back to the environment, which I began with, the forward progress in building a consensus around the world on how we can address global climate change; the shepherding of our relationship with Russia and the Gore-Chernomyrdin Commission; the

shepherding of our role in the transformation of South Africa with the Gore-Mbeki Commission; the removal of nuclear weapons from Ukraine and Kazakhstan and Belarus as part of the negotiated end to the deployment of nuclear warheads in the former Soviet bloc countries other than Russia. You know, give me a little time and I can complete the list.

Exhausted from taking notes, the reporter pointed out to Gore, "That sounds a lot different from Walter Mondale's approach of not taking any line responsibility as vice president and being a free-floating advisor to the president."

"Well," Gore replied, missing the scribe's point, "I've done that, too. Maybe that ought to be first on my list, because that's what I spend most of my time on."

So what is it with Gore's mechanized oration? I asked Washington political pollster Frank Luntz, who suggested I focus my attention on Roswell, New Mexico.

"What does Roswell have to do with Gore?"

"Aliens," replied Luntz.

"As in space creatures?"

On July 8, 1947, Luntz pointed out, witnesses claimed a spaceship with five aliens aboard crashed on a sheep and cattle ranch outside the New Mexico town, an incident they and many others claimed was covered up by the military so as not to cause widespread panic and mayhem around the world—if not the solar system.

Are you saying what I think you're saying?

"Nine months after that day, Al Gore was born," Luntz said.

I quickly made calculations—numerical and biological. Moments later, I rang the White House. Nobody there knew off the top of their head the exact date the vice president was born.

"Why do you want to know?" asked a Gore aide.

"I can't tell you—not now at least," I replied.

The Gore aide put me on hold. I told him to hurry.

"March 31, 1948," he came back to say.

"You do the figuring," I told readers of my column. "Then be sure to vote."

Chapter 13

Erin Brockovich—Of Course!

MY FAMILY WENT THROUGH HELL," said former President George H.W. Bush, after being trounced by Bill Clinton—and the media. "I don't understand why they are doing it."

Referring to sons Jeb and George W. and their quests for gubernatorial seats in Florida and Texas respectively. He could easily have quoted Will Rogers to his boys: "If you hear of anybody proposing my name for public office, please maim him and send me the bill."

Neither, it turns out, was listening.

"I think George W. is an excellent candidate," opined Texas Republican Senator Phil Gramm. "It's hard to believe that someone can be Barbara Bush's son and still be a redneck."

He wasn't entirely kidding.

A first lady in the traditional sense, the grandmotherly Mrs. Bush abided by one rule: never discuss politics. Okay, there was the time her husband's manhood was called into question—by a woman, no less—and Mrs. Bush shocked the world by labeling Geraldine Ferraro as "I can't say it, but it rhymes with rich." She later insisted she meant witch.

But unlike her successor, Hillary Rodham Clinton, Mrs. Bush was never confused about which half of her marriage got elected president. Which isn't to say the unassuming first lady didn't hold her own private summit or two with the world's top leaders, one of which she never revealed until leaving the White House.

As Mrs. Bush tells the story, during a state dinner with Boris Yeltsin, the Russian president leaned over and, through an interpreter, asked the first lady what it meant in America when, under the dinner table, a woman places her foot atop a man's.

In his country, Yeltsin continued, it means the woman "loves" the man.

"Without realizing it, I'd been grinding his foot into the ground with my foot," Mrs. Bush explained.

An obviously impressed Russian leader later scribbled a note to the first lady on a White House menu: "You stepped on my foot, you knew what it meant, and I felt the same way."

WHAT ELSE GOES ON UNDER TABLES and behind closed doors?

In 1996, I intercepted a "classified" State Department cable that I took the liberty to "declassify" (after reading it several times, I came to the conclusion that I wouldn't be revealing any state secrets).

The cable stated that the Russian president Yeltsin remarked during a meeting with President Clinton that Moscow could help Secretary of State Warren Christopher learn the Russian language by providing an attractive woman to instruct him twenty-four-hours a day.

The Russian leader's offer, which no doubt made you-know-who's ears perk up, was extended during at an antiterrorism summit in Sharm el-Sheikh, Egypt, just after Clinton handed Yeltsin a communique printed solely in English.

According to the State Department cable: "Foreign Minister [Yevgeny] Primakov said he could read it, and Yeltsin joked that since Primakov knew English Secretary Christopher should now learn Russian."

The U.S. cable quoted Yeltsin as saying: "The Russians would be glad to provide the secretary with a young attractive instructress who would work with the secretary day and night."

Clinton, the classified cable concluded, "joked that this would change the secretary's image in the United States." Clinton would know.

"Unfortunately," U.S. policy in the 1990s was "dominated by this obsession" with Yeltsin, says Congressman Curt Weldon of Pennsylvania. "We didn't want anything to rise to the surface that would embarrass Yeltsin, so we pretended it wasn't happening."

Strobe Talbott, for seven years deputy secretary of state and architect of the Clinton administration's policy toward Russia, revealed in his 2002 book, *The Russia Hand,* that U.S. officials regularly tracked Yeltsin's alcohol consumption during meetings between the two superpowers and actually adjusted their expectations for progress based on the number of shots that went down the Russian leader's chute.

Talbott added that Clinton never seemed bothered by Yeltsin's conduct or inability to govern. Then again, foreign policy wasn't the strength of the former Arkansas governor. I overheard Senator Bob Dole remark that Clinton's biggest international relations accomplishment was reducing the number of caning strokes in Singapore from six to four.

Any foreign policy weaknesses on Clinton's part weren't for lack of crossing the ponds. In his eight years in office, according to National Taxpayers Union Foundation records, Clinton made more visits to more nations—a record 133 journeys—than former Presidents Eisenhower, Kennedy, Johnson, and Nixon combined. And almost as many as former Presidents Carter, Reagan, and Bush combined.

And like the scandalized Richard Nixon before him, Clinton reached the peak of his overseas travel the year of his impeachment. I opined that the president "weathered his 1998 impeachment by getting out of Dodge," one of his escapes a forty-three million dollar African safari. All tallied, Clinton's travels were estimated to have exceeded half-a-billion dollars. The 229 days he spent abroad also is a record for any president, thus wherever he went, he was recognized and greeted by adoring mobs.

———————

THE SAME CAN'T BE SAID for Clinton's secretary of state, Madeleine K. Albright.

Certainly Mrs. Albright thrived on diplomatic housekeeping. But as I pointed out in 1999, she didn't take kindly to being mistaken for a housekeeper during the Kosovo peace negotiations. It was after midnight, Dukagjin Gorani, editor of a Kosovo English-language daily, recalled for the British TV broadcast "War on Europe," and Albright strolled into the Albanian delegation's room at the Rambouillet chateau in France.

"Give us five minutes and please go away!" one negotiator abruptly dismissed Albright, mistaking her for the maid. Albright became furious, Veton Surroi, another member of the delegation, was quoted as saying, "using explicit language which the translators never could translate into Albanian."

Hers wasn't the only case of mistaken identity. Take the time former Soviet President Mikhail Gorbachev was visiting Washington and the ample White House Press Secretary Marlin Fitzwater was literally hoisted off his feet and carried out the door of the Soviet embassy by members of the KGB Ninth Guards Directorate who mistook him for the average Joe.

But there was no mistaking Clinton, who at the close of his presidency was more a celebrity than commander in chief. In June 2000, for example, he was invited to address the Russian parliament. Later, the London *Times* reported that Clinton's "folksy tone" might have served him well in Arkansas, but his powers of persuasion fell far short of charming the Russian State Duma.

The newspaper's correspondent wrote that Russian deputies who bothered to show up for Clinton's address—there were several empty seats— calmly read newspapers or stared at their watches. Vladimir Zhirinovsky, deputy speaker of the Duma, confessed that the audience was packed with "cleaners and security guards" who were told to clap when Clinton arrived and departed.

But the real action was in the corridors, the correspondent wrote, when Clinton was ambushed by a Russian woman shouting, "Bill, drop your trousers and show us what a sex boss you are!"

———————————

"MY GOD, YOU CAN'T EVEN GET A VELVET ELVIS" for two dollars, said FBI Special Agent I.C. Smith, referring to a valuable oil portrait of Bill Clinton stolen from the rotunda of the Arkansas state Capitol and resold by a transient for two dollars.

It was a sign of the times.

As Clinton was packing his White House suitcases, the Arkansas highway department announced it was removing one hundred road signs posted along the state's borders boasting that Bill Clinton is a native son. Better yet, they would be willing to make them available to museums and other interested parties as "historical artifacts."

Time went by, though, and only ten or so requests for the signs were submitted.

"They're not our hottest item," admitted one highway employee. "We thought a lot of people would want them just for target practice."

The leftover signs were repainted with the message: "Buckle Up for Safety."

"Which, come to think of it," wrote Meredith Oakley, well-known columnist for the *Arkansas Democrat Gazette* and an early Clinton biographer, "that wouldn't have been bad advice for our boy Bill."

For lack of buckling up—and myriad other scandals—the Clintons left the White House clutching an eleven million dollar legal bill. And even though the couple would soon be raking in tremendous sums of money, they still appealed to Americans to foot the monstrous note. Amazingly, Americans responded.

Californians doled out the most money to the "Clinton Legal Expense Trust," followed by New Yorkers and residents of the nation's capital. And it wasn't just the upper-crust writing "sympathy checks," which totaled seven million dollars by January 2001. In Washington, records revealed everybody from bellhops to college professors were opening their hearts—and wallets—to the Clintons.

I found this astonishing, considering the reported eight million dollar advance Senator-elect Hillary Rodham Clinton had just landed for her memoirs, not to mention the millions of dollars Clinton would soon be pocketing for his sordid story and speaking tours (for sixty speeches in 2002, the former president earned $9.5 million).

And on top of that, there was not one, but two houses—his and her models—the Clintons purchased upon leaving the White House: a $1.7 million Dutch Colonial in suburban New York City, and a $2.85 million brick Colonial near Embassy Row in Washington.

All they needed now was furniture.

––––––––––

WHAT UPSET ONE FORMER HIGH-RANKING Reagan administration official I interviewed was the relative ease with which the Clinton camp, at the erroneous expense of Ronald and Nancy Reagan, tried to "legitimize" what the couple took with them from the White House to fill the two new estates.

"It's, you know, presidents all through the past have taken gifts," former White House Chief of Staff John Podesta tried telling ABC's *This Week*.

"The Bushes did—the Reagans took a $2.2 million dollar house," Podesta insisted.

Wrong, John.

"Well, but—you know," he tried again, "Mrs. Reagan took a million dollars' worth of—according to the *New York Times,* I just read that this morning—of jewelry and personal furnishings."

Take it from a "gossip" columnist, John, don't believe everything you read.

"There was a sudden burst of these charges about the Reagans' house over the weekend," said the Reagan official, who detected a coordinated effort by Clinton loyalists to divert attention from what had become—in the final days of the administration—yet another in an endless string of scandals.

"After the Reagans left the White House, they paid the purchase price and then some for the house," the official said. "It was not a gift. I know this because I observed the process quite closely, as did the White House counsel and other attorneys."

Democrats in Congress who were asked about the latest scandal suddenly realized that after eight long years of offering excuses for the Clintons they didn't need to anymore. ("I love liberals," remarked Washington pundit George Will. "They put up with this guy through perjury, suborning perjury, obstruction of justice, use of the military to cloud discussion of his problems. He steals the toaster and they say, 'That's it. We've had it with the man.'") Within days, legislation nicknamed the "Hillary Ban" was introduced, among the co-sponsors liberal Congressman Barney Frank. The "Members-elect Gift Ban Application Act of 2001" sought to impose gift rules on House and Senate-elect members before they take the oath of office.

"The purpose of that is to stop a future Hillary Clinton from escaping the restrictions on giving gifts to members of Congress between the election and the time when members of Congress are sworn in," explained Congressman F. James Sensenbrenner.

"I was appalled," added the Wisconsin lawmaker, "but not surprised at all of the types of gifts that were showered on the new senator from New York before the restrictions kicked in, and that was using the loophole in the law for personal benefit."

Ethics rules banning gifts were already in place for sitting senators, designed to protect the public from conflict of interest and influence peddling by wealthy business interests. And now that she is a bona fide senator, rest assured that rules bar both Mrs. Clinton and her husband from accepting individual gifts worth fifty dollars or more, or a total value of a hundred dollars from a single source. The rules also preclude lavish dinners and expensive weekends with those wishing to curry favors.

A far cry from 2000, when the Clintons set a record for accepting almost

$200,000 in gifts, according to the couple's financial disclosure statement released in 2001. By comparison, former President Bush received $52,853 in gifts in 1992.

To quell the swirl of impropriety charges, Mrs. Clinton in 2001 agreed that she and her husband would pay for half—almost $86,000—of the gifts they chose to keep. Among the more controversial: two coffee tables and two chairs worth almost $7,500 from Denise Rich, whose fugitive billionaire ex-husband was granted a last-minute pardon from Clinton (the president's second-to-last scandal). But the most ironic gift of all came from insurance magnate Walter Kaye, the infamous man who recommended Monica Lewinsky for a White House position. Kaye presented the Clintons with a cigar humidor.

Still, with every intention of one day retaking the White House, the Clintons haven't strayed far from Pennsylvania Avenue. No better told than by former Reagan political advisor Lyn Nofziger (and his alter ego) in the wonderfully written book, *Unbridled Joy: The Verse of Joy Skilmer:*

> I wonder if we'll ever see
> A country that is Clinton-free,
> A time when Hillary and Bill
> Have left us and gone o'er the hill,
> A time when they don't think they're meant,
> Each one, to be our president,
> To tell us all what's best for us,
> Defy us then to make a fuss,
> To insist they're meant to rule us,
> Sure, as always, they can fool us,
> A time when they at last have quit,
> Their drinking from the public teat,
> When Bill no longer wags his jaw,
> Instead, goes home to Arkansas,
> And Hillary no longer runs
> But takes to baking hot cross buns.

With Bill Clinton suddenly "husband" to a senator, there was a bigger, more immediate concern lurking on Capitol Hill.

"My biggest concern," confessed Senator Gordon H. Smith of Oregon, "is that Bill Clinton will be with my wife in the Senate spouses' club."

IF THERE WAS EVER A SLIVER OF HOPE that somehow he could miraculously resurrect his otherwise impressive campaign for president, Arizona Senator John McCain finally realized his race for the White House was over when his trustworthy bus driver, Greg, couldn't steer him to Philadelphia and the Republican National Convention.

Where's Greg?

Answered a somber McCain riding aboard the bus once dubbed the Straight Talk Express: "He's now driving Aretha Franklin."

ONE OF THE BEST THINGS about being a political columnist in Washington is you get to interview just about anybody you want. For me, Al Gore was always somebody else's interview. Still, I wasn't the least bit upset when the Gore camp suggested that, instead of the candidate, I interview one of Gore's biggest supporters, who was also a delegate to the Democratic National Convention.

"I can't remember a man so qualified to run for office," supermodel Christie Brinkley told me. "I can't understand why this race is so close."

Let's talk about George W. Bush, I suggested.

"You know, some women come up to me and say, 'Christie, I think Bush is cute.' I am insulted by that!" she said.

"Let me tell you about women today. If Bush gets ahead with women voters, it's because women are so busy adjusting to their hectic lives, getting their kids to school, being a good wife, a good mother. They're seeing only the periphery of this race right now, and so is the media—looking at the personalities instead of the issues."

And the issues are?

"The Supreme Court," Brinkley replied. "Right now four of the justices are getting a little bit older, and they happen to be four of the more liberal ones. George W. already said he likes judges in the vein of Clarence Thomas and Antonin Scalia, so these are really rightwing, scary appointments that will make our country leap back in time."

Are you excited that Gore has chosen Joe Lieberman as his running mate?

"You know, Bill Richardson got a bum rap," Brinkley didn't mind saying (an outspoken environmentalist, the model worked closely with the former energy secretary on nuclear issues).

"He would have made an amazing running mate with Al Gore. But Lieberman is an excellent choice as well."

What about Dubya's choice of Dick Cheney?

"Who in their right mind would vote for cop-killer bullets?" she spat.

But surely, I remarked, you must support the Second Amendment to the Constitution?

Silence.

You know, the right to keep and bear arms.

"I used to live in Mexico and go out in the jungle and shoot coconuts out of the trees," Brinkley replied. "I got pretty good at it. I could shoot a coconut down in one or two shots."

Shortly after publishing the model's take on the 2000 presidential campaign, the mail poured in.

"Doesn't it seem rather odd," reasoned R. Grimm of Houston, Texas, "that Ms. Brinkley would find fault with women being for George W. because he is 'cute?' Why does she think anyone would be interested in her opinion, because of her intellectual attributes?"

Good point, Mr. Grimm.

Mrs. Peter C. Appelbaump, administrator of a children's opera in Harrisburg, Pennsylvania, wrote: "I'm nobody special, but . . . since when does . . . Brinkley speak for me or any other mom who 'are so busy adjusting to their hectic lives, getting their kids to school, being a good wife, a good mother?'

"Are we all so stupid that we are 'only seeing the periphery of this race now, looking at the personalities instead of the issues?' I can assure you that I have taken a look at the issues—and the men who espouse them."

Linda Mathis griped, "You probably thought she was cute."

Yes, I've always thought she was cute. And talk about a figure.

Soon, I heard from Nina May, who heads Renaissance Women, a group of ladies whose goal is to give women an alternative voice to radical feminism. She'd read my interview with Brinkley and wanted me to know that her friend, supermodel Kim Alexis, was "so concerned for our country right now and the outcome of this election," that she was fasting—water only—every Tuesday until Election Day.

For the sake of balance, I knew I had to interview the starving Alexis.

"During the fasting days, I pray more frequently that the people in our great nation see the truth of who God wants to govern our country," Alexis soon told me. "A lot of people are turned off by this presidential campaign, and they do not feel like they want to vote. I believe that if the wrong man gets elected to our highest office then our nation will be set back in many ways. We are at a crossroads right now."

So who's the right man?

"I strongly support George W. Bush," she said. "I think he has much more integrity."

So there you have it. Beauty is in the eye of the beholder.

Tony Coelho, the former House Democratic whip who took command of Al Gore's fledgling campaign, disagreed. Coelho not only was driving Gore's 2000 bandwagon, he was working pro bono. Lucky for me, my cousin had worked for Coelho on Capitol Hill, and not only did he take my phone call, he made news by saying it would be tough for Gore to climb out of Clinton's dark shadow.

Not that it was Clinton's fault.

"History will show you that every No. 2 has had difficulty moving out of the image of the No. 1," Coelho said. "That was true of Nixon, true of George Bush, true of Walter Mondale. The more loyal you are, the more difficult it is. Especially when you have become part of a team to make things happen, when you are considered part of the principal operation. It's important for people to relate to who Al Gore is."

So will we see Clinton stumping for Gore?

"You may," Coelho said.

So the vice president wants him on his campaign trail.

"Of course!"

In light of Monica and—

"I'm not getting into that."

Into what?

"Into all those things. They're not important."

Oh, but they were.

———————

AL GORE WAS DESPERATE to become president. Seriously desperate. And who could blame him? When the ballots were tallied in the 2000 presidential election, he won the largest vote ever achieved by a Democrat running for the White House—far more than his contender—and still he was denied the presidency in the Electoral College.

"At 12:30 A.M. on the Friday after Election Day, the phone rang in the Tallahassee hotel room of Ron Klain, a top Gore aide," wrote David Kaplan in *Newsweek*.

"It was Al Gore, calling from Washington, D.C. Gore had not only been thinking about the problem, but he'd done something about it. He'd called Erin Brockovich. Not Julia Roberts, who played Erin Brockovich in the movie about a town's legal fight with a polluter—but the real Erin Brockovich."

No way.

With the Florida recount debate heating up, Gore thought "she should come to Florida and lead our efforts to collect affidavits," explained Klain.

The vice president told him: "What Erin Brockovich's good at is going to real people and getting them to tell their stories. That's her specialty. . . . I think Erin Brockovich would be great."

After Gore hung up the phone, Klain said he tried to go back to sleep, "bemused" as he was by his conversation with the stressed-out candidate.

"Barely two days in the post-election morass," *Newsweek* added in disbelief, "and Gore was recruiting somebody he'd heard about in a movie."

As Klain put it: "Bring in a camel with three heads. It just seemed like the whole thing's a huge menagerie at this point. Erin Brockovich—of course!"

I'D CAUGHT UP WITH JIM MARTIN, president of the 60 Plus Association, at the Capitol Hill Club. It was Martin, way back in 1967, who gave George W. Bush his first political job.

"George W. was our gofer," Martin didn't mind admitting, "because George W. doesn't mind admitting it."

Martin was the top aide to Congressman Edward J. Gurney, a Florida Republican seeking a seat in the U.S. Senate.

"We were looking for someone to get the media on and off the plane, into their hotel rooms, and back up again at 6 A.M.," Martin explained.

A political consultant named Jimmy Allison, who had just finished managing the winning campaign of a freshman congressman from Texas named George H.W. Bush, told Martin: "I've got somebody in mind, the congressman's oldest son. He's getting out of Yale, just like his father. He's getting his license to be a pilot, just like his dad."

"Gosh," Martin replied, "how much will we have to pay him, and how soon can he start?"

Martin went in and told Gurney about the younger Bush, and Gurney said he would welcome his addition. Soon, George W. was riding with a handful of reporters aboard a propeller-driven press plane, tailing "The Green Hornet" twin-engine plane carrying Martin and the congressman.

"I remember him as a very handsome twenty-one-year-old," Martin said of George W. "A clean-cut guy, very articulate, extremely bright, very gregarious, a hale fellow well met in that everybody likes him instantly. You shake hands with him, you like him. And he was very cordial with the press, too."

Gurney eventually won the Senate seat—capturing 59 percent of the Florida vote. The Florida vote thirty-three-years later would be much closer for George W.

AS FAR AS ELECTORAL VOTES GO, the 2000 presidential election was the closest in 125 years. It was the second closest in terms of the popular vote. The results might have been different—and certainly less controversial—had more than 50 percent of the voting-age population bothered to show up at the polls. But half stayed home. Welcome to modern America.

"Hardly an endorsement of the idea of electoral resurgence," concluded the Committee for the Study of the American Electorate (CSAE) in Washington, which has monitored a progressive generational decline in voting. Americans ages eighteen to twenty have reduced their rate of participation in the electoral process by more than 40 percent since they were given the franchise in 1972, both in presidential and midterm elections. Consider these additional CSAE findings:

- The rate of presidential voting participation of Americans ages 18-24 has declined 40 percent since 1972.
- The rate of participation for ages 25-34 has declined 32 percent since 1964.
- The voting rate for 35- to 44-year olds is down 23 percent since 1964.
- The voting rate for 45- to 54-year-olds is down 16 percent since 1964.
- There has been a 9 percent decline for 55- to 64-year-olds since 1964.

"Only those over 65 have actually increased their rate of participation," says CSAE. In fact, the number of Americans above age seventy-five casting presidential ballots has jumped 21 percent, partly because Americans are living longer.

What do these embarrassing numbers reflect for this country's future?

"This generational decline," CSAE predicts, "will not be reversed until some new generation gets different stimuli in the home, their schools, and in the macrocosm of American politics."

For the sake of the country, let's hope it happens soon.

Chapter 14

A New Era

H E'S A CALIFORNIA CONGRESSMAN and senior member of the House International Relations Committee. But in another life Dana Rohrabacher was in most bizarre company.

The lawmaker was a member of a small mujahideen unit in Afghanistan, engaged in battle against Soviet forces in and around the city of Jalalabad. Intriguing by itself, but there's more.

"We at one point came across a camp of tents," says Rohrabacher, who wore a beard like the rest of his mujahideen unit. In fact, like "American Taliban" John Walker Lindh, who trudged through the same desert but on a far different mission, you wouldn't know he was an American until he spoke.

That's why Rohrabacher was told to shut up.

"They were white tents, and you could see them in the distance," the congressman says, "and I was told at that point I must not speak English for at least another three hours."

Because?

"Because the people in those tents were Saudi Arabians under a crazy commander. Named Osama bin Laden."

Rohrabacher, now in his eighth term in Congress, was told by the mujahideen that "bin Laden was so crazy he wanted to kill Americans as much as he wanted to kill Russians."

"Thus, I must keep my mouth shut or we would be attacked by those forces under bin Laden," he said.

Rohrabacher did as he was told, and unlike three thousand innocent Americans on September 11, 2001, he avoided bin Laden's murderous ways.

SHOCK STIRRED THE SLEEPY COMMUTERS as they squeezed through the customary Pentagon bottleneck and across the 14th Street Bridge. Car radios that had been relaying disturbing word that a plane crashed into New York's World Trade Center now blared the unthinkable: a second plane, a second tower.

Obviously, these weren't accidents.

Seconds later, an orange-and-green America West jet rolled down the runway of Ronald Reagan Washington National Airport and took off into a clear blue sky. Through my sunroof, I watched the jet follow the course of the Potomac River, flying directly between the Pentagon and the White House.

How unusual, I thought, that the Federal Aviation Administration would permit a passenger jet to take off given the unprecedented horror unfolding in New York City. Certainly if those of us stuck in traffic knew something horrible had struck New York, the FAA had to know.

At that precise moment, American Airlines Flight 77, a Boeing 757 that departed from nearby Washington Dulles International Airport—supposedly bound for Los Angeles—was on its final, twisted approach. I actually felt the impact before hearing the loud "pop." Through my rearview mirror, I watched a fireball rise above the Pentagon. Only then did I realize that the United States of America—in most bizarre fashion—was under enemy attack during the height of the morning rush hour.

Abandoning my SUV on the shoulder of the highway, I raced ahead of the first responders to the burning military headquarters. As I ran, oddly enough, I thought of G. George Ostrom in Montana. He wouldn't be proud of his cub reporter on this suddenly historic day.

"A good newsman sleeps with his camera," George drilled into my head after I showed up at a torched Montana restaurant with only a notebook. These days, with an award-winning photography staff at the *Times*—they don't write, therefore we don't take pictures—my camera is relegated to sunsets and Irish castles.

Inside the Pentagon complex, military brass were glued to television sets watching the horror unfold in New York when sixty-four doomed souls (luckily, 78 percent of Flight 77's seats were empty) arrived unannounced. By the time I reached the grassy perimeter of the massive five-sided structure, the first casualties were being carried out and placed beneath the shade of trees.

Members of the armed forces not assisting with the evacuation stood helpless in their crisp uniforms, jaws agape, unable to fathom how the military headquarters of the most superior, technologically-advanced fighting force in the world could fall victim to enemy attack while sugar was being poured into their coffee.

Tricycles sat motionless at the Pentagon's daycare center, tiny riders scooped up and whisked away while the pedals were still turning. "Unlike Oklahoma City," I scribbled into my notebook, "at least the children were spared in this terrorist act."

It proved impossible to record all the emotion. Unable to reach the now-crumbling Pentagon by taxi, a doctor who had been staying at the Four Seasons Hotel in Georgetown rented a bicycle and pedaled across the Potomac River to offer his medical assistance.

Unbeknownst to me, a friend and former classmate of mine at Bishop Ireton High School in Alexandria was struggling to save himself and his comrades inside the burning Pentagon. The terrorist-hijacked plane crashed into the offices directly below the desk of Robert "Bobby" Hogue, deputy counsel for the U.S. Marine Corps.

"The story of what happens after is harder," Hogue would tell my newspaper one year later. "Life goes on in some respects in an ordinary way. You get up, go to work, go home. Yet what is going on here is complete upheaval. It matched what I was feeling inside. But things progressed to normalcy faster than I did."

From his fourth-floor office, Hogue and his staff watched the breaking news on television as one plane, and then another, slammed into the trade towers. He asked Marine Corporal Tim Garofolo to check on the security status of the Pentagon, worried that the building was increasingly vulnerable because "all eyes were glued to TV."

"Hogue went to talk to his boss, Peter Murphy, counsel to the commandant of the Marine Corps," the *Times* reported. "As he reached Murphy's door, an explosion threw him into the air."

In a memo he'd write later for military investigators, Hogue recalled, "The ceiling began to fall in; the lights came down. We could see the fireball rolling up past the windows."

He didn't know it at the time, but all the Pentagon personnel in the offices below him were dead. Four persons in Hogue's office made for the door, which he and Garofolo struggled to wrench open. When they were able to reach what remained of the hallway, it was filled with smoke. Unable to see, they ran in the wrong direction, the smoke getting thicker and blacker.

"We headed south into thick smoke, holding onto each other like blind mice," Hogue wrote in the memo. "We could feel the heat from the fire and see flames through the floor."

Doubling back, the five faced a critical dilemma: which risk to take? Then, through the choking air, they heard a voice tinged with sanctuary.

"[We] heard someone shouting from the north end to follow the sound of his voice—that there was a way out," wrote Hogue, who was suffering from a severe concussion. "We followed the voice—of a young naval officer and my new hero, whomever he is—and made our way to the interior."

Only then did Hogue peer behind him into the fiery, gaping hole from which he and the others just escaped. He could see directly into his boss's office. His own office had fallen to the ground.

SUNUP SEPTEMBER 12. As the first rays of a somber day filtered through the still-smoldering Pentagon, an older woman stood alone with her thoughts on a grassy knoll overlooking the blackened ruins. In her bony hands she clutched a pair of binoculars.

What are you looking for?

"I'm waiting for my husband to come out," she replied in the strongest voice she could muster.

She welcomed the opportunity to talk, explaining that her husband had recently moved into a newly refurbished office in the Pentagon's west wing. As terrible a tragedy as it turned out to be, it could have been worse. The section of the Pentagon that absorbed the impact of the crash was the first to undergo renovations, ironically enough to bolster the headquarters from possible terrorist attack. As a result, instead of potentially 23,000 victims, 123 had lost their lives.

The wife of one stood her lonely vigil until a friend came to take her home. She would look for her husband's car some other time.

Across the Potomac, Senator John Kerry of Massachusetts was on the phone with the husband and daughter of a close friend who'd been aboard United Airlines Flight 175 that crashed into the second tower.

"The pain and depth of loss in their voices was excruciating," I quoted Kerry as saying, "and the helplessness to do anything but to share that pain and offer comfort brought an even deeper sense of anger and resolve for the acts that have occurred. It is critical that all of us remember, as we talk about responses and war against terrorism, that our rhetoric be matched by our actions."

If the senator didn't remember his own rhetoric, President George W. Bush did.

Congressman Henry J. Hyde of Illinois, chairman of the House International Relations Committee, resurrected Abraham Lincoln in this time of need: "Our country represents the last best hope on earth. We must reestablish the identity of America and hope among the peoples of the world if we are to merit that description and, by doing so, secure our world for generations to come."

Meanwhile, the leader of the Democratic party, soon to be the personal target of another terrorist attack on Washington, was visibly incensed.

"As an American, as an elected representative, I am outraged," shouted Senate Majority Leader Tom Daschle of South Dakota, thrusting Congress into anything but ordinary session that morning of September 12. "As a husband and father, I am pained beyond words."

Pain and a new "reality" was no better described than by Amy Ridenour, president of Washington's National Center for Public Policy Research.

"The 21st Century has begun," she'd write. "Throughout the 20th Century, Americans felt safe at home. We weren't always safe, particularly after the dawn of the atomic age, but we felt safe. To 20th Century Americans, America was an invulnerable fortress. At home, we were safe. September 11 ushered in a new era. We're 21st Century Americans now. We know, not just in our minds, where we've long acknowledged it, but in our hearts, where we never did, that it can happen here."

THE DAYS LEADING UP TO SEPTEMBER 11 had been business as usual at the White House. President Bush was entertaining his good friend, Mexican President Vicente Fox, and as I noted in my column neither leader had "pressing" issues to discuss.

"We had an issue of avocados," I quoted Bush as saying. "For those of you avocado lovers, you'll be pleased to hear that we solved that problem."

Bush, to my knowledge, hasn't mentioned avocados since.

"Your point about our loss of innocence since Tuesday hit home," wrote Maggie Hittie of Algonquin, Illinois. "There is another thing those hijackers took away from us—trust and acceptance. Only an idiot wouldn't notice the terrorists all look pretty much like us. They walked among us, spoke English well, shopped in grocery stores, lived alongside and even accepted the hospitality of generous Americans. A lot of folks now do not trust anybody wearing a turban or shawl or sari, which is sad. They took that away from us—trust in one another.

"P.S. My Greek brother-in-law, who looks like a terrorist, shaved his beard last night."

On a more uplifting note, reader Kellie Ann Moore relayed, "My New Yorker Grampa Jackson and his World War II buddies are ready for war, manning their couch stations, military hats on their heads, TV remote in hand, making decisive executive decisions without hesitation—just like they used to. They are eager to enlist as 'experienced fighting men,' Grampa said. 'The country needs us.' These guys are in their seventies and eighties. One is in a wheelchair, and Grampa has an oxygen tank."

I was touched by a letter "respectfully sent" by Eugene Hill, a professor of electrical and computer engineering at Canada's University of Brunswick:

"Please let me first express the deepest sympathy and heartfelt sadness at the incomprehensible tragedy of innocent deaths in the United States this past week. Following from that, we in this idiotic country of Canada in which I live have just witnessed a day of prayer and a government-sponsored service during the National Day of Mourning in which there was no public prayer. In the same context, this past week the courage of the people of the United States, and the return of the people of the United States to their spiritual roots, was remarkable and in my opinion so appropriate and characteristic. But there remains a great mystery—how people and a country could for forty years, through their attitudes and courts, do everything they could to get every reminder of God, no matter how small or insignificant, out of the public domain and out of public sight and then suddenly, in a very public and government-involved way, seek God?

"The ACLU set aside, it does not seem possible to have it both ways and it is probably therefore very fortunate (for all of us, even in our everyday lives) that the Bible record shows God to be merciful, generous in overlooking our inconsistencies and faults, and ready to forgive."

Few column items had as much impact as a cockpit announcement from the captain of United Flight 564 as his plane prepared to depart Denver. Peter Hannaford, a Washington public affairs consultant and former advisor to President Reagan, quoted the pilot as saying, "I want to thank you brave folks for coming out today. We don't have any new instructions from the federal government, so from now on, we're on our own."

His passengers were all ears.

"Sometimes a potential hijacker will announce that he has a bomb," the pilot continued. "There are no bombs on this aircraft and if someone were to get up and make that claim, don't believe him. If someone were to stand up, brandish something such as a plastic knife and say, 'This is a hijacking,' or words to that effect, here is what you should do. Every one of you should stand up and immediately throw things at that person—pillows, books, magazines, eyeglasses, shoes—anything that will throw him off balance and distract his attention. If he has a confederate or two, do the same with them. Most important get a blanket over him, then wrestle him to the floor and keep him there. We'll land the plane at the nearest airport, and the authorities will take it from there.

"Remember, there will be one of him and maybe a few confederates, but there are two hundred of you. Now, since we're a family for the next few hours, I'll ask you to turn to the person next to you, introduce yourself, tell them a little bit about yourself, and ask them to do the same."

The conclusion of this remarkable address, Hannaford said, brought sustained applause from the planeload of passengers.

ON CAPITOL HILL, incredibly enough, I noted that embattled Congressman Gary Condit had suddenly resurfaced: to fight terrorism. Embroiled in suspicion surrounding the disappearance (she was later found murdered) of intern Chandra Levy, the California lawmaker was among four Democrats tasked by House Speaker J. Dennis Hastert to an elite subcommittee on terrorism and homeland security.

All the news wasn't coming out of Washington. FedEx Corporation founder, chairman, president, and chief executive officer Frederick W. Smith had been a Marine Corps aviator in Vietnam and before that a fraternity brother of George W. Bush at Yale. His company was among the first to pull advertising on the late-night TV program *Politically Incorrect,* after host Bill Maher unintentionally saluted the bravery of the September 11 terrorists.

"We have been the cowards lobbing cruise missiles from two thousand miles away. That's cowardly," said Maher, later regretting his choice of words. "Staying in the airplane when it hits the building, say what you want about it, it's not cowardly."

Commissioned in 2001 in Norfolk, Virginia, the guided-missile destroyer USS *Winston S. Churchill* is the only active U.S. warship named after a foreigner. As a show of goodwill with Britain, it is also the only U.S. military vessel to have a Royal Navy officer permanently assigned on board.

With great fanfare, this unique warship steamed out of U.S. waters for a goodwill tour of the United Kingdom—escorted August 23 into the British harbor of Portsmouth. Her tour ended abruptly on September 11, when the ship—like the rest of the U.S. Navy—went on high alert.

"Well, we are still out at sea, with little direction as to what our next priority is," an ensign aboard the ship wrote to his father. "The remainder of our port visits, which were to be centered around max liberty ... have all but been canceled. We have spent every day since the attacks going back and forth within imaginary boxes drawn in the ocean, standing high-security watches, and trying to make the best of our time. We have seen the articles and photographs of the World Trade Center and Pentagon attacks, and they are sickening. Being isolated as we are, I don't think we appreciate the full scope of what is happening back home, but we are definitely feeling the effects."

Then, this unexpected addendum:

"About two hours ago, the junior officers were called to the bridge to conduct shiphandling drills. We were about to do a 'man overboard' when we got a call from the 'Lutjens,' a German warship that was moored ahead of us on the pier in Plymouth, England. While in port, the . . . Churchill and the Lutjens got together for a sports day/cookout . . . and we made some pretty good friends. Now at sea, they called over bridge-to-bridge, requesting to pass us close up on our port side, to say goodbye.

"We prepared to render them honors on the bridgewing, and the captain told the crew to come topside to wish them farewell. As they were making their approach, our conning officer announced through her binoculars that they were flying an American flag. As they came even closer, we saw that it was flying at half-mast . . . and the entire crew of the German ship were manning the rails. They had made a sign that was displayed on the side that read 'We Stand By You.'

"Needless to say," the ensign told his dad, "there was not a dry eye on the bridge as they stayed alongside us for a few minutes and we cut our salutes. It was probably the most powerful thing I have seen in my entire life, and more than a few of us fought to retain our composure. The German Navy did an incredible thing for this crew . . . [and] after the ship pulled away . . . the officer of the deck turned to me and said, 'I'm staying Navy.'"

HERB WURTH WAS UP TO his usual practical joking when he telephoned his old Pentagon buddy Bill Clarke toward the close of September 2001. By the time they hung up, neither was laughing.

Wurth explained his experience in a letter to a friend, retired Air Force officer Frank Jennings, a longtime neighbor of mine in Alexandria who worked at the Pentagon (today, Jennings is a writer/historian living in San Antonio, Texas).

"You may remember Bill Clarke," Wurth wrote to Jennings, "who used to work in Pentagon Air Force Personnel and Public Affairs, who at one time was an F-4 pilot in Vietnam. He now lives in Raleigh, N.C., in retirement. While visiting Raleigh this past weekend, I called him, pretending (with my usual Wurth humor, which nobody understands but Wurth) to be a 'Sergeant Cunningham from Air Force Personnel in the Pentagon.' I asked him if he would be interested in coming back into the Air Force to fly F-4s at an undisclosed overseas location.

"He asked if I knew he was seventy-three years old. I told him that of course I knew that, as I had his personnel folder right in front of me, that his old record showed he was an Air Force pilot flying F-4s in the Vietnam War, we were going to 'demothball' a lot of F-4s, and that we needed F-4 pilots very badly and, as he knew, you couldn't train [pilots] overnight.

"I thought he might catch on and know that I was joking, but much to my surprise he said, 'Sergeant, if the Air Force needs me, I'll be up there in the morning.'"

Quite moved by Clarke's response, Wurth closed the letter by saying, "Of course, I then had to fess up."

OBSERVING ITS SIXTY-FIFTH REUNION, Yale's Class of 1937 issued a call for the ROTC—banned from the university since the undeclared Vietnam War—to be restored on campus.

"The new threat of a long, continuing antiterrorism struggle confronting our nation" was reason given by the class secretary, Rynn Berry, who with his surviving classmates dedicated the reunion to the memory of the 514 Yale men and other Americans who died in World War II.

Albert Bildner, a former Navy ROTC member also from the class of '37, argued that today's world and its inhabitants, "including the Yale faculty and students, are notably different in spirit and temperament than those of the late 1960s, when Yale banned the ROTC program in the throes of the Vietnam War.

"But forty years later, it is a more dangerous world," Bildner continued. "There is a need for ROTC at Yale, particularly after the surprise attack by Osama bin Laden, fueled by an ideology which sees the United States and Western culture as its mortal enemy."

Bildner then stated rather bluntly, "Yale should not expect other people to carry the burden of defending the country while Yale students do nothing in defense of the United States."

These advocates for marching the ROTC back onto the Connecticut campus recalled the rich and storied affiliation between the U.S. military and Yale, which once offered thriving ROTC detachments of every service. But the program was expelled from the campus in 1969 after Yale's faculty voted to revoke credit for ROTC courses.

"Perhaps worse," Berry noted, "Yale accepts ROTC dollars, but refuses to grant credit for ROTC courses." Today, Yale students who wish to participate in the ROTC can sign up for classes at the distant University of Connecticut.

Ideological waves frequently roll out of Yale. In 2001, I wrote about how 171 of Yale's faculty opposed awarding a special honorary degree to President George W. Bush, a Yale alumnus, because they felt it came too early in his tenure. So what if Theodore Roosevelt, Franklin Delano Roosevelt, and John F. Kennedy were all offered honorary Yale degrees during their first years as president.

In fact, the same faculty that shunned Bush as a newcomer in 2001 had no problem inviting "freshman" New York Senator Hillary Rodham Clinton to speak during the university's 2001 commencement weekend.

Days after recalling this higher-hypocrisy, I was pleased to receive a letter from a distinguished reader, former President George H.W. Bush. The nation's forty-first president, who graduated Yale in 1948 (President George W. Bush was in Yale's class of '68), wanted to weigh in on restoring ROTC at Yale.

"I read your column 'Yale's Turn,' and I just want you to know that I totally agree with the idea that it is time for Yale to restore ROTC to the campus," the former president wrote. "It is my strongly held view that ROTC should not have been kicked off the campus in the first place.

"I love Yale," the senior Bush continued, "but they sometimes, especially back in the sixties, seemed to try to jump out ahead of the radicals, totally turning off a lot of loyal alumni like me in the process. I honestly believe things are very different there now."

During his university days, Bush did more than his share to defend the country. As a World War II Navy pilot in the Pacific theater, he flew fifty-eight missions from carriers. He was rescued at sea not once, but twice, dodging Japanese capture within minutes. Rightfully, he was decorated for valor.

Shortly after Bush lost the presidency to Bill Clinton in 1992, two highly influential Yale alumni recommended he return to his alma mater as president. Even more ironic, right up until Election Day, Clinton's name was also on the short list being considered for the university's top post.

Shortly after I published Bush's analysis of Yale, another letter arrived on my desk. This one was from Kennedy in-law Sargent Shriver, who asked to "second" the remarks of the former president.

A member of Yale's class of 1938, Shriver, who went on to become director of the Peace Corps, wrote that he had served in the Naval Reserve upon graduation and became a Navy apprentice seaman in February 1941. But there's much more to his wartime experience, I was amazed to read:

"I was called to active duty in April 1941, at which time I was given thirty days' leave of absence to complete the requirements in order to become fully inducted as an operational ensign in the Navy," Shriver began. "As a consequence, I was put on active duty in June of 1941.

"As a result, I was the officer in charge of the entire Third Naval District which extended from Maine to South Carolina and out into the Atlantic Ocean. Thousands of sailors and officers of the U.S. Navy were on duty in that very large area.

"Miraculously," he continued, "I was on active duty on the day that Pearl Harbor was attacked; and I was, in fact, in charge of the entire unit despite my being the youngest officer. Thus, it was I, on Sunday, December 7, who issued a call to general quarters. All hell broke loose at that moment! Within ten to twenty minutes I had the two sailors working with me receiving phone calls from everywhere within the entire district. Many of the callers started off by swearing at me for issuing a 'general quarters' on a Sunday.

"But when I blasted back at them that the Japanese had attacked Pearl Harbor and killed our men and officers and sunk our ships, they shut up, and slammed down their phones. It will surprise no one, I believe, that within fifteen to twenty-five minutes of when I issued the general quarters' alarm, my office became filled with Naval officers, all of whom were ordering me to get out of the way, which I quickly moved to do."

Shriver, after that "infamous" day, remained on active duty until 1945.

––––––––––––

CITIZENS OF THE NATION'S CAPITAL were on edge for a month and counting. Around lunchtime on October 15, word quickly spread through the city that a letter opened in the office of Senate Majority Leader Tom Daschle contained a "powdery" form of anthrax.

At first, nobody seemed overly concerned.

In fact, the very next morning hundreds of congressional staffers lined up in Room 216 of the Senate Hart Office Building (downstairs in the atrium from where the deadly envelope had been opened) to be tested for anthrax exposure. One U.S. Capitol policeman, asked about the danger of people assembling in a building where anthrax spores had been released into the air, casually replied that the ventilation system was shut down.

But towards the head of the line a memo was distributed from the Capitol's attending physician, Dr. John F. Eisold. There will be "further testing of the ventilation system," he wrote to jittery senatorial aides. After the testing, each staffer was handed green packets containing six Cipro tablets—a three-day supply. It was the most effective anti-anthrax antibiotic known.

"Remember to return on Thursday for your results," staffers were reminded.

Some were so upset they cut into the front of the line to get tested, as if time was of the essence.

"Please try to relax," a medical assistant appealed into a microphone. "If you have a newspaper and some time on your hands, please sit down. And do not cut into line."

In retrospect, nobody should have sat down. Instead, they should have collectively stood up and run from the building. Testing for anthrax exposure should never have taken place in the highly contaminated building. Something in my head told me to get out of line, and it wasn't my daily deadline. The very next day, the same Hart Building, where half of the hundred U.S. senators have offices, was sealed shut. It remained closed for three months, undergoing one of the largest, most thorough toxic mop-ups in world history.

Still, lawmakers didn't seem to get it. On October 16, one day after Daschle was targeted with millions of anthrax spores, Senate Minority Leader Trent Lott of Mississippi and seven other senators on Capitol Hill hosted the first annual "Bipartisan Catfish Feed."

And talk about astonishing. Under the headline "Grab a Shovel," I reprinted a most sensational press release surrounding a most untimely groundbreaking ceremony on the West Front of the U.S. Capitol: "Speaker Dennis Hastert and his wife, Jean, under anthrax attack at the Capitol, rushed from a press conference on the Hill yesterday morning to do the groundbreaking for the new National Garden."

As for me (as millions of Americans would hear), I was too nervous to talk. Like others in a line we never should have been standing in, I was prescribed a course of Cipro. In fact, I went straight from getting my nose swabbed to the ABC studios in Washington, where for three-grueling hours I guest-hosted the *Rush Limbaugh Show.* One of my callers, it so happened, was a medical doctor. After I took the liberty to ask him about the adverse effects of the large white pills I rattled into the microphone, I dared not swallow one.

ONE OF THE MOST OUTSPOKEN Washingtonians in the wake of both September 11 and the anthrax attacks was former House Speaker Newt

Gingrich. In an interview with me on October 17, Gingrich blasted former President Bill Clinton for all but ignoring previous terrorist attacks orchestrated by Osama bin Laden against the United States.

"You had the World Trade Center attacks in 1993, the Khobar Towers bombing in Saudi Arabia in 1996, you had the U.S. Embassy bombings in Kenya and Tanzania Africa in 1998, and the attack against the USS *Cole* in 2000. So we had been at war for seven years," he continued. "And yet the Clinton administration insisted on treating this as a criminal justice operation, insisted on not funding the CIA adequately, not creating human intelligence capabilities. So we were crippled."

Bin Laden's mug didn't even appear on the FBI's Ten Most Wanted list until 1999, when five million dollars was offered for his capture. But Gingrich wasn't finished filling my column with what was choking his chest:

"Here we have a president who defended perjury, had the meaning of the word 'is' changed to fit his own definition. Instead, we fire sixty-six missiles in one day with no follow-up campaign. When I look at what the Clinton administration said—and did—it was astounding. I felt very sad when the planes hit the World Trade Center towers and the Pentagon, because it was possible to hunt these people down over eight years."

He was alone in his criticism. More than a month after the terrorist attacks, I quoted former Secretary of State Madeleine K. Albright as saying that the Clinton administration never had the "public support" it needed to uproot bin Laden from his terrorist training grounds.

"This Bush administration has the support to go forward in a way we did not," Albright told reporters in Cherry Hill, New Jersey. "We did everything we could based on the intelligence we had."

"You got my blood boiling this morning with the excerpt from Madeleine Albright," CIA career veteran Anne Allen later wrote to my column. "Albright didn't happen to mention, did she, Clinton's disastrous executive order, prohibiting the CIA from dealing with 'shoddy' informants?

"As a thirty-seven-year CIA veteran, recently retired, I see that as the most devastating blow to intelligence fathering in decades. And she didn't happen to mention, did she, the many steps short of military action which could have been taken to prepare this country for unknown but certain threats—linking FBI lists with airline manifests, providing for vaccines against bio threats, securing our borders, linking intelligence information to visa issuance, to name only a few?

"These are not steps known only in retrospect," Allen said. "We had repeated and ignored warnings throughout the nineties. National security is the primary job of a federal administration. This was a disaster in the Clinton administration, and now they don't even have the grace to keep their mouths shut."

It's too bad Allen, in the spring of 2004, wasn't called to testify before the National Commission on Terrorist Attacks Upon the United States, otherwise known as the 911 Commission. Given what the former CIA official told me, she would have refuted, in no uncertain terms, sensational charges leveled by former White House counterterrorism czar Richard A. Clarke that President Bush, unlike Clinton, did not take the terrorism threat seriously during his first months in office.

Although the CIA was caught off guard on September 11, the intelligence agency did know—and warn—about the deadly strike strategies of bin Laden and other anti-Americans of his ilk.

On December 7, 2000, I thought it extremely newsworthy when CIA Director George J. Tenet painted for his Town Hall of Los Angeles audience the "psychological terrorist profile" that, nine months later, would rear its ugly head.

"The kind of [terrorist] thinking that asks: 'How can I negate the overwhelming military force of the United States?' The kind of thinking that leads a terrorist group to seek a chemical or biological weapon. The kind of thinking that could lead a small nuclear power to blackmail us—not with the possibility of defeat, but with the threatened destruction of one of our cities," Tenet said.

"Today, Americans must recognize that ours is a world without front lines. That the continental United States—and not just our embassies and forces abroad—is itself susceptible to attack. And that the potential method of assault goes well beyond a terrorist with a truck full of conventional explosives."

Unfortunately, few of the nation's elected officials (many wanted Tenet fired after September 11) were listening when the CIA director concluded: "We in the intelligence community believe that the chances for unpleasant—even deadly—surprise [attack] are greater now than at any time since the end of the Second World War."

Now, several years later, Americans are paying closer attention to an unpleasant reality. Still, the CIA has additional warnings to pass along, which you might read now for the first time.

By the year 2015, the agency educates, there will be more than seven billion people on earth—a billion more than today. More than 95 percent of that growth will be in developing countries, which are least able to cope with the resulting pressures of population expansion. Take fresh water, for example—or lack of it.

A dozen years from now, nearly half of the world's population will live in "water-stressed" areas, where fresh water is consumed faster than it can be replaced. Worse yet, the CIA says much of the water shortage will be in the Middle East, where it will add to the current tensions. Similar severe shortages are also projected for Africa, East and South Asia, where it will complicate economic growth.

In addition, the CIA warns that emerging science and technology, which can be either tools for progress or weapons of evil, will grow tremendously in capacity. Consider advances in the miniaturization of circuits, which hold the promise to permit the near duplication of human intelligence in machines.

"Imagine," Tenet remarks, "what a dictator might do with power like that."

A New Era

THE MODEL OF THE NEW, TWENTY-FIRST CENTURY POLITICAL FIGURE is no better explained than by author Anthony J. Dennis in his book, *Osama bin Laden: A Psychological and Political Portrait.*

"He holds no public office. He communicates his decrees over the Internet. He instructs his followers by cell or satellite phone. And he lives in a small room in an underground bunker. And yet he commands more influence and exerts more military muscle than some governments."

———————

IN MID-NOVEMBER 2003, a frightening United Nations report was leaked into public view warning that despite the war on terrorism, the risk of al Qaeda's acquiring and using chemical and biological weapons continues to grow. It added that the terrorist network was busy developing new conventional explosive devices, such as bombs that can evade airport scanning machines.

Jonathan Schanzer, a research associate with the Middle East Forum, told me in an interview that President Bush, partly for political reasons and partly not to offend the Arab world, has chosen to ignore the real enemy—militant Islam—when referring to the "war on terrorism."

"This is the first time to my knowledge that any leader has declared a war against a tactic," Schanzer said, noting that it's difficult to fight a global war on "terrorism" when opposing sides, rightly or wrongly, all consider each other to be "terrorists."

As a result, not explicitly targeting "militant Islam" and its brutal totalitarian ideology has been costly to America, hindering everything from airline security to sensible immigration policies. Worse, it means not identifying potential allies, particularly the moderate majority of Muslims.

Bush "has opened a big can of worms," Schanzer concluded. "We need to identify our enemy. We are fighting radical Islamic groups and the terrorism they perpetrate. We are not fighting other 'terrorist' groups like the IRA or the Shining Path—we are going after al Qaeda, Hezbollah, the Islamic Army of Aden, the list goes on."

If there's any doubt of our enemy, Schanzer reminds that nineteen of the nineteen terrorist hijackers of September 11 were militant Islamists. The same fold overwhelms the FBI's Most Wanted list.

"We're afraid to offend, for politically correct reasons and because we're afraid of ticking off the Arab world," he said. "This is not a war against the 1.3 billion Muslims in the world. We know who the enemy is."

On May 1, 2002, I got hold of a telegram from the U.S. consulate's office in Jeddah, Saudi Arabia, addressed to Secretary of State Colin Powell, Defense Secretary Donald Rumsfeld, CIA Director George Tenet, and National Security Advisor Condoleezza Rice. It identified a "troubling streak of intolerance" that has emerged among certain Muslims in the Arab world and warned of a possible "convulsion" of the Islamic faith.

"The vast majority of Muslims are accepting of persons of different faiths," the cable stated. "However, in the wake of September 11, many observers have remarked on the existence of a troubling streak of intolerance that colors Islam as it is practiced and preached in Saudi Arabia."

The consulate's dispatch educated that a radical brand of Islam, called Wahhabism, arose in the eighteenth century in the rural and historically poor part of Arabia known as Najd, and by the early twentieth century had found fertile ground from Mecca and Medina to Mogadishu.

"Today, zealots in and around the holy cities see themselves as continuing the Prophet Muhammad's struggle to uproot and destroy all vestiges of the . . . polytheistic past. In so doing, they confirm early Islam's enmity toward the confessional comity that once characterized this region. Try as they might, [the Islamic faith] cannot credibly characterize Wahhabism as a freak sectarian aberration. The Najdis' intolerant message succeeds because it remains unchallenged; no Muslim Luther has summoned the courage to nail his propositions to the door of the Kaaba" (referring to the Holy Kaaba, the most sacred structure in Islam), the consulate wrote.

"There are those who express hope that Islam, drawing on centuries of experience of absorbing and ultimately de-fanging its radical fringe, can harness the Wahhabis' drive and apply it toward constructive purposes.

However, it appears equally likely that the as-yet-unchecked spread of Saudi Arabia's state faith could precipitate a convulsion such as that which engulfed the West in the sixteenth century and subsequently was termed the Protestant Reformation. Then, Christendom struggled to amend itself while parrying perceived Muslim predations. Five hundred years later the tables are turned, and it is by no means clear whether Islam will accommodate itself to the emergence of a secular society or withdraw further into obscurantism and intolerance."

I headlined the eye-opening telegram, "Coming Convulsion."

ACCORDING TO ANTHONY DENNIS, who before his psychological portrait of bin Laden authored, *The Rise of the Islamic Empire and the Threat to the West,* bin Laden wants Muslims to perceive him as "a modern-day Saladin the Great, who led the Muslims to victory over the Christian Crusaders during the Middle Ages.

"However, this dream of Muslim greatness founded upon the myth of military superiority is a fatal delusion in the nuclear age," he says. "The Muslim world will only be great when it finally decides to put down the sword, not when it takes it up."

In the meantime, Dennis says Americans cannot assume that any aspect of Western society "is safe from annihilation as long as the transnational Muslim fundamentalist movement still rages somewhere on the globe. Washington, D.C., and other large Western cities are obviously attractive targets for terrorists and will continue to be so until terrorism is expunged from the story of human progress and development."

LESS THAN THREE MONTHS BEFORE SEPTEMBER 11, on June 25, 2001, the American Embassy in Riyadh and the U.S. Consulate in Jeddah announced in Arabic to Saudi Arabia's citizens: "The U.S. Embassy in Riyadh is proud to announce the implementation of its new U.S. VISA

EXPRESS service for expediting nonimmigrant visa applications through-out Saudi Arabia.

"Now all Saudis and non-Saudi applicants may obtain visas at their own convenience by submitting their applications through any of ten designated travel/courier companies operating throughout the Kingdom of Saudi Arabia," said the announcement, a copy of which I obtained. "Applicants will no longer have to take time off from work, no longer have to wait in long lines under the hot sun and in crowded waiting rooms, and not be lim-ited by any time constraints."

No wonder the majority of the September 11 terrorist hijackers obtained their U.S. visas in Saudi Arabia. Uncle Sam all but packed their box-cutters for them.

Chapter 15

Awaiting Vice President Moseley

SEPTEMBER 11 WAS CRUEL ENOUGH. Days later, Washingtonians witnessed a rare and deadly tornado whirl past the Pentagon and across the Potomac River. On the twister's heels were the equally lethal anthrax attacks and a pair of deranged "Beltway" snipers that made it risky to pump gas. A crippling blizzard followed, curtailing everything but hardware shopping sprees by frantic soccer moms who tried to "duct-tape" terrorists out of their McMansions.

When warmth was never more needed, there came the "2003 Summer That Wasn't"—oddly cool temperatures and relentless rains, capped off by a monster hurricane that churned up a swollen Potomac and left thousands homeless. Those tourists Isabel didn't blow away would wake up to read in the newspaper that their chances of getting shot and killed were greater in Washington than in war-torn Baghdad.

It is for these reasons that I continuously strive on a daily basis to bring much-needed relief to Inside the Beltway readers. With so much depressing news, why make more?

Take, verbatim, the first two paragraphs of this hilarious 2003 newspaper article clipped from Indiana's *Journal Gazette* about one well-known congressman: "HUNTINGTON—Making his first trip to Huntington as the 5th District congressman, Representative Dan Burton discussed tax cuts, prescription-drug costs, and border patrols in a Town Hall meeting Monday.

"Burton spoke at Huntington High School to a crowd of about one hundred, many of them students required to attend as punishment."

––––––––––––––––

THEN THERE WAS THE INSTANCE in October 2003 when, hoping to curtail damaging leaks, President George W. Bush issued an order to senior White House officials saying they could no longer speak to members of the press if they insist on being identified as an "unnamed administration official."

So revealed an "unnamed administration official."

Another government memo suggests that only family members need apply to the GSA: "Roger Johnson, administrator of the General Services Administration, yesterday announced the appointment of Martha Johnson as associate administrator, to succeed Marlene Johnson."

Outrageous federal policy statements are always worth bringing to the public's attention, particularly those memos seeking to satisfy the swelling plank of political correctness:

"As federal employees, we must ensure that our communications, both written and verbal, are free from the appearance of any form of discrimination. Effective immediately, sexist language is not to be used. Terms such as 'the men,' 'man-hours,' 'man years,' etc., are not acceptable. Instead, terminology such as 'staff,' 'staff hours,' 'staff years,' and 'employees' are to be used."

Which had John Michael Williams, a reader in Maryland, wondering: "What do they call their men's room?"

At the expense of others, I call further attention to inexcusable newspaper corrections that aren't my doing. Take this doozy issued by the *New York Times:* "A brief article on Monday about a Connecticut legislator who revealed that he is gay misidentified the legislator. He is Representative Patrick J. Flaherty, a Democrat who represents Coventry, not Representative Brian G. Flaherty, a Republican who represents Watertown."

Too late, Brian. Word's already out.

———————

MARTIN MOREHOUSE, A READER in Seattle, made a good point when writing: "Sir, in your column today you mentioned the commerce secretary, who recalled that the 1990 census failed to count 4.4 million people. How does he know this, if the census failed to count them?"

When stumbling upon the following display of patriotic duty, I recalled the six "W's" of Journalism 101:

WHO: Two muscular U.S. Marines, bottle of Brasso, sponges, and cloths.

WHAT: Polishing brass base of flagpole bearing Marine insignia.

WHERE: The Vietnam Veterans Memorial, Washington.

WHEN: Dusk Sunday.

WHY: Because Marine insignia is dingy, tarnished.

WRAP: U.S. Park Service ranger, sporting goatee and wire-rimmed glasses, informs Marines they're violating SOP (Standard Operating Procedure); orders they cease and desist polishing; use of Brasso could harm brass base of flagpole; it's not the way we do it.

(What did the Marines do? They came back while the rest of Washington slept and spit-shined their insignia. And they still do to this day—or night).

The author of the following correspondence is unknown, however my Internal Revenue Service contact confirms the agency receives hundreds of hilarious letters like this one every tax season:

"Dear IRS: Enclosed is my 2003 tax return and payment. Please take note of the attached newspaper article and you will see that the Pentagon is paying $171.50 for hammers and NASA has paid $600 for a toilet seat.

"Please find enclosed four toilet seats (value $2400) and six hammers (value $1029). This brings my total payments to $3429. Please note the overpayment of $22 and apply it to the Presidential Election Fund, as noted on my return. Might I suggest you send the above mentioned fund a 1.5 inch screw (see attached article: HUD paid $22 for a 1.5 inch Phillips head screw.)

"It has been a pleasure to pay my tax bill this year, and I look forward to paying it again next year. Sincerely, a Satisfied Taxpayer."

It's not often I get the opportunity to write about family members, but I couldn't help it after telephoning my older brother Rob to wish him a Happy Father's Day. If anybody deserves one day set aside to honor dads it's my brother. Already blessed with two daughters, he and his wife Tami were keeping their fingers crossed for a son. Weren't they surprised when the stork dropped not one boy, but two, as well as another girl. Their complete set is now named Missy, Molly, Maddy, Mike, and Mark.

"So, what's new?" I asked my sister-in-law, an avid equestrian.

"Not much," came her usual refrain. "Oh, wait, I did lead Elian Gonzalez around on our pony."

Long pause.

"Elian Gonzalez?"

"Yes, the little Cuban boy."

Longer pause.

"On our pony?"

"Yes, Merrylegs," she said, obviously missing the international magnitude of this particular pony ride. (Every news reporter up and down the East Coast was trying to pinpoint Elian's whereabouts while Washington and Havana continued playing tug-of-war.)

"Elian Gonzalez was riding on Merrylegs?"

"Yes, and I probably shouldn't say this, but Elian's dad and his baby—what a cute little thing—also climbed up on the pony and the saddle started to slide off! Everybody was watching, all of their Cuban friends and lots of U.S. Marshals.

"So, did you want to speak with your brother?"

LIFE IS TOUGH ENOUGH. Imagine waking up one morning dead.

U.S. Army Col. Donald R. Condrill served with distinction in the military for thirty-two years. He is now retired and lives with his wife Margaret outside Washington.

When Condrill's father-in-law, Navy Lt. Cmdr. Donald F. Burns, passed away in 2002, the colonel promptly notified the military's Defense Finance and Accounting Service (DFAS) by telephone, then followed up with a letter—to make "doubly sure."

"I telephoned you that he had died," the colonel wrote to the DFAS, "and wanted to be sure that his retirement pay had ceased."

To assist authorities, Condrill provided his father-in-law's military service number, Social Security number, and date of birth.

Two weeks later, the colonel's wife, Margaret, received not one, but two letters from the DFAS expressing "sincere sympathy on the death of your husband, Colonel Donald R. Condrill. We realize that this is a difficult adjustment period, and wish to offer our assistance."

Assist they did.

"The DFAS decided that I am no longer alive and without warning has cleaned out our checking account of $9,300," Condrill told me. (The confiscated thousands covered payments made to the colonel after his "death" several months before.)

"It is simply incredible to me that this letter, which I signed, has been interpreted by DFAS as a notice of my death," he said.

To make matters worse, the colonel's previous wife, who was receiving direct bank deposits from the military, also had her checking account "raided by DFAS—again with absolutely no warning," Condrill said.

He immediately wrote to DFAS to inform them of their "gross error." Several days later he received a most incredible response in the mail: "You must go to a base, police station, or consulate and have them send a letter verifying that you are alive and well and entitled to payment."

Amazing as his story is, Condrill wasn't the only military veteran in limbo.

"I, too, have had a similar type incident to the tune of over fifteen thousand dollars," retired Army Col. William A. Ward of Niceville, Florida, wrote to me several days later. "Needless to say, it has put me in financial difficulties."

Ward contacted the Veteran's Administration, from which he was drawing VA disability compensation, and was connected to a specialist in the debt-management division. He explained that more than fifteen thousand dollars had been swiped from his account.

"What's this about?" the colonel was begging to know.

"Well, you're dead," came the response.

"If I'm dead, then how am I talking to you?"

"Then you're going to have to write a letter."

"If I'm dead, then how am I going to write a letter?"

"Don't get smart with me!"

I headlined the item, "Smart-Aleck Corpse."

FOR THE SAKE OF OUR CHILDREN—and this country's future—higher-ups at the National Education Association should turn off their television sets and, well, study.

After viewing NBC's popular prime-time show, *The West Wing*, this nation's top educators took the most bizarre step of issuing a news release headlined: "NEA Backs President Bartlet's Call for School Quality."

President who?

"Wednesday's *The West Wing* featured President Bartlet's plea for more teachers and better-funded public schools. NEA strongly agrees," the release stated.

The NEA, of course, didn't bother to mention that the actual president, George W. Bush, had just given a 38 percent increase in federal funding to the nation's teachers, part of his No Child Left Behind Act. Perhaps the NEA was still sore that hanging chads kept its chosen candidate out of the real West Wing.

I had to laugh when Al Gore and wife Tipper appeared together at a Washington bookstore to sign copies of their romance novel, *Joined at the Heart.*

"What's your name?" Gore asked one gentleman who'd been standing in line.

"Chad," the man replied.

Gore didn't blink.

Several people in line began to snicker.

"To Chad," wrote the former vice president, passing the book to his wife for her to autograph.

As the man turned to leave, a curious man next in line asked him if Chad was his real name.

"No," the man replied, and he walked away—no doubt anxious to accept bids that evening on eBay.

———————

AFTER VICE PRESIDENT GORE came Vice President Dick Cheney, who was on hand when the Hudson Institute presented the 2003 James Doolittle Award to his former boss—yes, boss—Defense Secretary Donald Rumsfeld.

"The true story," Cheney reveals of his first-ever 1968 meeting with Rumsfeld, then a Republican member of Congress from Illinois, "is that I flunked my first interview."

Cheney was a young congressional fellow working on his doctoral dissertation, with plans to return to the University of Wisconsin to teach. As part of his fellowship, he was to negotiate an employment arrangement—working for free—with the Capitol Hill lawmaker of his choice.

Rumsfeld had just spoken to the group of congressional fellows "and I was impressed, so I made an appointment to go see him," Cheney continues. "And the interview lasted about fifteen minutes, and I found myself back out in the hallway."

Cheney knew he didn't hit it off with Rumsfeld.

"He thought I was some kind of airhead academic, and I thought he was rather an arrogant young member of Congress," Cheney admits. "Probably we were both right."

As history had it, Rumsfeld was soon tapped by President Richard Nixon to be director of the Office of Economic Opportunity. Cheney, toiling pro bono for a less arrogant congressman, said he then "sat down one night, unsolicited, and wrote a twelve-page memo suggesting to [Rumsfeld] how he should handle himself in his confirmation hearings, and giving him some sterling advice on what he ought to do with the department once he got confirmed."

Weeks went by and Cheney didn't hear a word, not that he expected to. Yet the very next day after Rumsfeld was sworn in, Cheney got a phone call that the new OEO director wanted to see him. He remembers being led into the office, where the no-nonsense Rumsfeld had very little to say except: "You, you're congressional relations. Now get out of here."

"And that's how I was hired," Cheney said. "Literally."

Thus, ingenuity is how one grows up to become vice president. And perhaps one day there will be a Vice President Moseley.

"Greetings from Snellville, Georgia!" Chuck and Linda Moseley wrote in 2003 to Washington landlord Peter Kelley, his name found in a directory of apartments for Capitol Hill interns.

"Our son is a rising senior at the University of Georgia. He has been chosen as a full-time intern for [Georgia Republican] Congressman John Linder beginning Sept. 1, 2003, and ending Dec. 12, 2003. Please advise availability and any additional information you require. We will not be able to visit D.C. until after June 5, 2003, due to his classes. Thank you for your time."

A nice letter, obviously, from proud parents. Any landlord would be lucky to let a room to a promising young lad like Moseley.

"Hello Moseleys," Kelley wrote back. "Thank you for contacting us about your son staying at the 'Loj' during his internship. I'm usually very encouraging of young people doing congressional internships and staying here while they do them.

"However, I do have to say that as a full-time employee of an environmental group, and as someone personally quite alarmed about the direction that Congress and the president are taking with the environment, I have concerns about Representative Linder's record.

"He has a 5 percent score on the League of Conservation Voters environmental scorecard, and his Web site lists the following votes, all of which I deeply disagree with: Voted NO on raising CAFÉ standards, incentives for alternative fuels; Voted NO on prohibiting oil drilling & development in ANWR; Voted NO on starting implementation of Kyoto Protocol.

"I am torn," Kelley concluded, "because I hope that your son will have a wonderful experience in Washington and I know that working for any congressman, even one with Representative Linder's views, will be an invaluable experience that he will treasure his entire career.

"However, I would not feel right about having someone stay at our place who was working to advance views such as these, which I believe amount to abandoning our responsibility to future generations. And so I must decline your request for a room here."

STORIES, I'VE LEARNED OVER THE YEARS, materialize on the unlikeliest of stages. Take the 2003 commencement ceremony at Mount St. Mary's College and Seminary in Emmitsburg, Maryland, where not a single soul in the audience recognized the gentleman seated on the dais.

His identity became clear only when college president George Houston Jr. diverted from the written program to announce that he was awarding a presidential medal to Mohammed Odeh Al Rehaief.

Who?

The Iraqi lawyer who risked his life to save Army Pfc. Jessica Lynch of West Virginia.

"At first, there was stunned silence, it was a complete surprise," said Catherine Bartos, whose daughter was receiving her diploma.

"Then this small man stood up, and the place just exploded with applause—five minutes of sustained applause and tears that went on and on and on. It was wonderful. Finally, at least a part of the American public was able to thank him for what he did for one of our own."

Due to security concerns, the presence of Al Rahaief wasn't announced beforehand. Just days before, the Iraqi lawyer, his wife, and their five-year-old daughter were granted asylum in the United States and were living temporarily with a family of one of the Mount's graduates.

ENOUGH HEART-WARMING STORIES, you say?

During the summer of 2003, when I was in Paris reporting on the lack of Americans climbing the Eiffel Tower, President George W. Bush welcomed hundreds of fellow Yale alumni to the White House for a college reunion. (Keep in mind, Yale was an all-male institution when the president had run of the place in 1968.)

Unfortunately, I wasn't on hand to see the look on Dubya's face when one of his former college chums—now in a dress and heels—stepped forward to shake the president's hand.

"You might remember me as Peter when we left Yale," the *San Francisco Chronicle* quoted the woman as telling Bush.

The president didn't flinch. Instead, he grabbed his old college buddy's hand, looked her straight in the eye, and said in a most understanding tone, "And now you've come back as yourself."

Oh, to have been a fly on the White House wall that night when Dubya retired to the living quarters and told Laura what became of Pete.

Closing

Godspeed

ONE KNOWS WAR IS BREWING when unfamiliar flags fly over Washington. In the days and weeks before Iraqi dictator Saddam Hussein was blown from his tyrannical throne, the yellow and green Hezbollah flag was waved by America's more radical bunch. It didn't matter that the terrorist group claimed responsibility for numerous bloody attacks against innocent civilians, including the 1983 truck bombing in Lebanon that killed 253 Americans. Then again, many of today's protestors weren't born yet.

Also hoisted by defiant youth were the flags of Iraq, then a state sponsor of terrorism, and the Palestinian Authority, members of which publicly celebrated the murders of three thousand innocent Americans on September 11.

Yes, noted one observer, the U.S. flag was visible during the antiwar protests—wherever there was smoke.

"What do you make of the fact that millions of people across the globe have taken to the streets to protest your approach to Iraq?" a reporter asked George W. Bush.

"Two points," replied the president. "One is that democracy is a beautiful thing and people are allowed to express their opinion. I welcome people's right to say what they believe.

"Secondly, evidently some of the world don't view Saddam Hussein as a risk to peace. I respectfully disagree. Saddam Hussein is a threat to America. And we will deal with him. I owe it to the American people to secure this country. I will do so."

And he did, launching "Dubya Dubya III," as his critics called the U.S.-led operation in Iraq. In retrospect, it's unfortunate that Bush had to liberate the onetime prosperous country in the name of weapons of mass destruction. The fact that a modern-day "Hitler" and his lunatic sons were allowed to terrorize fellow countrymen for so long was sufficient enough cause for a regime change.

Now, rather than being commended for overthrowing a brutal despot and his offspring—rather than being saluted for his dogged pursuit of terrorists following the worst attack ever on U.S. soil—many Americans, rallied on by presidential wannabes in 2004, complain that Bush has given America a "bully" image.

It is true that a majority of people polled in nineteen of twenty-seven countries by the American Enterprise Institute for Public Policy Research no longer view Americans as passive, kind-hearted, law-abiding people. Yet it's unrealistic, if not ludicrous to think that one president, in office for less than one term, is behind America's decline in credibility. The thick-skinned Bush doesn't mind accepting blame for what he knew would be a difficult and unpopular mission. A captain, after all, is responsible for his ship. But he didn't create the ugly American.

"Thanks to Tony Soprano, *Sex and the City,* and young pop divas, Hollywood has given us our unflattering image," opines former House Speaker Newt Gingrich in a *Los Angeles Times* op-ed, his observations seconded by "practicing" Muslims in Kuwait.

After the Gulf War drew to a close in the early 1990s, I'd written about leaflets dropped on Kuwaiti doorsteps calling on citizens not to let "American culture and habits into your home."

"Do you know what these people's customs are?" the fliers asked. "Whether you are a father, a brother, a husband, take a vow not to let this device into your household."

The "device" was a satellite dish.

Gingrich labels as "astounding" the findings of Boston University's Melvin and Margaret DeFleur, who surveyed 1,259 teenagers from twelve countries about attitudes towards Americans.

"Few of those surveyed had any direct contact with Americans—only 12 percent had visited the U.S.," Gingrich notes. "But they did have access to American television programs, movies, and pop music, and based on that exposure most of these teens considered Americans to be violent, prone to criminal activity, and sexually immoral."

Mr. DeFleur himself concludes, "These results suggest that pop culture, rather than foreign policy, is the true culprit of anti-Americanism."

Others disagree. In November 2003, Charles V. Pena, director of defense policy studies at the Cato Institute, wrote that many people mistakenly assume that al Qaeda hates the United States for "who we are" as a country.

"But the reality is that hatred of America is fueled more by 'what we do'— that is, our policies and actions, particularly in the Muslim world," Mr. Pena says, arguing that "the United States needs to stop meddling in the internal affairs of other countries and regions, except when they directly threaten the territorial integrity, national sovereignty, or liberty of the United States."

Thus, he says Bush's national security strategy, which is based on the premise that the only way to ensure U.S. security is by "forcibly" creating a better and safer world, is actually undermining security and breeding vehement anti-American sentiment that could spark more terrorist attacks.

OBVIOUSLY, AMERICANS KNOW we aren't the bullies—or degenerates— many in the world make us out to be. Which is why it is crucial, given the growing hatred for America, that a continued war on terrorism—likely to last decades—be accompanied by an unprecedented public relations campaign touting the freedom-loving principles America stands for. But first, we as a country need to rediscover—if not learn for the first time—what being "American" is truly about. Not until we know ourselves can we be introduced to the rest of the world. A good place to start is around the dinner table.

"A majority of the young are growing up in homes whose parents don't vote; their schools don't emphasize civics, citizenship, and current events," acknowledges Curtis Gans, director of the Committee for the Study of the American Electorate in Washington. And unfortunately, he adds, the patriotic fervor generated by the September 11 terrorist attacks failed to translate into increased civic participation by Americans.

"[W]hat the citizenry was asked to do was to return to normalcy, consume material goods, and invest in the stock market, hardly clarion calls to civic involvement," Gans says.

Still, there is hope.

Thomas Donnelly, resident fellow at the American Enterprise Institute in Washington, has placed the controversial U.S. intervention in Iraq on his palate and painted a bright future for America, particularly as we are perceived in the rest of the world.

In his paper, "The Meaning of Operation Iraqi Freedom," Donnelly says the 2003 invasion of Baghdad "reflects the character of President Bush himself" and will become a case "where an individual makes a great difference to history . . . and, very profoundly, the nature of America, its power, and its principles."

As for naysayers who suggest peace will never take hold in Iraq, what with its porous borders and diverse cultural and religious backgrounds, Donnelly recalls our fathers and grandfathers saying that Japan and Germany were incapable of sustaining democratic values.

"Well, they were wrong," he points out. "The nation of Iraq with its proud heritage, abundant resources, and skilled and educated people is fully capable of moving toward democracy and living in freedom."

With little fanfare in the fall of 2003, the Gallup Organization released the first scientific poll assessing the postwar social and political climate of Baghdad. The groundbreaking study amassed 1,178 hour-long, in-home interviews in a cross section of Baghdad—including Sadr City, formerly Saddam City.

Among the findings, nearly two-thirds (62 percent) of Baghdad's citizens think ousting Hussein was worth any hardships they have personally endured since the invasion. Furthermore, two-thirds (67 percent) believe Iraq will be in better condition five years from now than it was before the U.S.-led invasion. Just 8 percent think it will be worse off.

Obviously, this rather upbeat Gallup poll was conducted before the rise in terrorist-related incidents in Iraq in 2004. And if that wasn't enough to cloud Iraqi optimism, photographs of prisoner abuse by military personnel at Abu Ghraib prison near Baghdad infuriated Iraqis and Americans alike.

As President Bush observed, "Human cultures can be vastly different. Yet the human heart desires the same good things, everywhere on earth. In our desire to be safe from brutal and bullying oppression, human beings are the same. In our desire to care for our children and give them a better life, we are the same."

AS I STOOD WATCHING the Pentagon crumble on the morning of September 11, my thoughts were, as Bush guessed, on my own child. The peaceful life Kerry and her classmates at St. Mary's School had always known vanished in the blink of an eye. For that matter, security felt by all Americans, young and old, was shattered in mere seconds. It pained me to think what the future held in store for our country.

At home that afternoon I wrote the most difficult column of my career, then realized I'd left Kerry alone downstairs watching rerun after rerun of the day's horrific events on television. As confused and frightened as I was, I couldn't imagine what was going through her mind.

I immediately recommended we take a walk, and as quickly as we stepped outside we smelled the smoke from the Pentagon, blowing as it was directly over our house. So instead of walking, Kerry suggested we take a take a drive.

When I was a boy growing up in Old Town, my next-door neighbor and part-time mother Nancy Ann Blount used to tell me that instead of a fireman or astronaut I'd grow up to be a newspaperman. With a purple bicycle as my transportation, I was always the first kid on the block to reach the scene of a bad car wreck or house fire, then promptly report back the gruesome details—often knocking on my neighbors' doors to do so. I'll never forget racing four blocks to inform neighbor Tom Dimond that the historic home he'd purchased only days before had been struck by lightning. He thought I was joking until he reached the corner and saw all the fire trucks.

Now, at my daughter's request on this bloody afternoon of September 11, we pulled up to the smoldering Pentagon.

Alone in her room that night, without my knowledge, Kerry wrote down her thoughts of the tragically historic day—innocent, yet profoundly optimistic observations that were later published in her school newspaper. To say her words gave her father the strength I needed is an understatement.

"Something was burning, only it wasn't a grill in somebody's backyard," she began. "We got closer to the Pentagon, and I started to see its outline in the smoke. We drove around it, and I turned to see the damage that had been caused. It was unbelievable. I had never seen anything like it in my short thirteen-year life, and I knew I would never forget it. Ever. I don't even know how to begin to describe it. It looked as if it was a gingerbread house and someone had eaten a huge chunk.

"As my dad and I were driving home, we listened to the news on the radio. I heard a quote that really meant a lot to me: 'It's a clear and sunny day, but one of the darkest days Washington has ever experienced.'

"It was true. I looked towards the Pentagon and saw the sky had been dyed grayish-black by the smoke that had come out of the disaster. But then I looked the opposite way and saw a crystal blue sky, as if nothing had happened. But something had happened, and it would be penned down by historians throughout the world, and added to history textbooks that would soon be read by our children and our children's children.

"But the blue sky meant something. It symbolized the people of our nation, the United States of America. We had been dyed by the grayish-black of the smoke, but soon we would turn the other way and see the bright blue sky ahead of us and think of our future. This is our world and we should do everything we can to improve it."

Godspeed, Kerry.

Acknowledgments

THE REAL AUTHORS OF THIS BOOK fill its pages. I consider it a privilege to retell their stories. In doing so, I thank my readers, co-workers and family for their patience and understanding while I neglected the present to disappear into the past.

This sojourn would not have been possible without the valuable assistance of *Washington Times* researcher Clark Eberly and fellow librarians Joseph Szadkowski and Amy Baskerville. Regretfully, I do not recall the name of the kind-hearted woman at Kalispell City Library who spent part of her Christmas holiday threading and re-threading microfilm while fellow librarians sipped eggnog and sang Yuletide carols.

It was veteran newsman and author Joseph Farah, former editor of the *Sacramento Union*, who sparked the fire beneath my indolent keyboard to produce this narrative. His enthusiasm was seconded by WND Books publisher David W. Dunham and WND editor Joel Miller. Patrice Taylor graciously supplied the publishing tools, and Susan Jacobsen the balm and nerve tonic.

I owe a special debt to my close friend and neighbor David Drake

ACKNOWLEDGMENTS

Hudgins, who in exchange for two pints of Guinness provided legal counsel in the preparation of this work.

I am similarly indebted to my computer technician, Ian Storm Taylor, thirteen, who, while too young for stout, navigated my neurotic mouse through myriad logistical and emotional breakdowns.

For being my constant eyes, ears, and anchors on both coasts, I am forever grateful to Chuck Rigney and Dick Hammett.

Finally, I am truly blessed to be the middle son of Robert W. McCaslin, grandfather to Finneas McCaslin and seven elder cohorts, who upon stoking his wood stove each morning sits down to read every word I write.

Sources

Adams, Jackie. "Grizzly Trees Tourists." *Hungry Horse News* (June 2, 1983).

Allen, Mike. "Sabato More Plugged-In as Usual." *Richmond Times Dispatch* (30 June 1994).

Arnold, James W. "Tim Russert: Feisty Host of Meet the Press." *St. Anthony Messenger* (October 1994).

"Baghdad's Citizens: Ousting Saddam Hussein Worth Personal Hardships," Gallup Organization (24 September 2003).

Bell, Christopher. "Clinton's Step-Nephew Has Klan Membership." *Huntsville Times* (23 July 1993).

Berthoud, John. "Security—at What Price?" National Taxpayers Union Foundation (June 1994).

Berthoud, John, with Demian Brady. "Bill Clinton: America's Best-Traveled President." National Taxpayers Union Foundation (March 2001).

Bhatti, Jabeen. "Dual Anniversary Dredges Up Emotional Scars." *Washington Times* (11 September 2002).

Birnbaum, Jeffrey H., with Rick Wartzman. "Hillary Clinton's Brothers Ask Firms To Finance Parties." *Wall Street Journal* (14 January 1993).

Brokaw, Tom. *A Long Way from Home: Growing Up in the American Heartland.* New York: Random House, 2002.

Chan, Swell. "Morgue Again Takes Turn for Worse." *Washington Post* (27 September 2003).

SOURCES

DeFleur, Melvin, with Margaret DeFleur. *The Next Generation's Image of Americans.* Boston University, 2003.

DeLoach, Cartha Deke. *Hoover's FBI: The Inside Story by Hoover's Trusted Lieutenant.* Washington, D.C.: Regnery Publishing, 1995.

Dennis, Anthony J. *Osama bin Laden: A Psychological and Political Portrait.* Lima, Ohio: Wyndham Hall Press, 2002.

Donnelly, Thomas. *The Meaning of Operation Iraqi Freedom.* American Enterprise Institute, 2003.

"For the Record." *National Review* (13 October 1997).

Gans, Curtis. "Preliminary Primary Report." Committee for the Study of the American Electorate (2 July 2002).

Gingrich, Newt, with Peter Schweizer. "We Can Thank Hollywood for Our Unflattering Image." *Los Angeles Times*, (21 January 2003).

Glasgow, William M. *Northern Virginia's Own.* Alexandria, Va.: Gobill Press, 1989.

Harvey, Tom. "Bear Autopsy Report Pending." *Daily Interlake* (28 July 1980).

Hitchens, Christopher. "District of Contempt." *Vanity Fair* (March 1998).

Hoeft, Mike. "Killer Bear May Have Evaded Trap"; "Rangers Resume Search for Killer Bear"; "Bears Claim 3rd 1980 Park Victim"; "Bear-Mauling Victim Spread God's Word on Earth"; "Dead Bear Was Killer, Says Autopsy." *Daily Interlake*, July-October 1980.

Isikoff, Michael. *Uncovering Clinton: A Reporter's Story.* New York: Random House, 1999.

Jones, Bob. "It's Good To Be King." *World* (28 July 2001).

Kaplan, David A. "Gore's Secret Plan." *Newsweek* (17 September 2001).

Sources

King, Larry, with Pat Piper. *Anything Goes! What I've Learned from Pundits, Politicians and Presidents.* New York: Warner Books, 2003.

Labash, Matt. "O.J. Simpson on Women and Clinton." *Weekly Standard* (25 May 1998).

Lardner, James. "The Anti-Network." *New Yorker* (14 March 1994).

Lee, Robert W. "Bipartisan Bigotry." American Opinion Publishing Inc., 1991.

Light, Paul C. "Problems on the Potomac." Brookings Institution (22 March 2002).

Limbacher, Carl. "Cleaning Lady." NewsMax.com (8 February 2000).

McCaslin, John. "Inside the Beltway." *Washington Times* (1992-2003); "Beltway Beat." *Los Angeles Times* Syndicate/Tribune Media Services (1999-2003); United Press International, KOFI-AM, KJJR-AM, KBBZ-FM, Bee Broadcasting, Inc. (1980–1984).

McClendon, Sarah, with Jules Minton. *Mr. President, Mr. President! My Fifty Years of Covering the White House.* Los Angeles: General Publishing Group, 1996.

McLellan, Diana. "And Then She Said . . ." *Washingtonian* (August 2000).

Murray, Joan. "Brother of Mauling Victim Attacked in 1979." *Daily Interlake* (25 July 1980).

Nofziger, Lyn. *Unbridled Joy: The Verse of Joy Skilmer.* Deatsville, Ala.: MND Publishing, 2000.

Oakley, Meredith. "Posterity, Not Potshots." *Arkansas Democrat Gazette* (11 December 2000).

Olsen, Jack. *Night of the Grizzlies.* Moose, Wyo.: Homestead Publishing, 1969 and 1996.

Ostrom, George. *Glacier's Secrets: Goat Trails and Grizzly Tales, Volume II.* Helena, Mont.: Farcountry Press, 2000.

SOURCES

O'Leary, Jeremiah. "O'Leary's Washington." *Washington Times*, 1991-1993.

Pena, Charles V. "Bush's National Security Strategy Is a Misnomer," Cato Institute, 30 October 2003.

Ridenour, Amy. "These Dead Shall Not Have Died in Vain," National Center for Public Policy Research, September 2001.

Russell, Andy. *Grizzly Country*. New York: Alfred A. Knopf, 1967.

Serra, Ray. "Night of Another Grizzly Recounted." *Daily Interlake* (29 July 1980).

Schumer, Charles. "Dad Explains." *New York Post* (26 January 1999).

Shapiro, Walter. "Boomer Report on Clinton Sex Dreams." *Time* (16 November 1992).

Sherrill, Martha. "Grave Doubts." *Esquire* (January 1996).

Simmons, Melody. "HUD Chief Orders Recall of Unshaven Mug Shots." *Baltimore Sun*, 10 June 1993.

Talbott, Strobe. *The Russia Hand*. New York: Random House, 2002.

Thomas, Bill. "Open Secrets." *The Hill* (9 July 2003).

Trulock, Al. "Findings on Grizzly Killing of Laurence Gordon." *Kalispell Weekly News* (29 October 1980).

Wannall, Ray. *J.Edgar Hoover, For the Record*. Paducah, Ky.: Turner Publishing, 2000.

West, Paul. "Destination White House Gore." *Baltimore Sun* (18 June 1997.)

Index

247

INDEX

INDEX

Index

About the Author

Syndicated columnist John McCaslin pens the award-winning "Inside the Beltway" column for the *Washington Times* and Tribune Media Services. A former member of the White House press corps, he was proclaimed "national ombudsman" for his knack at uncovering political shenanigans on both ends of Pennsylvania Avenue. One of Washington's favorite story-tellers, you've read his anecdotes in *Reader's Digest* and listened to him spin tales while substituting for Rush Limbaugh. Born inside the Beltway, he lives with his daughter Kerry in Alexandria, Virginia.